CHUCK SHELTON

LEADERSHIP 101
FOR WHITE MEN

HOW TO WORK
SUCCESSFULLY WITH
BLACK COLLEAGUES
AND CUSTOMERS

Chuck Shelton

MORGAN JAMES PUBLISHING • NEW YORK

LEADERSHIP101
■ FOR WHITE MEN ■

ISBN: 978-1-60037-472-2 (Paperback)

Published by:

MORGAN · JAMES
THE ENTREPRENEURIAL PUBLISHER™
www.morganjamespublishing.com

Morgan James Publishing, LLC

1225 Franklin Ave Ste 32

Garden City, NY 11530-1693

Toll Free 800-485-4943

www.MorganJamesPublishing.com

Cover/Interior Design by:

Rachel Lopez

rachel@r2cdesign.com

I dedicate this book to Dad, Mom, and Suzanne.
Every day your love shows me how to
choose the right,
nurture safety,
lead playfully,
and love long.

*"To whom much is given,
much is expected."*

LUKE 12:48

■ CONTENTS ■

LEAD AMONG COLLEAGUES

■ ACKNOWLEDGMENTS ■

I am deeply indebted to so many partners in the learning that fueled this book: family, friends, colleagues, clients, professionals in the written word, experts in diversity, and leaders from many settings. My heartfelt thanks extend to the following: Joe Albert, Cara and Ed Barker, Manie Barron, Sharon Bilgischer, Barbara Deane, Deb Fine, Tammi Jean Franklin, Rick Frishman, Bob Gilliom, Stacey Girdner, Laura Lee Grace, Richard Gray, Deborah and Lee Griffing, Stephen Guy, David Hahn, Bill and Marian Hall, Ben Hancock, David Hancock, Chitra and Tim Hanstad, Mallorie Hebert, Gary Kessler, Ed King, George Koch, Patrice Lewis, Lana Madison, Pat and Barb McDermott, Richard Mouw, William Pannell, Roy Prosterman, Sue Salget, Brenda Salter-McNeil, Lewis Smedes, Nancy Solomon, Dick Staub, Jeannine Thill, Megan Washburn, Claudia White, Woodie White, Susan Wright, and Scott Young.

I have been specially blessed by my amazing family: Suzanne Shelton, Melinda Shelton, Patrick Shelton, Mary and Beck Shelton, Joan, Hank, Chris and Michelle Broeckling, and Roger and Sharon Shelton. I hope you find that this book honors our family's heritage and future.

■ INTRODUCTION ■

Beyond Defensiveness

I once saw a poster promoting a gig by a rock band named White Male Guilt. I didn't go. And no, I didn't feel guilty about missing it.

Yes, I'm a white man, born and raised in America. I work as a leader. I've been married for thirty-plus years, and we have 2.0 children. I speak only English.

And sometimes diversity makes me defensive. It's tough to embrace diversity as an opportunity when it is used to shame white men for the behavior of our ancestors, who are often presumed to be slaveholders whether or not they were. It's hard to be diagnosed with symptoms of "dominance,", "oppression," and all manner of "isms" (racism, sexism) ad nauseam, like invisible diseases infecting only white guys.

Through a lifetime of learning and leading, however, I have discovered that white men generally are not hostile to people who are "different." We know that everyone is unique. Most white men in leadership enjoy productive relationships with women and people of color. We are usually willing to pursue the ways diversity can help our organization succeed.

Yet we are clear about what we don't want from diversity—to be the designated villain. As one white man, a weary veteran of corporate diversity intrigues, complained: "I just want diversity to leave me alone." That's unlikely; white males are now thirty-eight percent of all American employees, and white men who lead are just five percent of the U.S. workforce.

As a fellow white man who leads, I recommend that, since we can't run from diversity, we shouldn't hide from it either. We have to find our way beyond defensiveness. I have intentionally learned about differences in race and gender for most of my life. I've been taught the most about managing diversity by those who have suffered as a result of their distinctives: black people and others of color, immigrants, gay and lesbian colleagues, and white women. They showed me that their opportunities should not be truncated by personal attributes they did not choose, such as race, nation of birth, sexual orientation, and gender.

As white men, we know we need to learn more about leading among diverse stakeholders. In particular, the deeply rooted differences between white and black people continue to present us with powerful challenges. With all that's between us as white and black Americans—what's come before and what still separates us—it is time to get things right and make things right with our black colleagues and customers.

THE BOOK'S VOICE

Consequently, this book equips white men to lead. White women may also find some of these ideas useful as they seek to build stronger relationships with black women and men. And many of the lessons herein apply to all relationships, including people of colors other than black.

A note on language: while many black folks prefer the term "African-American," very few white people refer to ourselves as "European-American."

So I will generally use the term *black* as partner to *white*, and trust that African-Americans will understand my intent.

I focus in this book on working successfully with *black* colleagues and customers because there are ancient issues not sufficiently resolved between us. We need to continue the progress between black and white Americans, and also learn to lead effectively among people of other ethnicities and dimensions of diversity.

Not one black person you speak to about this book will agree with all my ideas. I suspect I've got some things wrong; I just don't know which things. Or maybe, as one of my black friends said about the book: "It's so very white." But their views should not cause you to discount my advice. I'm not speaking to black people. I'm writing about diversity as a white man who leads, and I'm talking to my own kind. I hope the book will equip us all to talk together more effectively. Constructive controversy is a healthy American tradition.

If you disagree with me, or what I suggest doesn't work for you, then find what does work to build stronger relationships with black colleagues and customers. That's what personal responsibility is all about. Use the book to do good and do well.

My Assumptions and Expectations about Diversity

I hope you will be encouraged or at least intrigued to encounter me as a white man who leads with tested convictions about how humans are alike and unique. It is important for you to know what I assume and what I expect from diversity:

• **Respect and reciprocity:** *Each person I encounter is unique and deserves respectful treatment from me. I expect the same from them. I assume the* *good faith of colleagues and customers. And if any person behaves in bad faith toward me or the people I lead, I will respond appropriately.*

- COMMUNICATION: *People sometimes receive my communication differently than I intend. I will try to close any gap between intent and impact, and I expect others to reciprocate. I will seek out, listen, and respond to feedback from leaders above me, my peers and employees, and our customers.*

- "DIFFERENT" DOES NOT MEAN "BAD": *I need to monitor and assign meaning to "difference" with more intelligence and openheartedness, and less bias. I will try not to negatively judge a person for being different in appearance, experience, temperament, or opinion. I reserve the right, however, to evaluate behavior as problematic.*

- WHITE MEN WHO LEAD WILL MAKE A DIFFERENCE: *Our leadership should serve generations to come, so we must rethink "differentness" as white men who lead in American organizations. Our particular advantages and choices, along with commonly held democratic and religious values, position us to contribute to an historic and global shift. Going forward, human differences will cause less conflict and produce more respect and opportunity in the marketplace and society.*

- MANAGING DIVERSITY CAN BE SIMPLE: *Working effectively with human differences can be simple enough, in that I need simply to apply the skills I already possess to new challenges among diverse coworkers and customers.*

- MANAGING DIVERSITY CAN BE COMPLICATED: *It is vital that I examine my own interests, values, biases, and behaviors as a white man who leads. I also need to learn what influences others to communicate and behave the way they do, so that we can achieve results together.*

I try to square my leading and my writing with these six core values.

OPTIONS FOR READING THE BOOK

Readers will open this book with diverse needs, expectations, and experiences. Consider several options for exploring the 101 essays that follow.

By all means, first study the Core Ideas in essays 1–13. And focus on the Conversation Starters at the end of each essay, as they offer a question or an idea to discuss with coworkers, family, and friends.

Reading Option One

Continue on through essays 14–101, reading one or two per day. Explore the Conversation Starters. The order of the book's nine sections equips you to lead on diversity from the inside out: Core Ideas, Start, Think, Learn, Manage Emotions, Respond, Talk, Act, Lead.

Reading Option Two

After essays 1–13, explore a critical path through seventeen additional essays, considering key concepts. Here's the trail I recommend:

#19 Distinguish between generalizations and stereotypes.

#23 The Advantage Complex: Unpack your power.

#24 The Advantage Complex: Appraise privilege.

#25 The Advantage Complex: Discipline your views of preference and affirmative action.

#26 The Advantage Complex: Evaluate opportunity with utter honesty.

#30 Invest heavily in due regard.

#36 Watch Yourself: Build the critical skill of self-monitoring.

#37 Deal with denial.

#38 Face the fear.

#39 Get past the guilt, and shed the shame.

#40 Metabolize anger constructively.

#45 Identify progress, but focus on joint achievement going forward.

#54 Constantly calibrate intent and impact.

#61 Trust-Building: Make promises, keep promises over time.

#76 Establish accountability with diversity-related performance objectives.

#93 Pursue the black marketplace.

#99 Lead with a transformative vision.

Then read for interest.

Reading Option Three

Review each section introduction, and then study what grabs you. For example, if you're looking for a structured approach to your diversity learning, essays 16–18 and 31–35 will help. Or if you'd like to drill into specific leadership tasks, consider essays 76–92.

It should be noted that, in some examples, names and other identifiers have been changed to protect the innocent and guilty.

Finally, remember that everything between white and black people is not about race, and everything between men and women is not about gender. It is simplistic and risky to attribute a difference of opinion to a difference in pigment or biology.

This book pursues a straightforward purpose: I want white men who lead to seize the personal and professional profit in working more successfully with black colleagues and customers.

May that be the return on your investment in this book.

CORE IDEAS

■ **1** ■

Diversity
Get it right, get it now.

iversity presents us, as white men in leadership, with a stark choice: human differences are either a distracting pain in the rear or a potent opportunity to improve. This book fuels the second option, by equipping white men to lead more successfully alongside black colleagues and customers.

White men have been a problem for black women and men for centuries. Some of *our* white male predecessors owned *their* black ancestors as slaves for more than 250 years. This is about making right out of what our kind got wrong.

And the challenge isn't just ancient history. We need to make it right, right now. Harvard psychiatrist Alvin Pouissant describes being black in today's America as "death by a thousand nicks."

1

Here's what it means to get diversity: white men who lead must do whatever we can to put a stop to this nicking, the tiny ripping in a black person's daily life that bleeds their joy and scabs over their potential.

Almost four hundred years from slavery's New World inception in 1619, white and black people still have a lot to learn and much to do—together. As white men, we're sick of being viewed as the problem. As leaders, most of us seek to become part of the solution. Here's how.

Get It Right

Women complain that men "just don't get it." Black people object that whites "will never get it." Employees have been known to observe that "my manager doesn't want to get it." As white men who lead, we seem to get it from every direction. In response, we mentally mutter several questions about "getting it."

What is "it"?

Here's the "it" we need to get: "the ability to distinguish among the attributes and cultures of your employees, peers, superiors, and customers, so that you encourage their contributions." I call this **due regard** (see essay 30). Our diverse customers and colleagues observe us getting it when our leadership shows that we care enough to involve them as individuals. They see us evaluate problems and opportunities from a culturally informed perspective.

We should acknowledge an irony here: we are confronted with the need to learn the significance of our own race and gender, while surrounded with legal and social mandates to act toward people *without regard* for their race and gender.

As white men, we are just now conducting a personal and interpersonal due diligence on diversity that black people have been compelled to practice throughout life. Remembering this will perhaps take the edge off our periodic need to whine about the difficulties in being a white man today.

Do I want to get "it"?

Managing successfully among diverse people yields profound personal and professional profit. See the "What's in diversity for me?" argument in essay 8, on **sustainable collaborative advantage**. This is an uncomplicated proposition: if you want to get diversity, you will. In doing so, you will secure remarkable benefits. It is a simple case of getting it before not getting it gets you.

Does my organization want "it"?

The business case for diversity is well tested and persuasive (see essays 7, 74, and 75). Explore why your organization should pursue diversity as a strategic advantage. Sadly, many corporate diversity commitments bog down into compliance ("don't get sued, avoid bad press") or celebration ("ethnicity of the month"). A company's diversity strategy will sustain results only when

- it positions the organization to compete for talent and customers;
- a growing number of white male managers actively support it.

How do I go about getting "it"?

The method for getting it may be summarized in a word: **teachability**. This means being ready, willing, and able to learn diversity's lessons fast and well, so you develop the reputation for instructability among people who are different from you. You'll be amazed at the insight and grace black people will extend as you responsively learn, in mind and heart, side by side with them.

Your customers buy and your employees work in an environment teeming with human differences that matter. As a white man who leads, your success hinges, in part, on your ability to learn about diversity at work.

GET IT NOW

Is it ever *too* late for a white man who leads to learn about diversity? In this case, late isn't much better than never. If you don't seize the advantages in leading effectively among diverse stakeholders today, you will lose promotions to other white men and diverse colleagues who know how to do that right now. And if your organization struggles to leverage the power of diversity, you can be certain that competitors are pursuing a diversity strategy to win market share, talent, and capital.

In any case, as white men who lead, we have a lot to learn and it's going to take us awhile to learn it. It's time to commit. Diversity: get it right, get it now.

CONVERSATION STARTER: *What don't you get about diversity, and how will you get these questions answered?*

CORE IDEAS

■ **2** ■

Define differences.

L et's be honest. Diversity is often a code word for differences in race and gender. I'm okay with that, as long as we intend such a code to communicate that racial and gender differences are essential to understanding the humans we lead. Gender and race matter; universally residing in our DNA, these aspects of difference are also suffused with historic meaning and current impact.

But it is more useful to us as leaders when we pursue diversity as a truly inclusive paradigm of human difference. It's about race and gender—and more. **Diversity**, simply put, is a concept to differentiate all the qualities that distinguish us from one another. Race and gender are vital currents in the human river, but there are other differences that leaders must navigate.

Over the years, my work with managers has led me to focus on the workplace impact of twenty **dimensions of diversity**. This book focuses

5

primarily on **race** (skin color and other physical traits that influence complex social meanings and practical knowledge) and **leadership** (an occupational role secured through opportunity and professional skill), with some attention to **gender** (being female or male, with the accompanying physical and social experiences).

The twenty dimensions of diversity are listed below (alphabetically, not in priority order). My purpose here is to define human differences to make them easy for the reader to use. If my definitions seem simplistic or inaccurate to you, please formulate your own.

AGE AND GENERATION: *How old you are and the influence of the time period in which you were born.*

APPEARANCE: *Your individual look, from physical attributes to chosen image.*

COGNITIVE TENDENCIES: *How you tend to think and learn.*

COMPETENCE/EXPERIENCE: *The degree of understanding and skill you demonstrate, as influenced by your background.*

DEMEANOR: *Your natural styles of personal conduct, communication, (e.g., outspoken/quiet, serious/easy-going), and collaboration.*

ECONOMIC AND SOCIAL STATUS, OR CLASS: *The money and resources you or your family of origin have, your social affiliations, and the opportunities those relationships provide to you.*

EDUCATIONAL ACHIEVEMENT: *Values and options you possess through completing levels of education and training.*

ETHNICITY: *A cultural group of which you are a part that may be distinguished by such common traits as appearance, demeanor, family, geography, language, race, and religion.*

FAMILY: *Your current family relationships, family of origin, and ancestry.*

GENDER: *Being female or male, with the accompanying physical and social experiences.* (Note: Some scholars use the word sex to refer to inborn physical traits, and gender for culturally learned attitudes and behavior. I have found, as I work with men, that the word sex connotes behavior, so I take the liberty of using the term gender to include innate and learned attributes.)

GEOGRAPHIC ORIENTATION: *Connection to place; where you grew up (city, suburb, town, rural area), and where you live now.*

HEALTH: *Your physical and mental well-being, and the well-being of those for whom you care.*

LANGUAGE: *The tongues you speak or understand.*

LIFESTYLE: *The personal activities that are important to you and in which you participate (music, entertainment, sports, hobbies, clubs, and so on).*

NATIONALITY: *Your nation of origin or adoption, including military service.*

OCCUPATION: *Your fields of knowledge and effort, and your professional role.*

POLITICAL INTERESTS: *Your opinions on and affiliations with issues, elected officials, and government.*

RACE: *Your skin color and other physical traits that influence complex social meanings and practical knowledge.*

RELATIONAL ORIENTATION AND ATTRACTION: *Your tendencies and inclinations to people or tasks, friendship, sexuality (the gender to which you are physically attracted, and the way you manage that attraction).*

RELIGIOUS COMMITMENT/SPIRITUALITY: *Your faith or spiritual interests.*

No doubt there are other aspects of diversity that could be added to this list, and certainly there are more complete definitions of these categories. But such accessible definitions equip us as white men to think, speak, and lead with clarity.

But what if defining differences this inclusively is really a smokescreen that obscures diversity's real issues? Black professionals have complained to me that white people prefer to define diversity this broadly so that we can avoid dealing with race. I have seen that this can be true: in a popular management handbook, *The Boss's Survival Guide*, the three white male authors completely ignore race while exploring other dimensions of diversity. To advise managers on diversity and never mention race is breathtakingly ignorant.

That being said, the book you hold uses the dimensions of diversity concept as a paradigm for all the human differences that leaders must learn to manage, while investigating race as a critical area for concern and growth.

This dimensions of diversity approach is a practical tool for leading from the inside out as a white man. It will serve you well.

CONVERSATION STARTER: *Which dimensions of diversity most influence who you are? Which dimensions least shape who you are?*

Introducing
the Fundamental Filter

I n 1950, two Harvard professors, Clyde Kluckhohn and Henry A. Murray, edited *Personality in Nature, Society, and Culture*, a groundbreaking anthology on what makes humans tick. These editors provided us with a tool for sifting through human differences. I call it the **Fundamental Filter**, and we can use it to distill meaning in three levels of human identity.

Each one of us is:
Like All Others,
Like Some Others, and
Like No Other.

To say we are *Like All Others* speaks of universality, the ways that all humans are similar. What we share in common as humans is astounding and wonderful and precious. Our sameness is real and powerful, even when we don't see it or feel it. Our alikeness is the garden where our differences can grow in health.

To note that we are *Like Some Others* speaks to our social character. Here is an inescapable truth: we are joiners, relational creatures who innately need to associate with those *like* us. This is about the richness and comfort and inevitability of culture, group identity, and organizational life.

And to declare that we are *Like No Other* just affirms the obvious—individuality is core to our existence. All the dimensions of diversity, universality, and group identity weave together to form each of us as one-of-a-kind. That's awesomely good. The catch to individuality? We are solely answerable for ourselves and our work.

To equip you to distinguish among universal traits, group identities, and individuality, let's scrutinize each membrane of this Fundamental Filter.

Like All Others:
Identify and treasure similarities.

Our most basic common link is that we all inhabit this small planet.
We all breathe the same air. We all cherish our children's future.
And we are all mortal.

PRESIDENT JOHN F. KENNEDY

11

UNIVERSAL TRAITS

White male managers have been known to voice the concern that emphasizing our differences can drive employees apart, rather than helping us work together. So how do we focus on differences without deepening the divisions?

One way to do this is to recognize and understand—the action words of awareness—that people are fundamentally similar in many ways, even when our differences are so apparent.

To illustrate this from my own life, let me tell you about Brenda, a colleague and a dear friend. We don't look much alike or come from the same place: she's a beautiful black woman from New Jersey, and I'm a fast-aging white guy from Seattle. We differ in many other ways as well, but let me offer up some of what we have in common:

- We worship the same Lord, and faith is core to our lives.
- We earned advanced degrees (okay, she's Rev. Dr. Brenda; I just can't keep up).
- We're passionately committed to racial reconciliation.
- We are a bit loud.
- We laugh a lot (sometimes at each other).
- We like to speak in public.
- We sing.
- We are married to psychologists.
- We each have two children, a boy and a girl.
- We write books.
- We struggled through the loss of a parent and came out stronger.
- We tune in observantly to people around us.

- We enjoy thinking deeply, and we try to apply our deep thinking to our lives.
- We are not rich, but we have enough.
- We enjoy relatively good health, but we don't relax enough.
- We're brave most of the time.
- We like Cuban food.
- We are … friends.

It took me less than five minutes to come up with this list. But many people, observing the two of us together, would note only our differences. Brenda and I are profoundly different, and we are wonderfully alike.

Sift through this filter of commonality by responding to the following exercise. Discuss the traits below with family, friends, and colleagues. Refine your own view of how humans are alike.

As human beings we generally:

	True of Me	True of Almost Everyone
Enjoy laughter	○	○
Want to make a contribution through our work	○	○
Love our families deeply	○	○
Feel threatened by people who are "different"	○	○
Expect respect	○	○
Like to learn	○	○
Find change stressful	○	○
Can be brilliant and stupid on the same day	○	○
Aren't as self-aware as we need to be	○	○
Find that our physical, mental and spiritual health shapes everything we do	○	○
Derive satisfaction from successful work relationships	○	○

Figure 3

Such traits characterize and unite us—girls and boys, women and men—across every race, nationality, physical ability, sexual orientation, and language. As we explore the reality of diversity, embrace and believe in the power of what we have in common. To do so is to see ourselves in others. This potent connection prepares us to live with integrity and lead effectively.

> *Whenever I meet people I always approach them*
> *from the standpoint of the most basic things we have in common.*
> *We each have a physical structure, a mind, emotions.*
> *We are all born in the same way, and we all die. All of us*
> *want happiness and do not want to suffer. Looking at others*
> *from this standpoint ... allows me to have a feeling*
> *that I'm meeting someone just the same as me.*

TENZIN GYATO, THE FOURTEENTH AND CURRENT DALAI LAMA

Each one of us is *Like All Others*.

CONVERSATION STARTER: *What human attributes do you believe are universal? How could this belief change how you think about and relate to black people?*

Like Some Others:
Clarify what's cultural.

Each one of us is:
Like All Others
Like Some Others, *and*
Like No Other.

To identify and treasure similarities (Like All Others) encourages our connectedness. But cultural diversity tests our sense of self and the way we lead. We are often challenged and troubled by group-related differences.

Cultural Identity

Culture may be defined as "the assumptions, values and behaviors a group of people develop as they share experiences over time." Our unique individual identity evolves from our inborn hardwiring, personal experience, and the profound influence of all the groups we encounter. Examples include the cultures of

- your company
- your profession
- your team
- your coworkers
- customers and clients
- your home and family
- both genders
- American culture.

You and your coworkers and customers live in and are influenced by such cultures. You will lead more effectively as a white man when you grow aware of and skilled at handling human differences that manifest at a group level. Illustrations like the following demonstrate how awareness of cultural alikeness serves a manager's interest.

- *Group difference by language:* Key Bank discovered an increasing number of Spanish-speaking customers entering their branches in the eastern half of Washington State. In five years Hispanics will compose more than forty percent of the region's people. The first bank system to deliver bilingual customer service will seize market share.

- *Group difference by geographic orientation:* From its inception, Wal-Mart focused on the need in small towns and rural areas for greater product choice at the lowest price. This business model has expanded to edge suburbs, but has steered clear of urban markets.

- *Group difference by social status, gender, race:* The executive team (all white men) at a New York company instituted a casual Friday dress code, specifying khakis as preferred clothing for men, and prohibiting denim for all. Their well-intended policy hit the fan: some criticized the senior managers as Ivy Leaguers pushing their upscale informality, women wondered aloud why their denim options were foreclosed, and people of color had no intention of dressing down and running the risk of appearing less professional.

- *Group difference by demeanor and cognitive style:* A Microsoft project manager realized that his most poignant diversity challenge was the differing collaborative styles among team members. Half his programmers expected to work by themselves in their offices with someone else integrating their work (individual orientation), and the other half wanted to team together in the same large workspace (group orientation). He had to deliver team results with all of them.

- *Group difference by political interest:* Employees in a liberally minded HMO joked that in their organization it was "more acceptable to be a lesbian than a Republican." This turned out be true (and controversial) when an initiative that outlawed gay marriage reached the statewide ballot and caused conflict in the workplace.

- *Group difference by family, health, generation:* In a Fortune 100 company, senior leaders were disturbed to discover through a consultant's research that the store managers held up as success stories (virtually all middle-aged men) suffered from consistent sixty-hour work weeks, high divorce rates, and poor health. Many high potential assistant store managers (younger women and men) observed the price these store leaders paid, and did not pursue such positions.

We are surrounded by cultural differences such as these. We need to see and honor group differences in order to lead effectively.

THE RISK OF GROUPISM

Many who speak, write, and teach about diversity tend to emphasize the ways people are shaped by groups. They stress the power of cultural diversity (our *Like Some Others* filter). But we need to beware of what I call **groupism**, which is the unthinking presumption that cultural connections determine individuality rather than shape individuality.

It is true that each one of us is influenced by the norms and behaviors of people with whom we share distinctives. But group influence does not *determine* our individuality; that's what stereotyping teaches (see essay 19). Diversity work in some contexts suffers from an "us versus them" mentality. Leaders need to avoid this groupthink trap. As a manager, you work to build a team and an enterprise with diverse persons, where individual enablement should reign.

GROUP DIFFERENCE BY RACE, GENDER, AND OCCUPATION: WHITE MEN WHO LEAD?

As white men who lead, we don't tend to identify ourselves as part of the group technically known to others as "white guys." It is easier to avoid examining the culturally derived advantage that accrues due to our whiteness and maleness. In subconscious peripheral vision, our own race and gender tend to be defined by what they aren't; being white can be "not black," and being a man can be "not like a woman." We need to explore the culture of white men who lead (see essay 48), since they are some of the others we are like!

For now, permit me to offer you this guarantee. Your black colleagues need you to understand your own cultural connections: the cultures of race, gender, and occupation that shape you.

CONVERSATION STARTER: *By dimension of diversity, of which cultures are you a part? How does being in this group shape you and your choices?*

CORE IDEAS

■ 5 ■

Like No Other:
Seek to turn loose the contribution of uniqueness.

Each one of us is: Like All Others
Like Some Others, and Like No Other.

INDIVIDUALITY

Common sense teaches that each one of us is unique. And many white male managers focus intensely on individuality. Perhaps we've internalized the John Wayne–ish image of ourselves as independent and self-actualized men.

There's truly good news here for us as white men: we "get" individuality, so we are particularly well suited to turn loose the contribution of the utterly unique people we lead. Many of us seem to lead with the innate sense that since each direct report decides how they will follow us, we need to lead them one at a time.

The real challenge for us comes when we try to lead in a way that calls out each person's uniqueness, while also honoring each person's cultures (Like Some Others) and similarities (Like All Others).

A white male VP at Fuller Theological Seminary did this well. The two female managers in his unit tended to remain quiet at team meetings. Instead of assuming that he knew why, he talked with them individually. One, a newer member of the team, indicated her preference to get to know the others better before she participated more. The other woman was deeply frustrated because she "couldn't get a word in edgewise," while the men seemed to interrupt one another, tussling for airtime.

One of the most effective ways to individualize your leadership is to gather direct feedback from individuals. On the one hand, this manager knew that some women found it difficult to contribute in meetings, when the men appeared to verbally compete for control. On the other hand, he didn't want to assume the women would respond identically because they were women. So he supported the first woman, as she made her own decisions about participating. And to help the second, he facilitated a more inclusive communication style among team members. Everyone benefited.

Each person you serve is *Like No Other*. Keep these tips in mind:

- Monitor your stereotyping, in which you see an individual as the personification of a group ("They're all like that, and she's one of them, so she's like that."), and miss their uniqueness.

- Take stock of your biases, in which you (often unconsciously) judge a difference as bad. Such bias limits your capacity to connect with people as unique contributors. A small and subtle example: one time a white male manager expressed to me his severe discomfort with the dreadlocks worn by a black man reporting to him. You limit your success by permitting such reactions to restrain relationships.

- Factor appropriate cultural information into your account of an individual. When we learn how a black colleague is shaped by black culture, it gives context to our rapport. Check out essay 30, on due regard. It's a sweet method for individualizing.

- Start with the mirror. Some of the traits that identify you as *you*—that is, your individuality—are readily observable. Other attributes stay behind the "seens," invisible. Understanding others requires understanding yourself. Schedule time to think through your own story around each dimension of diversity.

Manage differences to individualize, rather than divide. Does the very act of spelling out our differences separate us rather than unite us? It won't if we are clear about why we focus on similarities and differences. As managers we need to

- *focus on similarities*—not to influence others to become like us, but rather to build mutual trust and common commitment;

- *focus on differences*—not to divide, fragment, or reinforce bias, but rather to give due regard to the individual traits that shape our colleagues and customers.

Managing differences and similarities is a powerful method for recognizing individuality. You do this because each person deserves such respect, and because it will evoke their best contribution to the team's results. In so doing you also distinguish yourself—you demonstrate your own unique excellence as an effective leader.

> *Each one of us is:*
> *Like All Others*
> *Like Some Others, and*
> *Like No Other.*

Here's the chief utility of the Fundamental Filter: these phrases are tools we can use to view each person we encounter with a consistent approach. The saying helps us evaluate alikeness and difference with intelligence and positive expectation. And *that* is one highly effective antidote for racism, sexism, and every other "ism" that degrades a difference into a fight.

Use these three filtering ideas to identify and treasure similarities, clarify what's cultural, and turn loose the contribution of uniqueness.

CONVERSATION STARTER: *What is it about you, precisely, that makes you unique? What is unique about each person you lead?*

CORE IDEAS

■ 6 ■

Build

Your Diversity Point of View.

Establish your **Diversity Point of View** by applying the three levels of the Fundamental Filter to the twenty dimensions of diversity. Okay, if you understood that sentence, you've been paying attention to the previous essays.

Log onto www.leadershipforwhitemen.com, select Diversity Point of View (DPOV), and download My DPOV. You'll build your own journal, similar to the format you see here.

To establish your Diversity Point of View, each dimension of diversity is considered from four angles:

1) How do I describe me?

2) What do I believe/observe to be true about all people? (Like All Others)

26

3)   What do I see to be generally true about people with whom I share this dimension? (Like Some Others)

4)   How am I unique among people I am like? (Like No Other)

Quiet reflection is a learning style often appreciated among white men. So use this tool to assess where you personally stand with each dimension of diversity, or at least with the differences that interest you the most.

Build your DPOV from the inside out. Answer the four questions based on what you observe and believe. And don't shortchange your self-assessment work by moving to action prematurely. Finish your deep-thinking foundation first.

Here's my DPOV on race, ethnicity, gender, and the occupation of leadership.

RACE: SKIN COLOR AND OTHER PHYSICAL TRAITS THAT INFLUENCE COMPLEX SOCIAL MEANINGS AND PRACTICAL KNOWLEDGE.

How do I describe my racial makeup?

I'm just about as white as they come. To my knowledge, three fourths of my ancestors hailed from Britain, and one quarter came from Germany.

How are all people influenced by their racial traits and experience?

Race seems to matter when another race is present, and when there is an interracial difference in power. So it matters that people of other races see me as white. Race-related traits and experiences serve all people as markers of difference.

What words generally describe people who share my racial background?

> With regard to white people, the word "pre-aware" comes to mind
> (see essay 17). We don't expend many calories learning about
> our whiteness. I also generally experience white people as hard
> working, friendly, family oriented, future focused, and calm.

In what ways am I unique/unusual among people of my racial makeup?

> I explore for myself what being white means, I seek to learn about
> the people of other races, and I'm always ready to engage my own
> kind in considering what it means to be white.

ETHNICITY: A CULTURAL GROUP OF WHICH YOU ARE A PART, WHICH MAY BE DISTINGUISHED BY SUCH COMMON TRAITS AS FAMILY, GEOGRAPHY, APPEARANCE, DEMEANOR, LANGUAGE, RACE, RELIGION, AND ECONOMY (SEE ESSAY 27).

How do I describe my ethnicity?

> If I have to hyphenate myself, I'm European-American. But my
> earliest ancestors arrived in North America in the 1630s, and the
> most recent came in the 1850s. So, while my tribal DNA is white and
> European, and while I understand that *American* is my nationality,
> American also seems to describe my ethnicity more accurately.

How are all people influenced by their ethnicity?

> This mix of traits is a powerful aspect of our self-identity. Ethnicity
> = tribe, and the "Like Some Others" experience is critical to our
> sense of belonging in the world. It's about being connected by
> likeness. Ethnicity is a key category for social comfort.

What words generally describe people similar to me ethnically?

> I would describe European-Americans and Americans as informal, committed, pioneering, helpful, and insular.

In what ways am I unique/unusual among people who share my ethnicity?

> I'm louder than most white Americans, I think more (sometimes too much), and I focus on values more and money less.

GENDER: BEING FEMALE OR MALE, WITH THE ACCOMPANYING PHYSICAL AND SOCIAL EXPERIENCES.

What gender am I, and what does that mean to me?

> I am a man, and to me that means trying to live in a manner that demonstrates my commitment to *integrity* (a courageous congruence between who I want to be and how I act) and *intimacy* (the disciplined focus on connectedness in relationships).

How are all people influenced by their gender?

> For me, gender is the most critical dimension of diversity, the core biological and social fact of life from birth to death. We find both identity and limitation in the attributes society defines as masculine and feminine.

What words generally describe people of my gender?

> I experience men as people who are focused on getting things done, physically active, not as quick with words as women, prone to a teasing sort of humor, and often not fluent with their emotions.

In what ways am I unique/unusual among people of my gender?

> I was once called an "honorary woman" because I like to talk, and
> I tune into emotion (my own and others) more than many men.
> I think they meant it as a compliment; I had mixed feelings.

OCCUPATION: YOUR FIELD(S) OF KNOWLEDGE AND EFFORT, AND YOUR PROFESSIONAL ROLE.

How do I describe my occupational commitment?

> I am a leader. For years I have worked to define **leadership** in ten
> words or less. My current definition of the occupation: achieving
> results by developing people though work.

How are all people influenced by their occupation?

> I believe work is an opportunity from God; the chance to exercise
> our gifts, pursue our interests, and earn our way in the world.
> That being said, millions of people do not enjoy meaningful or
> gainful occupations. Every human's choices are influenced by
> how much they earn.

What words generally describe people who share my occupation?

> I often experience leaders as smart, committed, results focused,
> time conscious, caring, irritatingly shortsighted, with weaknesses
> skewered masterfully in Dilbert cartoons.

*In what ways am I unique/unusual among people whose occupation is similar
to mine?*

I am less patient, more likely to laugh, more focused on people, better at the big picture and how to get there, worse at detailed follow-though, and less technically proficient.

To lead with diversity in mind, you actually need to have diversity in your mind. Your Diversity Point of View is a private tool that helps you clarify what you believe, what you have experienced and still need to explore, and what you do and don't want from diversity.

CONVERSATION STARTER: *When will you devote time to journaling on your Diversity Point of View, and who will you discuss your DPOV with?*

Learn to articulate
the business case for diversity.

ax DePree, the retired CEO of Herman Miller, Inc., author of *Leadership is an Art*, and white himself, tells a story of being invited into a large organization to speak to the senior management team about leadership. When all the executives had arrived in the boardroom, the company's CEO nodded to Max to let him know it was time to begin his presentation. Max ignored the gesture. Several silent and awkward moments passed, and still Max paid no attention to the CEO's attempts to urge Max to start. Finally the frustrated CEO walked over to Max, bent down, and whispered, "Mr. DePree, everyone is here. We're ready to begin." Max replied, "No, we're not ready; not everyone is here. There are no women and no people of color around this table. No, not everyone is here; we are not ready to begin." Max then introduced them to the imperative to create a diverse workforce and leadership throughout the organization.

We must see the business necessity of diversity clearly, like Max, so that we can explain it and persuade "our own kind." Here's why: without our partnership, colleagues of color and women have been making the most cogent, data-based, results-driven arguments for diversity, yet receiving less than a full hearing. There are two explanations for this. First, white male executives may dismiss the factual business case for diversity as simple self-interest coming from those making the argument. Second, white male decision makers may wonder if diversity will advantage women and people of color over them or their sons.

We are the antidote to this resistance, when we join our diverse colleagues in actively articulating the business benefits of working with diverse employees and customers.

The business case for diversity can be distilled into five business trends and seven business motives.

Business Trends

- *Demographics:* In our most populous state, California, there is now no ethnic majority, and that will be true nationally before 2050. Population change is destiny, and every passing year will bring competitive advantage to organizations that invest in reaching the diverse customer base and labor force.
- *Education:* Today, America struggles to prepare students to compete in the global marketplace. Diversity issues include overcoming multilingual challenges, educating both boys and girls effectively,

addressing economic and quality disparities among public schools, and ensuring access to/affordability of higher education.

- *Opportunity:* Legal protections and public policies (e.g., equal opportunity and affirmative action), and corporate practices such as strengthening relationships with women- and minority-owned vendors, seek to ensure advancement and economic opportunity for increasingly diverse employees and business partners.

- *Participation and economic clout among American women*: In 1975, women composed twenty-three percent of all managers in America, and today that figure is thirty-seven percent. Women make eighty-three percent of the buying decisions and collectively control more than $5 trillion in economic activity. Women-owned businesses employ more people than all the Fortune 500 firms combined. American business now devotes more attention to women's growing participation and economic clout.

- *Globalization:* American business generally understands its stake in working successfully with differences in culture, language, and nationality. But the power and pace of worldwide economic change transcends these dimensions of diversity. As Thomas Friedman argues in *The World Is Flat*, technology is reformulating how individuals and their organizations work and succeed across the planet.

BUSINESS MOTIVES

- *Compete in the diverse marketplace:* Organizations now segment markets by gender, age, location (urban, suburban), race, language, and other dimensions of diversity. They seek to understand and tap into the buying power of their customers' cultures.

- *Select, grow, and retain a diverse workforce:* There is now a pitched battle for talent—finding, developing, and keeping the diverse employees needed to reach diverse customers. The research shows that good pay and great benefits aren't enough. Employers seek to build an environment where all people have the chance to do what they do best, every day.

- *Improve processes:* Excellence in managing diversity strengthens key business behaviors in communication, decision making, conflict resolution, continuous improvement, and customer service. When inclusion is used effectively as a strategy, diverse stakeholders innovate and solve business problems faster and better, and at lower cost.

- *Leverage team results:* Diverse teams produce better results. Companies like Apple, HP, and 3M build innovative capability by seeking to employ more women and people of color. Heterogeneous groups, with shared goals and values, can avoid groupthink and deliver superior products and services.

- *Strengthen relations with suppliers, community, government, media, and labor:* Many companies now relate to external stakeholders with an intentional approach to diversity. As a consequence, they improve revenue and reputation, decrease costs, and manage risk, through profitable vendor contracting, enhanced community connections, a constructive engagement with regulators, a positive relationship with the media, and favorable labor relations. And all these benefits help them find diverse candidates for open jobs and secure new customers.

- *Succeed internationally:* A proactive engagement with diversity is critical to personal and competitive success in a marketplace burgeoning across the nations of the earth, by language, cultural characteristics, and other aspects of diversity. Another advantage: multicultural skills also help organizations reach people of the world who come to the United States.

- *Avoid litigation*: Handling human differences competently helps to prevent what every white male manager fears: claims of discrimination based on gender or race, or violations of other protections such as reasonable accommodation. Avoiding diversity-related lawsuits is a worthy goal; just ask any leader who has been sucked into such a fight. But when litigation avoidance serves as the primary objective of a commitment to diversity, the organization squanders the value that diverse colleagues and customers offer.

For more detailed information on these trends and motives, see essays 74 and 75 on the underpinnings of the diversity imperative.

If we do not help our colleagues establish a compelling business case for diversity, other white male managers will tend to tolerate, ignore, or resist diversity's contribution, putting themselves and our organizations at risk.

CONVERSATION STARTER: *Specifically, what is the business case for diversity in your organization?*

Seize

the sustainable collaborative advantage.

WHAT'S IN DIVERSITY FOR ME?

When diversity is for us, we're for it. When diversity lines up against us, we avoid being the nail sticking up, so we don't get pounded. It may be painfully obvious to you how diversity is against you as a white man who leads: always on the verge of getting blamed for history's injustice, concerned about giving corrective feedback to a person of color, discouraged about competing for a job for which a white man may not be preferred.

Beyond the blame and shame game, what's in diversity for you? Why should you develop the competence to manage diversity? The bottom line is simple: **sustainable collaborative advantage**. Consider the many tangible benefits that accrue to the white male manager who invests in developing his diversity competencies.

As you work more effectively with diverse people, you will:

- Correct the performance of diverse employees with confidence, instead of withholding your feedback for fear of putting them off.

- Communicate respectfully with all employees, producing the impact you intend.

- Delegate more appropriately to develop your people.

- Deepen your insight and hone your skills to win, grow, and keep diverse customers in global markets.

- Motivate higher productivity, creativity, quality, and continuous improvement from your diverse team.

- Resolve conflicts before they escalate.

- Relax and enjoy people as individuals, rather than suffer under stifling, make-nice censorship. Are you tired of walking on eggshells around certain people, unclear about how to avoid offending them by what you say or do?

- Decrease your risk of harassment or discrimination claims.

- Gain appointment to teams and assignments that would benefit from a white male manager who "gets it."

- Multiply your diversity learning by living it out with your family and friends. Help the next generation learn to handle human differences; it will be important to their success. And your community needs more people with the capacity to build a society that works for all citizens.

- Understand yourself better, and lead with boldness and humility. Learn to lead from the inside out, grounded in your character and values.

- Show your boss that you're smart and talented enough to get with the diversity program. Such an ability to work successfully with human differences will factor into outstanding performance reviews and better compensation.

- Build a reputation as a promotable leader in a company that takes diversity among employees and customers seriously. The honest truth? Such a reputation will give you an advantage over the many white male managers who still ignore or resist diversity.

There are too many rewards from managing diversity to tolerate the blame and shame game. Use this book to make diversity work for you.

SELF-INTEREST AS MOTIVATION

Diversity is "the right thing to do" when it is the right thing to do for you. When you experience the benefits of working with diverse people, you seek more. Self-interest is a powerful motivator. It is the means by which a collaborative advantage becomes sustainable. That we will pursue our own self-interest is as certain as the increase in health care costs.

Of course, the self-interest in diversity for white men who lead is not self-evident. When diversity seems to exclude you, you will not support it with enthusiasm. People do not thrive by participating in behaviors that threaten or neglect them. This is a central tenet of diversity work, and it applies to white men and others alike.

The **self-interest in diversity** may be defined as a healthy attention to your own motivations and needs, as you work with diverse people. In this context, self-interest is not a selfishness that calculates every action only in terms of personal benefit. Instead, mature self-interested managers coordinate a variety of interests: helping colleagues and subordinates succeed, meeting performance objectives, satisfying the customer, pursuing the financial success of the department and company, all while still finding time for family and the rest of life. Some self-interests mesh, while others compete. You may have to choose, for example, between allowing a diverse team the time it needs to accomplish work as delegated, or getting more involved than you would prefer in order to meet a deadline.

Coworkers (whether boss, peers, or employees) bring their own interests to each meeting, hallway chat, phone call, golf round, and email. Again, the interests of team members may dovetail or collide. Manage effectively by operating with a clear sense of what *you* need and want, in order to negotiate successfully with similarly self-interested colleagues.

Increasingly, colleagues and customers differ from you in pigment, gender, relational orientation and attraction, physical ability, and spoken language. This diverse business environment requires every manager to negotiate among competing self-interests shaped by all the dimensions of diversity.

Here's the proof that self-interest is a useful dynamic to manage: every employee is a unit of one, whom you must lead individually. So you have to lead in a way that works for you, too.

You will work successfully with black colleagues and customers only if you develop your tangible self-interest in doing so.

CONVERSATION STARTER: *Specifically, what's in it for you to build your competence at leading among diverse employees and customers?*

Commit

to personal response-ability.

hen I was thirteen, I attended a racial reconciliation workshop at Blaine Memorial United Methodist Church in Seattle. This was 1967, and interracial conflict was burning its way across America. I have always remembered what Reverend Woodie White (a black pastor and now a retired bishop) taught me.

- Black people resent being viewed as a "problem," when white people are often the main problem black folks have.
- Since being black in America is hard enough, many black people tire of the expectation that they should teach white folks about race.

- White people must learn how to accept responsibility for being white.

Let me be clear: the point is not to label you as a "white man who leads." A manager once scoffed to me: "I've just been hyphenated—now I'm a European-American!" This book does not pander to racial politics or set you up for another round of the blame game.

Instead, I hope you're reading this book because you want to accept personal responsibility and whatever comes with it—the good and the painful—in twenty-first-century America. As a white man who leads, investing in diversity will deliver positive returns.

I implore you to accept this challenge as your own: lead as the best white man you can be. Fuel your professional success with personal development, hold yourself accountable in a way no one else can, and remove from black people the burden of teaching you about race. Educate yourself. Renew the courage of your convictions by speaking up as a white man who leads.

We also pursue a critical social responsibility when we learn about our whiteness. White supremacists (and black leaders if they stereotype white people) must be overruled as the arbiters of what it means to be a white American. Since whiteness is our nation's historic racial norm, as white people we are much less likely to see how our skin color shapes our life experience. But we must not simply acquiesce to the dangerous oddballs of the Klan and their ilk. The crazy cousins shouldn't be allowed to speak for the family. It is mortifying that white racists earn media coverage with their spew and misbehavior, while white America's commitment to equality quietly putters along. We need to speak up. Dr. Martin Luther King Jr. said: "Our lives begin to end the day we become silent about things that matter."

The heart of personal responsibility is owning who we are as a person. For years I wondered why our whiteness, so utterly visible (the epidermis, after all, is the body's most visible feature) and so obviously an advantage to us, has remained so habitually unexamined. Why do we hide from our whiteness?

We hide from our whiteness because it hurts to pull it out, let the sun shine on it, and claim it as our own. We avoid the chance to learn about our racial selves and connect our identity to our race, because whiteness is inescapably, publicly, and frequently linked to blame, shame, guilt, fear, and ignorance.

We hide from our whiteness because an inquiry into our racial selves can feel irrelevant. When two out of three Americans are white, it's the others who are set apart.

We hide from our whiteness because our silence keeps the whole set-up working. As it turns out, the profound benefits of being white best accrue and are retained by not identifying them out loud. (I'm blowing our cover here.) There's an unspoken yet powerful "us versus everyone else" presumption among us white folks. We can see it in the unmentioned but utterly tangible impulse to whine about so-called political correctness and reverse discrimination. It is easier to ignore, deny, neglect, and generally resist the whole reality of racism's impact, on us and everyone else.

We hide from our whiteness because we intuitively fear that an unflinchingly honest attempt to understand our race could unravel the entire Advantage Complex (see essays 23–26). This is our racial ecology, with its "natural" features of merit, achievement, preference, privilege, and power. Being a white man in a leadership role works pretty well, in America and globally; from the time we were boys, many of us have taken our advantages for granted. We believe in enjoying life because we are used to doing so, we deserve to, and we've earned it through our accomplishments. This is not about blame; in fact, I believe our Creator wants every person to enjoy life. It *is* about becoming aware of the advantage that comes with being a man who wears white skin. It is simply easier to hide from our whiteness than it is to courageously discover how whiteness provides advantages psychologically, economically, educationally, and socially.

Taking responsibility for being a white man won't be easy. But it will be good—for us and for our black colleagues and customers.

CONVERSATION STARTER: *If your manager was watching for evidence that you are personally responsible for leading with diversity in mind, what behavior from you would demonstrate such a commitment?*

Own
your whiteness.

ON BEING WHITE

F or the purposes of this book, consider yourself white if you are Caucasian with European ancestry (even if you know your pedigree is mixed). Under the white umbrella, of course, we are ethnically diverse: English, German, Irish, Italian, French, Jewish, Scandinavian, and so on. In *Whiteness of a Different Color: European Immigrants and the Alchemy of Race*, Matthew Jacobson plots the experience of European immigrants, as America transformed some of our ancestors from lower-class non-Anglo to white Caucasian through the "alchemy of race."

Whiteness in America counts. Race (and racism) is primarily about three things:

1) The pigment of skin, and other physical features.

2) The meanings that you, other people, and history attach to such features.

3) The behaviors that demonstrate these meanings.

Beyond skin color as an immutable trait, the meaning of race is endlessly debated by physicians, sociologists, political scientists, psychologists, and diversity professionals. Take the following, for example:

- *Is race a social construct rather than a physical fact?* In an article in the *Annals of Internal Medicine*, Ritchie Witzig, MD, argued that race is not a medically significant category, but rather a social construct that affects health care decisions. Yet other medical professionals point to illnesses suffered disproportionately by black patients.

- *What is the precise relationship between race, ethnicity, and nationality?* A friend and colleague, organizational psychologist Claudia White, PhD, was born and raised in Jamaica, and pursued higher education and now lives in California. Her skin is black, and she hails from an island nation that is part of the Americas, but she does not consider herself culturally African-American.

- *To what degree does race influence personality?* Suzanne Shelton, PhD (my wife and a clinical psychologist), believes that personality is the sum of all twenty dimensions of diversity (with race as one factor), combined with our brain organics and our Creator's good intentions for our lives.

- *How do economic values drive our race related ideas and actions?* Slavery in America was a system grounded in the economic exploitation of people with black skin. It was raw capitalism, designed, funded, and led by white men. One hundred and forty years after the Civil War, history's impact lingers. Many black people still struggle with substandard education and health care, suffer from higher rates of unemployment and incarceration, and experience lower rates of home ownership, savings, and investment. Want to quantify the value of our whiteness? Read *The Color of Wealth*, by writers from United for a Fair Economy. Chapter six details white advantage in wealth accumulation, contrasted with chapter three, entitled "Forged in Blood: Black Wealth Injustice in the United States."

No single book can answer our all our questions about race. To guide further inquiry, see the Resources section and www.leadershipforwhitemen.com.

For now, let us stipulate that race involves a host of issues. Here we seek to equip white men who lead to focus on the personal and behavioral aspects of race.

While we learn to lead with race and gender in mind, we do well to learn from black people as they sort through lessons around race. Many black people have to work harder than they want to at "being black," because the world seems organized to take their skin color into account.

Yet as we learn more with them and about them, our most important lessons will be about ourselves. When white Americans step up and pursue a new degree of personal responsibility for being white, I suspect that the burden of racial attentiveness will begin to lift from our black colleagues and customers.

Explore this key fact in your life: vital meaning ensues from the whiteness of your skin. For example, your whiteness shapes your opportunities in education and employment, and influences some black people to doubt your ability to grasp diversity issues. Exploring your self-evident racial identity ("So what if I am white?") will produce powerful returns in your personal life and leadership.

And when you hear the phrase "it's nothing personal; it's just business," don't believe it. Business is personal because humans are involved. I invite you to take personally the business of succeeding as a white man who leads.

CONVERSATION STARTER: *What does being white mean in your life?*

Decide what it means

to be a good and connective man.

For many men, what it means to be a man is defined in contrast to perceptions of who women are: "Women are emotional, I'm analytical." "Women are relational, I'm action oriented." "Women are collaborative, I'm decisive." And so on.

Such thinking is doubly mistaken—men are more than the absence or antithesis of the feminine. Such gender-alizations confine men and women in stereotypical traits and rigid roles. Define your masculinity positively, and take personal responsibility for leading as a man of honesty and integrity.

How do men define men? Here are typical descriptors generated by white men in my training courses over the years. When asked to generally describe men, they say that men

- work long and hard to protect and provide for their families;
- care about giving and receiving respect;
- solve problems well;
- can get so caught up in work and achievement that they lose sight of their relationships;
- teach their children and others about courage and risk taking;
- like to learn how to make things work;
- build trust by making and keeping promises;
- enjoy food, sports, sex, and laughing (not necessarily in that order);
- find change stressful;
- are shaped by their physical, mental, and spiritual health;
- may feel threatened by people who are "different."

Granted, the phrases above also describe many women, and not all men. And the list does not emphasize all-too-common caricatures of men (greedy, emotionally stunted, clueless), because we are already fed that demeaning diet. Washington Mutual recently ran a series of ads skewering a herd of stodgy white male bankers; WaMu's investment in inclusion should produce a higher rate of return.

Here's the point: you need to define your own masculinity. Women in your life may tell you what to think, how to be, who to be. (I'm not sure why they do this; they seem to feel we need a lot of help.) Advertisers and pundits are more than ready to portray masculinity with a negative twist. You need to understand on your own terms what it means to be a good and connective man. You are the boss of you, and only you can generate your own clear purposes as a man.

My personal take on being and leading as a "real man" involves two key practices: **integrity** and **intimacy**. *Integrity* is the congruence between who I want to be and how I act, it's about making and keeping promises, giving and receiving respect, leading with courage and following with honor, getting clear on and staying true to my values, speaking the hard truths constructively, pursuing accountability, living with spiritual discipline, seeking wholeness and balance. *Intimacy* is about focusing on connectedness in relationships, living in a spirit of play, owning my part of being in love, nurturing safety and touch, adventuring and laughing, listening and responding, working through conflict with confidence, looking for creative opportunity, expecting growth. Women and men of all races tend to reciprocate when I show up as a man of integrity and intimacy.

Kevin Costner, the director and actor, leads with a clear view about what it means to be a good and connective man. Find the DVD of his film *Open Range*. The movie portrays integrity and honor, respect and intimacy among men and women under stress. His commentary as the director profoundly illustrates how he led the project from the inside out.

Another thing I know: black women can be great teachers. I remember walking into work with Brenda Salter-McNeil, a black colleague (yes, the Brenda in essay 3) at a client's office in Colorado Springs. Normally the door was opened by the one coming to it first. However, each morning at this project, Brenda waited for me to open the door to the building, even if she got there first and I was carrying more. It seemed odd, but I dutifully pulled it open. Later I asked her about it. She smiled at me for noticing and then explained that she was practicing the discipline of receiving respect from men. She went on to explain that there were instances of young men disrespecting women in the black community, and she was in the position of advising both women and men about expectations around respect. So she was practicing receiving respect from me in the form of door-opening, to prepare for leading elsewhere. And I thought it was just a door to go through!

Brenda helped me learn more about being a man. A good and effective man stays teachable while he defines his own masculinity.

And one more thing: as white men, Diversity 'R' Us. Here's a multiple-choice quiz question: *Put twenty white guys who lead in a room together, and what do you have?*

1) Four golfers, four video game guys, three runners, a b-ball player, a swimmer, a tennis wannabe, and six who think the rest of us get too much exercise.

2) Too many opinions and a lot of interrupting.

3) A striking assortment of hair loss, sore muscles, fashion blunders, and bad jokes.

4) A power struggle.

5) Twenty utterly unique individuals.

Answer: #5, yes   #1–4, maybe

A battalion of white men in business suits features awesomely diverse characters.

One purpose for this book is to help you, a man *Like No Other*, to leverage diversity so that you will get better at what you do, and be better at who you are.

CONVERSATION STARTER: *What does it mean to you to be a "real man," and how does your gender influence your leadership?*

CORE IDEAS
■ 12 ■

Consciously and appropriately
integrate race and gender into your leadership work.

I n the previous essays, I've been speaking about race and gender challenges. Now let's move on to the other main topic of this book: the work of leadership. My definition of a **leader** is a person who achieves results by developing people through work.

I use *leader* and *manager* interchangeably. Don't make too much of distinctions between "leaders do the right thing" and "managers do things right," A *leader* can emphasize strategy, values, and vision, and attend to high-level external relationships, and he will still fail if he neglects execution. Over time, a *manager* can only succeed with the team he guides when their day-to-day performance actualizes the company's values, vision, and strategy. So this book equips you as a white man to factor human differences (like race and gender) into the way you lead and manage.

Here are a few examples of such leadership:

- A department VP leads when, after helping to design a talent management strategy, he requires candidate searches to produce diverse and qualified candidates. Then he holds fast to the company's practice of hiring or promoting the right candidate, even when that means selecting a white male over a white woman or person of color.

- The middle manager leads by finding new ways to mentor and coach all high-potential personnel, when his previous tendency to discuss and attend sporting events with up-and-comers excluded women.

- The front line supervisor leads when he hires bilingual staff members and secures training in retail Spanish for his English-only staff, in response to an influx of customers who speak more Spanish than English, and who can shop at the competitor's store down the street.

- The CFO leads when, with diligence and courage, he directs a process that determines that the company can afford to extend benefits to same-sex and unmarried straight partners.

For the effective twenty-first-century leader, diversity requires a three-skill daily discipline.

- *Give human differences their due regard.* Attend to diversity appropriately in each situation, respecting each individual. The practice of due regard positions you to lead in a way that accounts for what's actually going on with diversity, while avoiding the two extremes of ignoring differences (without regard) or exaggerating differences (with excessive regard). For more on this key practice, see essay 30.

- *Collaborate.* **Collaboration** means to co-labor, to achieve business results with your colleagues, for your customers. Here's what collaboration looks like. As a diversity consultant, I was brought into a public agency to work with the senior leadership team on race-related dynamics. The initial scope of work focused on black versus white issues among the executives, but quickly steered off in an unexpected direction. As it turned out, a crucial conversation that had never occurred was between two African-American groups: the veteran black employees who had suffered from racism in the agency over the years, and the younger generation of black leaders who had experienced almost no racist behavior during their employ in the past five years. The collaboration needed to happen among these black employees, and I got to be the facilitator.

Picture my task: lead a productive dialogue among twenty black employees from two generations. There was plenty of diversity by experience between them, and they all had a lot to say! It was a memorable day of co-laboring for me. They did a fine job of airing their concerns, honoring one another's perspectives, and arguing honestly. And they made plans to build a new black network to help the organization move ahead and enhance their career opportunities.

The good news about managing diversity is that it offers you the chance (sometimes unexpectedly) to collaborate effectively. Deepen and demonstrate the leadership skills you already possess—the work of planning, organizing, leading, and accountability—with people you perceive as different.

When your co-laboring skills become habitual over time, you will sustain the professional advantages in diversity. Two truths will grow more relevant in every passing year of your professional life: collaborate with people and move ahead, or seek to control them and risk your career.

Leverage the dimensions of diversity among colleagues and customers to achieve business results. The LEAD section (beginning with essay 74) focuses entirely on this leverage.

CONVERSATION STARTER: *How can you integrate your growing diversity competence into the way you collaborate with employees, peers, and clients?*

Deepen the particular participation of white men who lead:
diversity work that adds measurable value.

O nce the personal and professional case for diversity is established, another critical issue arises for the organization: diversity as a business strategy must make business sense. To survive as a company strategy, it must add value. And diversity must deliver to sustain commitment among us as white men who lead. Why? Because, to generalize, we are wired for results.

Perhaps we will admit that many of us, as white male leaders, tend to focus on action over contemplation, task over relationship, results over process. So we grow as leaders when we join our diverse colleagues in thinking longer and clearer, investing more in our relationships, and recognizing that inclusive process produces superior results.

But while we improve on our shortcomings, we should also insist that our strengths continue to contribute. As white men who lead, we are people who excel at getting things done. Embedded in our inclinations toward action, task, and result is the accountability for delivering on promises that our organizations make to our customers and employees. Diversity must add demonstrable value to the work and results of the organization. Otherwise, we rightfully view it as a narrow concern with limited utility.

Many corporate diversity initiatives during the last twenty years have not effectively included white male managers (see Frederick R. Lynch's book, *The Diversity Machine: The Drive to Change the "White Male" Workplace*). Such exclusion communicated a shortfall of integrity—a gospel of inclusion that left us out. Worse, excluding white men prevented us from contributing what we could best invest in the diversity commitment: holding diversity accountable for adding practical and measurable value to the work and results of the company.

This is not to say that, as a group, white male managers are as excluded as women and people of color. That would be a lie, and a perverse twist of the exclusionary practices inherited from our white male forefathers. I merely highlight a simple fact: a diversity commitment that excludes the contribution of white male managers will fail, for lack of integrity, support, and value.

As white men who lead, we need to participate in diversity's success, as individuals and as a group skilled at leading for measurable results.

What diversity metrics matter? For a start, there are discrete and critical measures that correspond to each of the seven business motives for diversity in essay 75 (e.g., targeting and securing diverse customers, selecting and growing diverse talent, expanding internationally). White men who lead must insist on, develop, and leverage diversity-related performance objectives (see essay 76). And we need to lead by calculating diversity's return on investment (the ROI; see essay 98).

A CEO in a Chicago financial services company refused to develop any business metrics for his firm's engagement with diversity. Instead, he announced: "We pursue diversity because it is right—not because it will pay (although it may), not because the law requires it (although we will comply), not because it is trendy, but only because valuing differences is morally correct." While I applaud his ethical inclination, five years later his commitment to diversity produced positive media attention, but very little in measurable business value for employees and customers. When diversity does not serve the interests of the organization to win and retain employees and customers, a critical competitive advantage has been squandered.

Diversity: get it right, now. "It" isn't fancy footwork on "afraid you might offend" thin ice. You won't get it right by lining up behind diversity as a Human Resources fad du jour. Engage diversity as a vital leadership strategy for working with black colleagues and customers, and with every other stakeholder to your success.

CONVERSATION STARTER: *What measurable results must be produced in order for diversity to add value to your company? How will you help to develop and use these metrics?*

Start

When I watch the start of the men's 100-meter race at the Summer Olympics, I'm always struck by the final preparations of the runners. Before entering the blocks, each one has his own method for getting ready: stretching his muscles, jumping in short leaps, glaring at his opponents, visualizing how he will explode off the gun, going inward for focus.

These world-class athletes don't just crouch and take off. They have trained for this moment, and they persevere with the fundamentals right up to the start.

Leading as a white man is more like a marathon than a sprint, but the readiness principle is the same. In this section, we will consider several preparatory concepts that will launch your success as a leader on diversity.

First, we'll dig into two key issues standing between white and black people: the power of pigment, and divergent views of our shared American story. Second, we'll shape expectations for your diversity learning, and plunge into awareness. Finally, we'll clarify the difference between generalizations and stereotypes.

With these six essential essays as a tailwind, you'll hit the ground running, in service to black colleagues and customers.

■ **14** ■

Explore

the pigment paradigm.

To honor Dr. Martin Luther King Jr., my daughter Melinda's third grade class sang "We Shall Overcome" for the gathered parents. I'm a child of the '60s, and seeing my innocent and precious little girl singing that song made my eyes water (God help me ... I couldn't actually cry in public!). What particularly touched me was Melinda's question later in the day: "Why does everybody make such a big deal about the color of somebody's skin?" Why indeed?

So while grade school children ask that precisely right question, we as adults permit ourselves to "mature" like rotting fruit into accepting the notion that different = bad. Why *does* everyone make such a big deal about the color of someone's skin?

The talking heads on television answer with more heat than light. Here's my take: human cultures have used, and still use, differences in skin color and gender to order relationships, distribute resources, and regulate opportunity. Globally during the last five hundred years, white European men and their male descendants have participated in such order, distribution, and regulation to our advantage.

Pigment is paradigmatic: our white skin is powerfully advantageous to us, and we tend to live inside the pattern without seeing it. Meanwhile, society's basic bias presses people with black skin to the margins. Marking them by their melanin, our white culture assumes black people less capable, in order to keep them in their place in the social order. Racism self-perpetuates after four centuries in America, and between many tribes and nationalities through four millennia in human history. Even today, color remains an efficient force to order, distribute, and regulate, long after the ideology of white supremacy and its implementation in slavery has been discredited and discarded.

This pigment paradigm operates in our lives as a heritage from ancient days. There is so much momentum in our whiteness that we don't need to generate advantage ourselves. As white men who lead, we do not rise in the morning with the thought: "Today I think I'll dominate the earth, because, after all, I'm a white guy." It's not a conspiracy, it's an ecology. We're fish who don't know we're big and wet.

And, sadly, even when people of color denounce us as racists undeservedly, they reinforce the absurd power of pigment. The daily news chronicles this ceaseless back and forth across the color lines.

A person with black skin certainly recognizes that their pigment puts them at a disadvantage. *New York Times* journalist Lena Williams writes: "This society makes blacks think constantly about being black ... every now and then I imagine how wonderful it must be to go out in public looking any way one chooses and be treated and accepted as a first-class citizen." This is such a telling testimony to the price of the pigment paradigm, coming from a black professional who embodies, in her own achievements, how far America has come.

On our side of the black-white divide, the pigment paradigm offers us a very different cost/benefit ratio. Andrew Hacker writes in *Two Nations* that "all white Americans realize that their skin comprises an inestimable asset. It opens doors and facilitates freedom of movement. It serves as a shield from insult and harassment." And this asset of white skin is even more valuable for men who hold position power as leaders.

Yet the tide turns: this historical advantage accruing to white men is now eroding, as demographics change the workforce and marketplace. White men in leadership jobs compose only five percent of employed Americans; there is now no ethnic majority in California; and every American will be a "minority" before 2050. Our grandchildren's experience of the pigment paradigm will differ dramatically from our own.

But let's not travel too far into America's future, because we need to take a hard look back into the legacy of the pigment paradigm. As it turns out, diverging views of history are pivotal for the white man who seeks to lead more successfully among black colleagues and customers. That's what the next essay explores.

CONVERSATION STARTER: *Why does everyone make such a big deal about the color of somebody's skin?*

START

■ **15** ■

Close
the history rift.

B lack and white Americans tend to think about history differently. White men who lead for a living, in particular, need to understand this difference.

We white people know the stories of our family lines. We understand that much of what we enjoy today may be traced to the courage, choices, love, and hard work of our parents, grandparents, and other relatives back into the past, mostly in America and Europe. Our ancestors struggled mightily (almost all of my family, five and six generations back, came west on the Oregon Trail), and we stand on their shoulders.

While we deeply appreciate our heritage, we don't dwell on the past. We tend to order our identities and daily lives around individuality, our immediate family, and our expectations for the future.

But yesterday shadows today among black Americans. To be black in America—so I've been told—is to know every day that your skin color alone puts you at risk. It is to remember (at least in the back of your mind) that black people have paid that price since 1619, when people of Africa were enslaved and forced to these shores. For twenty ensuing generations, black American's courage, choices, love, and hard work shaped and produced the African-Americans we know today.

Consequently, black individuals identify with their "group" and their cultural history in a manner and to a degree that we as white people neither share nor comprehend.

There is a history rift between black and white Americans, and we need to do what we can to close it from our side. Consider a few historical examples after 1860 that put this gap in perspective:

- Many black citizens view the Civil War as a tragic but belated necessity, the promise of which has yet to be fulfilled, since white men are often *still* their problem. For white men who know Civil War history, it rankles if black people castigate all of us as a group, because we remember that 620,000 white men died in the struggle over slavery.

- Between 1882 and 1964, according to records kept by the Tuskegee Institute, white men lynched 3,445 black men. If you do the math, you will find that men who looked like us hanged three black men per month for eighty-two years running. My own family's contrasting path in the same timeline: my maternal grandmother was born in 1883, served as one of the first female teachers in Kittitas County, Washington, and raised a family with my pioneer-stock grandfather. By 1964, both *my* parents had graduated from college and lived in the suburbs with their three healthy children. Black men died, while my family thrived.

- White people may long for "the good old days." Black folks may view such nostalgia as a wish for a time when black people did as they were told. The history rift is alive in our midst: when U.S. senator Trent Lott offered a tribute to segregationist Strom Thurmond in 2002, he lost his Senate leadership role and received a public rebuke. Apparently the good old days weren't good for everyone.

- White America should be shocked about the level of agreement within the black community on the case for reparations for slavery. In a Gallup poll, fifty-five percent of blacks agreed that the government should provide a cash reparation for the ongoing effects of the slave system. Ninety percent of whites disagreed. Here are numbers to quantify the history rift!

When we mutually address our divergent views of our common story and our present situation, we will more effectively move to improve the quality of life among suffering black citizens. Here's one thing you can do: buy a copy of Manning Marable's *The Great Wells of Democracy*, and read chapter nine, entitled "Forty Acres and a Mule: The Case for Black Reparations." It will rock your view of history and teach you about the history rift we need to close.

I hope black Americans will accept the advice of Holocaust survivors: "forgive and remember." While black people do this hard, daily work of forgiving, what can we, as white men who lead, do from our side of the history rift? I've been trying these three things since 1987, and they seem to be working for me:

1) Acknowledge to myself that black people may expect me to be ignorant about history and arrogant about opportunity. If they do, I want to prove them wrong.

2) Learn about black history and how my own history has worked to my advantage. Share this learning with black and white colleagues and friends, as appropriate. This includes a disciplined refusal to grow defensive when accused of having ancestors who owned slaves. In my case and to my knowledge, that is not true. But I'm learning to see the history rift as the real point. The trump card implication that "your people owned my people" is about opportunity denied to black people and accrued by white people, and how we move forward.

3) I try to surprise African-Americans, if they expect ignorance and arrogance, by instead giving deference and welcome, validating their view of history and the limits it places on them today, acknowledging that I derive resources and advantage by hailing from a white family, looking them in the eye with respect and a hospitable attitude, and seeking mutual opportunity.

We can make very practical behavioral choices to begin closing the history rift. To actualize our national motto, *E Pluribus Unum* (Out of Many, One), we can explore and heal these divergent views of and experience with the American story.

CONVERSATION STARTER: *What can you do to understand and close the history rift between white and black Americans?*

■ 16 ■

Travel the Transformation Curve:

From Pre-Awareness to Relative Expertise.

L earning to lead with diversity in view is a daunting and exciting chance to grow transformatively. **Transformation** is dramatic growth in an individual or an organization's character and performance. Join me in traveling the Transformation Curve, the five stages for growing your competence with human differences. Each stage offers a new level of learning about how to lead through the dimensions of diversity.

This essay introduces the entire Transformation Curve. The first level, Pre-Awareness, is considered more fully in the next essay, and the other four stages are presented in essays 31—35.

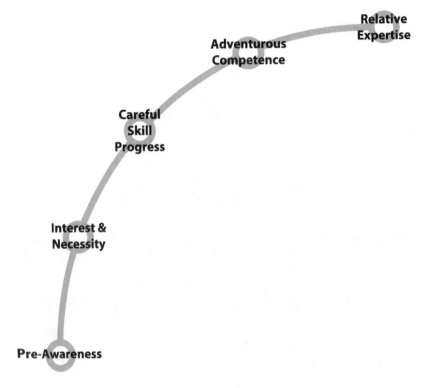

Figure 16

DEFINING THE FIVE STAGES

You progress through these stages in order. You can't skip one. And your learning curve is different for each dimension of diversity. For instance, you may have learned your way to Relative Expertise on gender, and still be pre-aware about race.

- *Pre-Awareness*: Ignorance and naivete operate freely here; "I don't know what I don't know." In this phase, you are not yet aware of diversity's significance to your leadership work. (See essay 17.)

- *Interest and Necessity*: Here's where engagement kicks in. Your values and circumstances compel you to deploy awareness, to recognize and understand individual and cultural differences and similarities among colleagues and customers. In this stage, you want to learn and you need to learn. (See essay 31.)

- *Careful Skill Progress*: At this stage, you experiment cautiously. Your expanding relationships, knowledge, and skills can get you into trouble, and can also get new things done. You evolve your leadership skills through an unpredictable mix of awkward attempts and confident skill building. (See essay 32.)

- *Adventurous Competence*: This is the point where your investment in leading among diverse colleagues and customers starts to show real results. You effectively diagnose differences at work, problem solve with sensitivity to diverse needs, and proactively manage multiple dimensions of diversity. (See essays 33–34.)

- *Relative Expertise*: You are recognized by diverse stakeholders as an expert, and you mentor others through the previous stages. "Relative" means you hold your expertise with humility; you lead across differences from your side, always remembering your limits so that you honor others' experience and evoke their contribution. (See essay 35.)

Within each of the five stages, there is a natural order for learning. There's a dynamism to this process, as we build relationships by increasing knowledge and skill. Here's the formula:

Relationships   When you explore differences with specific, diverse colleagues and customers ...

Knowledge	you are motivated to learn what you need to know, and ...
Skills	then you apply your knowledge to achieve results through your relationships.

Here's the point: your connection to real people drives your transformation. I am truly pleased that you are reading this book. And it's not enough. Learning about diversity without building skills in actual diverse relationships is like studying the operating manual for a car and then thinking you know how to drive. To lead with human differences in view, your knowledge and skills must grow among actual humans who differ from you.

To illustrate: a college asked me to debate a white male professor on the question, "Is affirmative action a justifiable and useful public policy?" The professor and I had a lively dispute about affirmative action's true impact and botched reputation (see essay 25 for my views). It became clear to me that while he was well versed in facts and arguments, he did not possess any of the nuanced compassion and honest data that accompanies actually knowing real people who have benefited from affirmative policies and practices. So I asked him, point blank, if he had ever talked directly to a black person (there at the college or anywhere else) who had gained opportunity through affirmative action. I suspect he knew I was preparing something devious with my question, because he paused. But he answered honestly; he had never spoken about affirmative action with one of its beneficiaries. My response: to advocate a public policy position, it is probably advisable to actually know the public as well as the policy.

Embed your growing competence with human differences in your merging relationships with "different" humans. They will prove to be invaluable partners as you move from ignorance to expertise along diversity's learning curve.

CONVERSATION STARTER: *With regard to race and gender differences, in which stage of the Transformation Curve are you?*

■ **17** ■

Transformation through Pre-Awareness:

Acknowledge that you don't know what you don't know.

The greatest of faults, I should say, is to be conscious of none.

THOMAS CARLYLE, SCOTTISH HISTORIAN

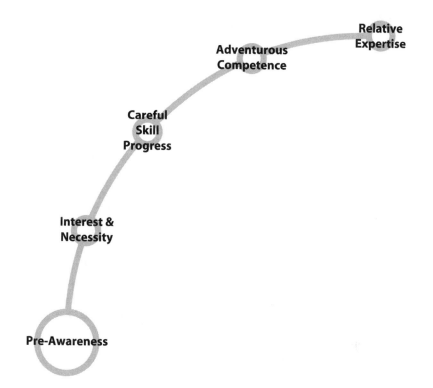

Figure 17

D o we actually have a problem if we're not aware of it? You bet. Sometimes our problem is that we don't know we have one.

Pre-Awareness, by definition, is the state of mind prior to awareness. I prefer the term Pre-Awareness to the ever-popular "clueless" as a descriptor of white men. It blames less and encourages more, by locating ignorance as a starting point for learning, rather than an unchangeable state. Pre-Awareness can lead you to *awareness*, defined as recognizing and understanding individual and cultural differences and similarities among your colleagues and customers.

Perhaps ignorance used to be bliss for white male leaders, but these days incomprehension can be the mother of much misery. What you don't know can hurt you bad. When you, as a manager, do not recognize and understand human differences at work, you may unintentionally

- offend, harass, or discriminate against others;
- lose excellent employees;
- hurt your team's results;
- drive away customers and suppliers.

The outcomes of Pre-Awareness can sting, and every manager is vulnerable. Here's a true example.

Lewis was the facilities manager in a growing hospital. To create a family-friendly setting, a committee he chaired renamed the four elevators Zebra, Orca, Eagle, and Lion. Unfortunately, Orca (as in whale) served the unit caring for obese patients and their families, who were deeply offended. Lewis's attempt to improve customer service backfired. Pre-Awareness strikes again.

Here are five warning signs that you may be suffering from Pre-Awareness of diversity-related issues:

- You are taken by surprise by some aspect of diversity, and mystified about what happened.
- The protest "I couldn't have known that!" leaps into your mind.
- You sense a strong impulse to defend some aspect of who you are (e.g., as a white person, a man, an American).
- You prefer to work with people who are like you (by race, gender, language, sexual orientation, age, and so on).
- You find yourself making off-the-record comments to other white men or your spouse, defending your actions or blaming diverse people.

Teachability is the only known solution to Pre-Awareness. When you are "ready, willing and able to learn diversity's lessons fast and well", the inevitable outcome is awareness (see the next essay). And awareness can lead to right action.

In receiving the anger of the hospital patients, Lewis suffered the sort of vard, pre-aware episode that bushwhacks many managers. Taken by a nasty surprise, he wondered "How could I have known?"

When your leadership falters, it is time for teachability, the chance to show that you can learn diversity's lessons fast and well. When you find yourself protesting—"But that's not what I meant!"—use the energy of the situation as motivation. Grow more aware of the needs and distinctives of the people you serve.

Watch for surprises. Scan for clues. They offer the chance to become aware of something you didn't know, so you can make a better decision next time. You might as well redeem the mortifying moment by showing your instructability.

In Lewis's situation, inclusion could have prevented the pain. The higher the stakes and visibility of the work at hand, the greater the need to include stakeholders. When you are making a decision (like naming an elevator) that is public, expensive, or hard to reverse, identify the people who will be affected by the decision, and then call a meeting, host a focus group, or send out a survey so you can

- explain the decision that needs to be made;
- ask for questions, comments, and ideas;
- ask if there's anything you need to know that you haven't considered;
- ask if there are others from whom you should seek input before you decide.

When you don't know what you don't know, talk with people who might know!

Our Pre-Awareness may originate from simple unfamiliarity. If so, we apologize, learn from our mistake, and make sure people see our teachability. But a more insidious aspect of Pre-Awareness is being willfully uninformed; we don't know what's going on because we've subconsciously expended some effort to make sure we ignored reality. I have observed in black Americans a growing willingness to interpret white male Pre-Awareness as purposeful. It has been more than forty years since landmark civil rights legislation, they note, so the "I just didn't know that!" defense about many racial matters just doesn't cut it.

For white men who lead, choosing to remain clueless about diversity may prove a career-threatening decision. Fortunately, we can instead pursue a simple strategy for human learning: acknowledge your Pre-Awareness, and awaken to awareness of diversity at work.

CONVERSATION STARTER: *Think of a time when you were caught pre-aware. What could you do to avoid future Pre-Awareness?*

■ **18** ■

Awaken

to awareness.

I know I'm often unaware—but at least I'm aware of my lack of awareness. ©

Ashleigh Brilliant

In the context of managing human differences, awareness is recognizing and understanding individual and cultural differences and similarities among your colleagues and customers.

The empathic awareness of human differences undermines ignorance, resistance, and denial. And awareness begets knowledge, understanding, and right action.

Moments of awareness may intrigue. For example, in 1984 I was directing a refugee resettlement program in California (I'm the gray-suited thirty-year-old right in the center of the team photo).

Figure 18

I remember learning how two of my employees, Channary and Vaneth, were such utterly different individuals, even though their similarities loomed large to me. Both were short in stature with dark skin, spoke the same native language (and my Khmer wasn't too strong), came from the same rice village, and survived the Cambodian nightmare concurrently. In their new country, they lived only a few blocks apart in Long Beach. Channary, a gifted accountant, tracked our books with remarkable precision; her financial skill made me look good. Vaneth, an irrepressible entrepreneur, cut deals for jobs programs without worrying much about implementation; he helped us grow.

Like financial and sales people everywhere, they didn't always get along. I had to manage them as gifted individuals on the same team – it was a potent lesson in individual and cultural awareness for a young manager.

Awareness can also hatch humiliation. I will never forget a major consulting project that I designed and launched with a large technology company. The company lead and my team lead (whom I had mentored as a subcontractor to my firm) conspired to cut me out of the project, to fuel their own ambitions. I ignored the early evidence of their dishonesty, and by the time I realized their betrayal, these two women had persuaded some of the stakeholders that I was incompetent. I mistakenly assumed that this colleague and this client would collaborate with me *because* they were women, unaware of their individual willingness to operate in bad faith by excluding me. I was certainly aware of my distress over the mess, but, as project manager, I should have recognized and understood much more about who they were, and how they operated.

Awareness can bring a rude awakening. While insight may intrigue us, sometimes it feels like "aware-mess." Awareness is like playing in big ocean waves: one minute it exhilarates, the next you're spitting sand.

As a fellow sand-spitter, I believe it is fair to say that most white male managers recognize and understand less about human differences at work than their diverse coworkers. This deficit in discernment derives largely from the overlooked normativity of being a white man who leads in America. In essay 20 we explore how being white and male is a leadership norm. Suffice it to say that a white man's skin color and gender has not generally proven enough of a disadvantage to embed in him a finely honed awareness of diversity at work.

On balance, most of us as white male managers invest less time and energy on diversity than our diverse colleagues. We therefore generate less insight about human differences, and suffer a narrower knowledge and experience base from which to lead.

Here's a resource to help us catch up: find a copy of Judith Katz's *White Awareness*, a pioneering and practical book on being white.

Awareness is the call that wakes us up, sharpening our ability to observe and respond to the distinctive traits and behaviors of our coworkers and customers. We need to awaken from this slumber of not knowing. Our advantages have rendered some of us sleepy and some of us comatose. We can wake up to the possibility of moving from Pre-Awareness to effective management action.

Awareness is a vital motivator as we concentrate on diversity in our leadership work. And the good news and bad news about awareness is identical: once you grow aware, you cannot return to Pre-Awareness. Once you wake up to the challenges and opportunities of leading with diversity in mind, the nap is over for the pale guy in charge of stuff. That would be you and me.

We snooze, we lose.

CONVERSATION STARTER: *What exactly are you doing to awaken to awareness, to recognize and understand individual and cultural differences and similarities among your colleagues and customers?*

Distinguish

between generalizations and stereotypes.

To make sure you start strong as a white man who leads, follow where awareness leads. To do so, let's distinguish between generalizing and stereotyping. Consider these definitions:

GENERALIZATION: *A useful but imprecise statement about widely observable tendencies among a group of people. For example: "White male managers tend to focus more on getting the job done than on the people doing it." This is generally observable among white men as a group.*

Bias: *An interior inclination that opposes (or supports) a person or idea. For example: "White men don't care about people of color." Such a presumption is bias, which often involves a negative judgment, a "steering against" a person or idea.*

Stereotyping: *Applying a generalization with bias to an individual, as in: "This person is one of them, so this person is ..." (we assume something about who they are), or "This person will ..." (we predict how they will act). For example: "My manager, John, is a typical white guy: only the results matter to him. He sees people as a necessary evil. He doesn't care about people of color, and he certainly isn't going to give us the chance to succeed."*

The relationship between these three terms may be expressed in a formula:

A **Generalization**

plus **Bias**

produces **Stereotyping**

It stings to be stereotyped, doesn't it? Stereotyping hurts even more when the applied bias accumulates over a lifetime. Black Americans endure stereotyping from childhood, and such experience can make it harder for them to distinguish intentional discrimination from miscommunication.

Stereotyping is a symptom of Pre-Awareness, that malady afflicting many white men who lead (and others, to be sure). We scuttle behind our stereotypes when we don't know how to handle intergroup differences. And if we don't understand black culture, at least we know "they are not like us." So we assign biased generalizations to "them."

This is easy to do. This seems natural. This is also profoundly counterproductive for leaders.

Stereotyping destroys the credibility and trust a leader must possess to succeed. Not one employee or customer deserves to be treated as the embodiment of a group, even if their group influences them directly and they identify with it.

Consider this illustration. For a diversity conference, I was asked to join a panel on issues related to race and gender in the workplace. They vetted my background carefully. The organizer openly wondered whether my experience would make me "compatible" with the other panelists: a black woman who directed an affirmative action office for local government, a white female attorney who litigated sexual harassment claims, and a Latino official from a large local union. Compatibility seemed like an odd thing to worry about at a diversity conference, so I got my hair cut and wore a suit and my favorite tie.

Long story short, the black female panelist took one look at me, and it was like a dog staring at steak. She "knew" who I was the minute she laid eyes on me. My background and experience didn't matter (she openly doubted it). My attempts at common ground were rebuffed (she was biased against me). And she frequently referred to me in "them" talk (my favorite was when she pointed at me and spoke to the audience: "Now they even dress up and show up at our diversity conferences claiming to be experts!").

To be completely candid, I was not in my happy place. I was sacrificed on her altar of stereotyping. My appearance made it easy to generalize about me as a white man; my tormentor had never met a white man like me, and did not believe I could be who I was. So she felt free, in public, to rip into me with impunity, without regard for me as an individual and her potential ally.

So there's the formula at work: a generalization applied with bias to an individual equals stereotyping. When we stereotype, it says more about us than the person we caricature.

All humans are tempted to stereotype. That being said, take my illustration with a grain of salt. Black people are much more often at the receiving end of stereotyping from you and me and other white men. And the humiliation of that panel remains fresh in me more than a decade later. I simply cannot imagine how a lifetime of such indignities would shape who I am today.

I find myself wishing for some high-tech virtual reality device that could project directly into our minds the devastating effect of our behavior on the person we stereotype. But until a microchip can deliver such accountability, we must rely on our own devices to nullify stereotyping.

It is a subtle process as we mentally flit at light speed from generalization through bias to stereotyping. By the time we express a stereotype in word or action, this entire internal process has taken us unawares. That's why awareness helps.

Why do we generalize in the first place? Nature and nurture shape us.

THE INFLUENCE OF NATURE

Psychologists tell us that the human tendency to generalize reflects our need to organize and remember information that helps us decide how to act when we encounter others. This is a social and survival mechanism wired into our makeup. It makes perfect sense to evaluate whether an individual we meet is likely to

- help us by providing safety, comfort, and affiliation;
- hurt us by acting like those who have harmed us previously;
- threaten us because they look like people we have been taught to fear.

But there is a limited utility in the way we generalize and maintain biases. As leaders we must verify what is actually true about each follower. We must not prematurely judge (prejudice is to pre-judge) a colleague or customer. We need to avoid misperceiving them as the embodiment of a group or culture we do not understand. See essay 78: Individualize the way you lead.

THE INFLUENCE OF NURTURE

We also internalize information about human differences through our family of origin. I have often heard white people reflect on the biases they heard and still hear from family, usually their elders. We also learn to interpret diversity while we participate in other cultures that influence our values, like school and church, teams and clubs, towns and nation.

By the time we begin our careers, data about differences is embedded deep in our brains. Some of these messages are healthy, and some are not. Throughout life, we are shaped by positive and negative experience with diverse people. Nurture carries clout.

So nature and nurture produce in us a rich mélange of generalizations and biases, a mix as unique to us as our fingerprints. These ingredients for stereotyping stand ready to appear, unbidden, when we are under stress, and when we are not concentrating on respectful communication. Sometimes, for no cause we can discern, out pops a generalization applied with bias to an individual. This is technically known as the Moment of Owie.

The antidote? In each moment we can learn to

- monitor our generalizations;
- discipline our biases;
- make better choices about how these messages affect our words and behavior.

CONVERSATION STARTER: *How do you know when a generalization turns into a stereotype?*

Think

You're a leader. You don't need me to tell you how to think.

In this section, then, I take the liberty of recommending what you should think *about* as a white man who leads. Your black colleagues and customers deserve your maximum mental effort. As it turns out, there's a good deal to consider.

So invest some thorough thoughtfulness in the following topics:

- White men as the leadership norm
- The lessons of your boyhood
- "Political correctness"
- Advantage: power, privilege, preference, and opportunity

- Ethnicity and racist assumptions
- The illusion of color blindness

This section closes with one of the book's key concepts in essay 30, "Invest heavily in due regard." This method helps you diagnose and dial in on diversity at work, escaping ignorance and avoiding excessive regard.

The French philosopher Rene Descartes famously wrote: "I think, therefore I am." As white men who lead, our cognition surely causes character.

It truly matters what you think about.

THINK

■ **20** ■

Consider
the normativity of white men.

(America's) problem isn't just "race" in the abstract ...
it's the idea of the "white race" as the social norm in particular.

ERIC LIU

The Accidental Asian

"NORM" AND "AL"

If one thousand people who represented the globe's demographic mix gathered in a room, there would be only one white American man who leads for a living. White American men in leadership jobs are six million among six billion.

90

Yet in our hearts we may still feel like the beloved and beer-guzzling character in television's *Cheers*, who, when he walked through the door, was greeted by all with a hearty "Norm!" We need to recognize and avoid the trap of thinking we are "normal."

As white men who lead we enjoy normative status. Our opportunities often emerge from social, historical, psychological, and economic circumstances of advantage.

A **norm** is a standard or model operating in a group. Normative American leaders have been and remain white men:

- Enacted in 1790, the nation's first immigration law provided for "free white persons" to become citizens. "In practice the idea of citizenship had become thoroughly entwined with the idea of 'whiteness' and maleness, because what a citizen really was, at bottom, was someone who could help put down a slave rebellion or participate in Indian wars." (Matthew Frye Jacobson, *Whiteness of a Different Color*)

- Today, white men compose about thirty-eight percent of the U.S. workforce, but we are more than ninety percent of top Fortune 500 executives, and two out of three managers in many organizations. Even with Mr. Obama's rise, eighty-four percent of our senators and sixty-eight percent of our congresspersons are white men, though white males are less than forty percent of the electorate. White men predominate as leaders in sectors such as technology, financial services, manufacturing, law enforcement, military service, and in the church.

One byproduct of normativity is Pre-Awareness; as the norm, a white man is more likely to be the fish that doesn't know it's big and wet. (While some characterize white male managers as sharks, bullheads, or piranha, I prefer to visualize us as the strong yet friendly kingfish … but I digress.)

As white men we personify the identified standard of leadership, and the workplace is deployed to operate the way most of us prefer. Take the following as examples:

- The communication style of a typical team permits the quick exchange of ideas, with plenty of interrupting and sports-related language.
- Decision making tends to be logical, linear, and focused on quantitative measures.
- Informal mentoring for us from white male leaders occurs naturally at the office, or informally in the community. No special program is required.
- Company security guards do not scrutinize us because of our skin color.

Look for expressions of normativity such as these at work in your environment, reinforcing your status as the norm. When you embody the rule, you have less experience as an exception to that rule, although other dimensions of diversity (such as living with a wheelchair) propel some white male managers outside the norm. And there are organizations in which women predominate.

In contrast, those who are not "normal" are exceptional: black women and men in leadership, for instance. They are intensely aware of the environment in which they work, the water in which they swim. To survive and thrive, they become experts at coping with being "different." Different from whom? From the norm of the white male manager.

A second outcome of being the norm: as white men who lead today, we were raised with the opportunity to achieve. I grew up expecting to attend college as my parents did; it was a given that I would join ninety percent of my high school classmates in pursuing higher education. When I graduated from college, I was told that one percent of the world's population holds a college degree. I was on my way to graduate school; it just seemed normal.

I don't mean to universalize my own background, since white male managers hail from varied social and economic settings. But comparisons with those beyond white maledom elicit more instructive contrasts. For example, it is still not unusual today for a young black American to be the first in his or her family to earn a college degree.

The expectation of middle-class achievement is integral to growing up white and male. Our unexplored assumption of merit fails to recognize that many people outside the white male norm do not presume their road to be paved with opportunity. White men who lead expect to hit some homeruns in life, and we feel good about crossing the plate. Non-norm colleagues may believe that when the white guy in charge steps up to bat, the base path shortens, the fence moves closer to the infield, and the pitches are slow and sweet. That doesn't make it true, but you can see the challenge in the perception that we have it easy.

A caveat here: starting with the post–World War II generation, the complete normativity of white men is moderating, evidenced in the business trends and motives for diversity (see essay 7). Women represent thirty-seven percent of all management personnel today, and in many disciplines, they are a majority of all undergraduate and graduate students (e.g., fifty-two percent in medicine, fifty-one percent in business). The development of the middle class among people of African, Asian, Hispanic, or Native heritage shows that Americans of all colors can succeed.

These signs of progress, however, do not gainsay the fact of white male normativity. Let's face it: while white men who lead are about five percent of the workforce, we hold more than eighty percent of the senior leadership positions in America.

For generations to come, white men, far beyond our proportion in the population, will lead in American organizations.

CONVERSATION STARTER: *How does the normativity you enjoy as a white man impact the way you lead?*

THINK

■ **21** ■

Hunt

through the lessons of your boyhood.

The boy is father to the man. We come of age as men by maturing as boys. Each of us, as men, issue from a young lifetime of natural talents and limitations, the love and influence of adults, and our unique experience. So we can learn about leading as white men by unpacking the lessons of our boyhood.

Explore how the boy you were influences the man you are becoming. Ask yourself the three questions below. I offer up my own responses to encourage you to find your own answers.

What did I learn about gender, race, and leadership from my parents, other people, and experience?

My mom and dad were remarkably intentional Christian parents. There was a lot to learn about race and gender in the 1960s, and they sought the schooling. They did not allow anyone to teach me bias or hate.

My mother was an early volunteer when Head Start was launched, and she volunteered me, too. From age ten to fourteen, I went into the city with her, spending days playing with a bunch of four-year-old black boys who didn't care about the color of my skin.

I gave up a season of high school football when I transferred from the suburbs into an urban high school in Seattle, because I wanted to experience a racially and economically diverse school. I sensed that I needed to learn things that my white, upper-middle-class community could not provide.

Equity between women and men was never an issue in our home. My parents were free to be themselves, they loved each other dearly, and there was no hint of hierarchy. I've always been comfortable calling myself a feminist, because I came to define **feminism** as the belief that God gives all humans, male and female, the freedom to be authentic and gifts to share with everyone. I wanted to live free, express my giftedness, and hang out with other people who lived that way. There was a powerful attraction to the gifts and challenge and joy that the female kind offered. As a boy, I saw no advantage in the idea of male superiority.

My leadership lessons were legion:

- Mom found a way to lead and influence in most rooms she entered; she was value focused, good with words, warm and caring, and group oriented. She also was elected to the school board, where she served as chair.

- Dad's leadership style was quieter, honed as an accounting manager at Boeing for thirty-seven years. He led more by deed than word, and when he spoke, people listened. He held a man's power playfully, gently, thoughtfully. When a job needing doing, he facilitated others getting it done, or he did it himself.

- My own tendencies to lead were also shaped by coaches and teachers, pastors and family friends. The first time I remember feeling like a leader was when I was six; my neighborhood boys (Danny, Kenny and David) usually followed where I led.

How does this learning as a boy shape how I view race, gender, and leadership today?

This book answers the question. I am committed to being part of the solution and not part of the problem for black people. I was raised to care and think about race and gender, so I have been trying to be a better man and a more useful white person for more than forty years. I have been a leader my entire life, learning from mentors and experience that if you want something done, you have to get organized and equip the people who will help you do it. That approach to leadership still works for me.

How do these boyhood lessons about race and gender affect the way I lead today?

I learned that leadership is a way to make things better with people who want better for themselves. I learned that differences aren't bad; they're intriguing, and they offer the chance for learning and excellent arguments. I learned that leading on diversity tests my values. My four professional skills—communicating, coaching, training, and consulting—are grounded in what I learned as a boy. The true influence of my childhood should be evaluated today in the way I lead and the results that my leadership helps to deliver.

I understand that my boyhood was different from most of the other white boys who also grew up to be leaders. I was exposed to strong faith-based values against racism and sexism, and I have an unusual orientation to diversity among my own kind. That's what's true for me, and the origins of this book are in that backstory.

But the purpose of these three questions is to equip you to understand your own story. Are you ready to hunt through your boyhood learning on race, gender, and leadership? It could help you understand where you lead from today.

And remember: as it turns out, boys won't be boys. They'll be men.

CONVERSATION STARTER: *What did you learn about gender, race, and leadership from your parents, other people, and experience? How do these boyhood lessons about race and gender affect the way you lead today?*

THINK

■ **22** ■

Steer clear
of "political correctness."

My goal in this essay is to dissuade you from using the term political correctness (PC). Additionally, I want to equip you to respond effectively when claims of PC challenge your leadership. And I should warn you up front, I've granted myself permission to rant a bit, but only on this topic!

It is my unscientific estimate that ninety-six percent of all people who complain about political correctness are white. This alone should give us both pause and food for thought. My main complaint about political correctness is that the way people use the term often stifles the very conversation we need to have.

The idea of **political correctness** alludes to the inherent tension between speech that avoids giving offense, and speech that is free and candid. On one side, the stifling "PC police" willingly risk censorship for, they claim, the sake of inclusion. On the other side, self-appointed defenders of individual opinion threaten relationships to protect free speech. Such liberal and conservative advocates care more about dominating with their opinions, and less about being useful or showing respect. Consequently, they generate enough smoke over political correctness to choke many Americans.

Both of these extremes offend me as a leader and as a citizen. I have no interest in a perpetual tussle that pits two historic American values against each other (free speech versus respectful speech), while silencing critical conversation in my organization at the same time.

Our success as leaders depends, in part, on our ability to manage this conflict between respectful and straightforward speech in the workplace. Speech that respects employees evokes their contribution. Such respect helps to secure from those we lead their commitment to produce; that's what following is about.

Candid talk is indispensable to the effective manager who corrects performance and leads through change. We must be able to speak the direct and unvarnished truth to employees, peers, and those who lead us—and be able to receive it from them.

So we cannot accept the false choice between sensitivity and honesty offered up by political correctness. I heartily encourage you to drop the term from your vocabulary as a leader and citizen.

Here are some options as you navigate this enduring clash between growing diverse relationships and building a climate where people openly speak their minds. To lead effectively among diverse people, both respect and freedom must flourish.

When . . .	You Could . . .
Someone attempts to dismiss an issue with an accusation of "political correctness"	Point out that it is actually a tension between respect and candor, and hold them accountable for both
One person blames another for an unintended slight	Remind them both that we all need to feel safe, and mistakes should be resolved with mutual respect
Respectful or free speech is inhibited or violated	Recognize the shortcoming as an invitation to diagnose interpersonal and organizational problems
Confronted with handling an employee who speaks their mind without apparent regard for relationships	Answer: Was the offense intentional? Coming from ignorance? Well-meant but inept? Respond appropriately.
You recognize your own tip-toeing on eggshells for fear of offending	Ask: What could I be missing in this situation or relationship? Reaffirm: I cannot abandon straight talk.

Figure 22

In the article "Rethinking Political Correctness" in the September 2006 edition of the *Harvard Business Review*, authors Robin Ely, Martin Davidson, and Debra Myerson offered this insight: "Setting the standards for civility and respect (can also) hinder the employee's ability to develop effective relationships ... Feeling offended or threatened in an interaction provides an important signal that invites inquiry."

So avoid the trap of political correctness. It's a smokescreen that chokes off the conversation we must have. Build a work environment where respectful talk and free speech thrive in creative tension.

CONVERSATION STARTER: *In what situations are you tempted to use the term politically correct? What could you say that would be more accurate and useful to the issues at hand?*

Introducing
the Advantage Complex

T he next four essays were a challenge for me to write, and may be hard for you to read. With clear-eyed precision, we will explore the advantages accrued by white men who lead, and how we metabolize these advantages.

We usually overlook the advantages that tend to accompany being a white man in a leadership job: power, privilege, preference, opportunity. Such advantage is like oxygen; we take its presence for granted, until we meet someone who is struggling for breath.

I'd like to ask a favor from you. Monitor your defensiveness, and open your mind and heart to this discussion. This isn't about blame. You are free to think your own thoughts. You know my views on political correctness if you read the previous essay. And remember essay 19 on generalizations and stereotypes; we're considering what is observably true about us *as a group*. It's up to you to evaluate if and how it applies to you as an individual.

As white men who lead, we need to become experts at diagnosing advantage as we truly see and experience it, and as others perceive it in us. Why? Two reasons.

First, we only come to be part of the solution when we decide for ourselves how we may be part of the problem. That's what it means to be a man who takes responsibility for his impact in the world. Second, people who don't look like us will continue to project power and privilege onto us, until we're prepared to engage them in honest conversation about what that might mean.

So we have a lot riding on this investigation of the Advantage Complex.

THINK

■ 23 ■

The Advantage Complex:

Unpack your power.

Accepting personal responsibility for *the power we possess* is at the heart of diversity for white men who lead.

Do you resist the previous sentence with the thought: "I don't have power because I am a white man who leads. What is he talking about?" Just checking in on that favor I asked of you! Remember to monitor your reactions to this cluster of essays, and distinguish between disagreement and denial.

Consider this value-neutral definition: **power** is the opportunity and ability to see, make, and carry out choices. When power is defined this way, it is fair to generally describe white men who lead as powerful people.

Quick Quiz: True or False?

	True	False
I am responsible for hiring and firing people.	○	○
As a man I am welcome almost anywhere I want to go.	○	○
My position of leadership gives me choices that non-exempt employees do not enjoy.	○	○
As a white person I can go almost anywhere I want to go.	○	○
I'm responsible for important decisions at work.	○	○
I can be fairly sure my voice will be heard in a group in which I am the only member of my race or gender.	○	○
I am free to consider professional options without wondering whether a person of my gender or race would be accepted for the work.	○	○
My job includes appraising employee performance and making promotion decisions.	○	○

Figure 23

Admittedly, power is relative. We can point to people with more advantages and choices, and some of these people are women and people of color. Yet by any meaningful measure, we identify, make, and carry out choices as white male managers.

By definition, power is synonymous with management. It's your job as a manager to envision and actualize choice. And power should be defined positively, because it is essential to capable leadership. It is the quality of the choices we see, make, and carry out that render power positive or negative.

I have often heard black people speak of power in terms of what is done *to* them, as if "power" is the name of an illness infecting white people. Perhaps this comes from the fact that we generally have more choices. But everyone would benefit from a clearheaded discussion of power and its use in management work. Four types of power are available:

- *Personal power* ("power within," empowerment): Personal power is always available because we can generate it internally. It fuels choices based on what we want, what we're confident about and motivated for, and how we engage our limitations. Personal power is the energy of self-efficacy.

- *Position power* ("power-over," authority): Position power is conferred by an organization. It positions a person for choice by virtue of the leadership role to which they are appointed. This power is formal (e.g., hiring and firing duties), and such power is useful when wielded responsibly. It is also limited; a consistently coercive exercise of power-over may cause compliance in the short run, but the overuse of position power engenders resistance among followers. Then they leave.

- *Collaborative power* ("power with" direct reports, peers, and customers): Collaborative power is critical for white men who want to lead successfully. Collaboration includes people in decision making, even if you decide in the end. (See essay 81 on inclusive decision making.) Delegation fuels the development of followers, and delivers results you could not produce on your own. This realm for choice making involves mentoring between peers and handling challenges without having to prematurely involve superiors. In *The Power Principle*, Blaine Lee links power and honor, where people participate with and follow from a heartfelt respect for the leader.

- *Choices when you're not in charge* ("power under," influence): This is all about influencing up. When position power is held over you, and when collaborative power requires too much time, you still have choices. We all know that we "manage our boss" sometimes, and as leaders we can be receptive to effective influence from those reporting to us. A great resource for more information on this topic is Geoff Bellman's *Getting Things Done When You Are Not in Charge*.

The most powerful among us are able to choose which forms of power to employ in response to a situation.

Evaluate the power you possess in each of these four types. Practically speaking, what does it mean for you to be able to see, make, and implement choice?

If you fail to answer this question for yourself, you may tend to deny the choices you do oversee when someone assumes that you have power. It is futile to deny possessing power that others perceive you to hold. Instead, such a perception should cause you to share how you think about power, and involve your colleagues in choice making.

As a white man who leads, you may fail to see your own power, because you're acutely aware of the power that higher-ups wield over you. White male culture assumes "power over." Yet "power with" collaboration reigns in these times of outsourcing, continuous improvement, team-based projects, and globalization. While you learn to envision and actualize choice with your colleagues (the exercise of the power you possess), you may still have to cope with those higher-ups who lord it over you rather than include you. It's not easy to lead in a manner different from the way you're being led. Personal power is pivotal in such situations.

Wielding power is not some original sin among white guys. But we are gifted at ignoring its possession. Handling choices, instead, is our profound responsibility. To see, make, and carry out choices that benefit black (and all) colleagues and customers is, as they say, "the opportunity of a lifetime."

In another lifetime (1826 to be exact), British prime minister Benjamin Disraeli said: "All power is a trust ... and we are accountable for its exercise."

Eighteen centuries earlier, an even more powerful leader named Jesus said: "To whom much is given, much is expected." Wait ... was he white? I know his Father isn't.

CONVERSATION STARTER: *In what ways do you agree or disagree with the following statement? "I understand and know how to use the power I possess as a white man who leads."*

THINK

■ 24 ■

The Advantage Complex:
Appraise privilege.

White skin brings with it a birthright of status and privilege.

LENA WILLIAMS
*It's the Little Things: Everyday Interactions That Anger,
Annoy and Divide the Races*

Ｗe defined power in terms of choice previously. **Privilege** is a related concept, and may be defined as access to special advantages, benefits, and opportunities.

Remember, we're not playing the blame game. But we could learn something important if we appraised the privilege others believe we enjoy. We might view ourselves in a new light; we might lead more effectively as a result.

For several years I've been asking black Americans how they would define the privileges of white men who lead. They were honest enough to provide quite a list of our "access to special advantages, benefits, and opportunities." All the perceptions below will not be true about you—I know they don't all describe me—and not all black people would agree with the list. But we live and lead more effectively among people when we permit their point of view to teach us, so keep an open mind.

Ｗʜɪᴛᴇ ᴍᴇɴ ᴡʜᴏ ʟᴇᴀᴅ ʜᴀᴠᴇ ᴀᴄᴄᴇss ᴛᴏ sᴘᴇᴄɪᴀʟ ᴀᴅᴠᴀɴᴛᴀɢᴇs, ʙᴇɴᴇꜰɪᴛs, ᴀɴᴅ ᴏᴘᴘᴏʀᴛᴜɴɪᴛɪᴇs ʟɪᴋᴇ ᴛʜᴇ ꜰᴏʟʟᴏᴡɪɴɢ:

1. They can accept a job with an affirmative action employer without having their new colleagues think they got the job because of their race or gender.

2. Their parents are often college graduates, and they grew up confident that they would attend college.

3. They can look at any house they are interested in buying, and never worry that the real estate agent will try to steer them to a more "appropriate" neighborhood.

4. They can speak in public without putting their gender or race on trial.

5. They can walk into any golf clubhouse in America, and no one will look at them twice.

6. They rarely stay quiet in meetings out of a concern for being viewed as pushy, uninformed, or not a team player.

7. They may get paid more for lower-quality work.

8. They expect diverse people to adapt, so they don't have to work so hard at adapting to people who differ from them by race, gender, nationality, or other dimension of diversity.

9. They can afford to move their families to communities with strong school districts and safe streets.

10. They will question black people on their educational background and work experience, but they would bridle at being questioned in a like manner.

11. Their network of friends from school, church, and work are equally well situated, and much opportunity emerges from their social network.

12. They rarely doubt there will be money to cover their family's health care needs.

13. They can focus on task over people, results without productive process, and not be held as accountable as women or people of color for team conflict or employee retention.

14. Their skin will not attract unwanted attention from the police.

15. Their gender seems to ensure opinions will be taken seriously.

16. Their leadership status increases their lifetime earnings.

17. The strangest benefit of all: privilege is so woven into their lives that they seem blind to just how privileged they are.

Trust me, this list could go on. Check out *Privilege, Power and Difference* by fellow white guy and professor Allan Johnson. In chapter three he lists more than thirty examples of privilege accruing to white men. Frances

Kendall has also written a truly useful book on the subject: *Understanding White Privilege.*

How maddening it must be to black people when a white man accuses them of thinking they are "entitled" to benefits or preferences. From their point of view, a white man can operate with a breathtaking sense of unexamined privilege.

Of course, the fact of our Pre-Awareness does not validate black people's perceptions of our privilege, nor does it confirm their entitlement. Still, as white men who lead, we remain part of the problem until we take a long look at the advantages, benefits, and opportunities handed to us. Our privilege is forged, in part, from our race, gender, and occupation.

That's why I call this the Advantage Complex.

Power—seeing, making, and carrying out choices
PLUS
Privilege—access to special advantages, benefits, and opportunities
EQUALS
A Pretty Sweet Setup in Life.

I know that's not what we think when we look in the mirror, but it is a cluster of possibilities and perceptions we should examine to verify or dispel. And if, along the way, we find that we possess more power and privilege than we understood, such learning will surely lead us to stronger and more honest relationships with black colleagues and customers.

CONVERSATION STARTER: *On the list above, only 8 and 10 (and I pray 7) do not apply to me. What about you?*

THINK

■ 25 ■

The Advantage Complex:

Discipline your views of preference and affirmative action.

I n this context, **preference** may be defined as selecting one person over another. Enough said, right? The practice of preferring some people over others contradicts a commitment to inclusion, plain and simple. To prefer is to exclude, by definition. This logic works. Especially if all we want is an argument.

But if we want to stop being a problem for black people, we should strictly order our thinking about preference and affirmative action. As we learn to do this, we monitor any tendency to engage in word games ("reverse" discrimination, quotas), rather than digging into the real issues. Intriguingly, the whole debate also prods our emotions, so we must take stock of our gut reactions as well.

Scan back over essays 14 (pigment paradigm), 15 (history rift), 23 (power), and 24 (privilege). Now let me frame the real issue with preference and affirmative action: To ensure opportunity for all, and to make things right, how will we come to agree on issues around "qualifications"?

Here's how Dr. Cornel West answers the question in *Race Matters*: "Affirmative action policies were political responses to the pervasive refusal of most white Americans to judge black Americans … on the *quality* [emphasis added] of their skills, not the color of their skin … Given the history of this country, it is a virtual certainty that, without affirmative action, racial and sexual discrimination would return with a vengeance."

Here's the paraphrased answer I've heard from many white men who lead: "We understand that the playing field must be leveled, and that we should compete with everyone else on the basis of *qualifications*. But when affirmative action is driven by numbers (code word: quota), when being white and male is a defined disadvantage, then it's not about qualifications and opportunity—its about 'making things right' by discriminating against white guys."

The surprising good news: both sides seek opportunity on the basis of qualification. But there's not much agreement beyond that.

Affirmative action would win a contest for the most botched brand in American life. Rarely has a social commitment achieved so much while so unpopular.

Across the country, opportunities in education and employment have opened to people previously locked out. White women, in fact, are the chief beneficiaries of affirmative action. Our increasingly diverse population is better reflected in higher education and the workforce. Affirmative action, as one tactic in the national pursuit of inclusion, has contributed to three heartening results:

- A larger percentage of leaders in America are women (near forty percent) than in any other nation (Sweden rates next, under thirty percent).
- Our organizations are more responsive to diverse customers than they were prior to the implementation of affirmative action.
- We have developed a multicultural middle class that is the envy of the world.

We grow stronger as laws force inclusion—forty-plus years after landmark civil rights legislation, the Supreme Court continues to interpret our laws and values regarding equality. America's progress toward equal opportunity, driven in part by affirmative action, is a success story unique in history.

Concurrently, a minority of affirmative action efforts clumsily assigned "extra points" for gender and race. Some people got special consideration because they were a female or person of color. This can also appear in the language of proportional representation: "We need employees who look like our customers." As a strategy, this has merit. But the employment decisions that implement such a strategy are tactical. Is representing a racial group part of the job qualifications?

White men show a general distaste for such preferences. We're not inclined to support turning our race and gender advantages into disadvantages. We tend to question a person's qualifications when they appear to receive extra consideration because they differ from us by gender or race.

Yet for us as leaders, defending or ending affirmative action misses the point. Resolving issues swirling around "qualification" is the more productive effort. Advocates of affirmative action have usefully defined *qualified* in terms of meeting the stated selection criteria. Affirmative action opponents counter that it's not just qualified that counts, but "most qualified." *It really boils down to how we define qualified, and how we apply that definition when we choose between candidates.* That's the fight worth having.

To ensure opportunity for all and to make things right, how will we come to agree on issues around qualifications? You need to lead by helping to engage this issue constructively in your organization. The following two questions will help you discipline your views of preference and affirmative action.

1) When a job posting is written, and when decisions on selection or promotion are being made, how clear-thinking and honest and brave will you be with issues around preference, qualifications, and representation? On such matters, the silence can be deafening from white men who don't lead.

2) How will we manage "merit stigma" that causes people, typically white men, to question a diverse person's qualifications? Our own bias may operate in this space. This stigma cannot be entirely blamed on affirmative policies, since newly selected black employees often face such white doubt even when their qualifications are objectively superior to any white candidate's experience.

To lead effectively as a white man, you have to be ready to speak with confidence when issues of preference and qualification come up. Prepare yourself for straight talk that attracts talent and builds relationships. That's one way to ensure opportunity, and make things right for black Americans, for white Americans, for all of us.

And that's putting your power and privilege to good use.

CONVERSATION STARTER: *What will you do to prepare yourself to ask and answer the two questions above?*

The Advantage Complex:

Evaluate opportunity with utter honesty.

No one achieves singularly.

Daphne Muse, Editor

Multicultural Resources for Young Readers

With open minds, we're working our way through the Advantage Complex, examining how power and privilege interact with qualifications and opportunity. White men who lead work hard, and we're right to be proud of our accomplishments. Our achievements stand on their own. Or do they?

The places we were nurtured (family, community, teams, church, schools, and clubs) opened opportunity's door for us as white boys. Such doors probably continue to swing wide for us as white men who lead for a living.

We should reevaluate the degree to which we are the self-determined individuals we imagine. At birth, we were dealt a hand containing power and privilege cards. There's no fault in playing the hand you're dealt to its fullest potential. I am certainly trying to do just that. But others in the game want to see that we understand that not everyone starts with or keeps getting dealt such advantageous cards. Our accomplishments do stand, but not on their own. It is easier to win the race with a head start.

Integrity requires us, as white men who lead, to reevaluate our beliefs about our opportunities, in view of the privilege and power we possess.

I don't know what such a private audit of your own power and privilege will produce. You can draw your own conclusions about how the Advantage Complex operates in your life. But we can be confident that colleagues, customers, and fellow Americans who are black need us to find courage for this task. Here are some ways that accounting for my own power and privilege has influenced the way I live and lead.

My Opportunities, Rethought	Life Impact
Educational Achievement College was expected; 1% of the world's population has a college degree; I got a Masters, too	Previous generations valued education, and they leveraged it into careers and income that opened doors for me; I extend this to my children
Moving into Management My education, experience and nerve got me into my first management job at 21	I gravitated to management jobs; was selected to lead a 30-person unit at 29, perhaps before I was qualified
Personal Safety My daily sense of physical safety isn't an achievement, but women feel at risk constantly, and are limited by that	I go where I want without much thought for my safety, assuming I can take care of myself; I can't imagine feeling at risk every day
My Income I never worry that I am making less than women or people of color for comparable work, but I know they wonder about it	I want to make as much as I can, and I try to ensure that people are paid comparably; I carefully respect those with less money than me
Career Choice At an early age, I started learning that others don't have a lot of the opportunities I have	Knowing how much I have (and that others had less) pushed me to choose my life's work; I didn't want to give up my opportunities, though
My Children's Opportunities My wife and I chose strong schools and safe streets for our kids, although that has limited their social exposure	We were not willing to sacrifice their safety and good education for more diverse friendships; we've raised them with a strong social consciousness
Freedom to Travel a Distance My friends of color have to ensure their safety by planning their driving routes and servicing their cars before leaving	I never calculate my safety on the road as a white man; it pisses me off that they are still not truly free to go anywhere they want, anytime
Burden of Diversity Learning Sometimes I imagine how nice it would be to ignore diversity; I could choose to retreat into uncaring advantage	I won't choose to hide; my values are too deep, the learning is too intriguing; the chance to make a positive difference is too big
Doubt About My Merit I know how hard I work, but I see many black Americans working at least as hard, with a tiny percentage of my advantages	I know I'm good at what I do, and I've earned a lot; but that's not close to justifying how much more I have than many black Americans; it shames me
Status as Leader My ego enjoys my status as a developer of leaders; it is personally and professionally satisfying to stand up in front and lead	I feel pressure to leverage my status and power to benefit people who do not enjoy my opportunities; "to whom much is given, much is expected"

Figure 26

In *By the Color of Our Skin,* authors Leonard Steinhorn and Barbara Diggs-Brown say: "Many blacks feel that no matter how much they've earned or achieved in life, they are subject to the whims of a white society that either patronizes or tolerates but rarely respects them." That could not be further from my experience as a white man who leads. It makes me wonder if more opportunity comes my way than I deserve.

I encourage you to recalibrate how you view your opportunities, in light of your power and privilege.

CONVERSATION STARTER: *When you consider your power and privilege, what insights emerge about your opportunities, about the way you live and lead?*

THINK

■ **27** ■

Analyze
your ethnicity.

(There is a) luxury that most white Americans enjoy: ethno-banality.
Roots without costs. The Sons of Italy, Daughters of Ireland and so forth:
whites can wear or remove their ancestry like a pendant.

Eric Liu

The Accidental Asian

P
reviously I defined **ethnicity** as a cultural group of which you are a part, which may be distinguished by such common traits as family, geography, appearance, demeanor, language, race, religion, and economy. As we learn how ethnic identity evolves,

we are more likely to understand diversity as it operates in our organization, and in the global economy. The root word here is *ethnos*, Greek for a "racial group or nation." So ethnicity is a category of "Like Some Others," with key similarities in genetics, geographic origin, and cultural practice.

For white Americans, analyzing our ethnicity can be challenging. Generally *white* serves as the racial umbrella for ethnicities with a common European heritage. Ethnicity serves as a meaning marker for the immigrant experience: the first few generations in America bear the stronger connection to the country of origin.

This dynamic varies among white Americans by region: the traditions of European ethnicities are stronger with the Irish in Boston, the Italians in New York, the Poles in Detroit, the Germans in Pennsylvania.

As ensuing generations grow distant from their family's entry into America, an ethnic link to Europe becomes essentially voluntary. As Eric Liu points to in the quote above, that is partly the result of whites (from any immigrant nationality) becoming America's ethnic norm. Evidence for this white norming is laid out beautifully in Matthew Jacobson's *Whiteness of a Different Color*, which tracks the historical process by which various European ethnic groups were joined into whiteness. One key motive for the coalescence: to distinguish themselves from and organize themselves against people stolen from Africa, whom white American men had already declared *black* through the slave system.

Our ethnicity is further shaped by geographic distance in the American experience. The movement westward developed its own heritage; pioneering shaped identity and diminished the meaning of European roots. So, while my DNA originates from England and Germany, all my ancestors arrived in America between 1630 and 1850, and their descendants (my forebears) traveled west on the Oregon Trail. I am a European-American technically.

But to me, my ethnic identity is really just American. I've talked with many Americans in the West who think the same, although it is useful to note that such consensus has been among white people. It is a challenge to sort out our American-ness. When ethnicity and nationality merge in white people (like me), it can come across as exclusionary for people whose ethnicity and nationality are two distinct identity markers (as in African-American).

When we analyze our ethnicity, we understand more about where we've come from and how others may perceive us.

As far as I've been able to determine, for many American-born black people, the terms *race* and *ethnicity* are basically synonymous. Because of the unspeakably violent circumstances under which black people left their homeland, it has been much harder to learn about their ethnic (tribal) background. Liu's "ethno-banality," a parlor game that many white Americans can play, shows up as a cruel joke for many black Americans, whose very surnames may descend from white slave owners. One intriguing development that testifies to the power of analyzing our ethnicity: individuals in the black community can now pursue genetic testing as a way to identify their tribal origin in Africa.

Consequently, in the black community, ethnicity and race are more important as organizing principles for individual identity. Their blackness sets them apart by our design—as whites we are the norm—so being black may matter more to them than being white counts for us. There are also ancient cultural dynamics at work here; individualism was more prominent in the tribal cultures of Europe, in contrast to African ethnic groups in which the will of the community loomed larger.

And consider one final feature of ethnicity at work today: economic activity. Check out Joel Kotkin's *Tribes: How Race, Religion and Identity Determine Success in the New Global Economy*. He argues that ethnic networks (he calls them "global tribes") drive international commerce, and will prove key to economic growth worldwide in this century.

The fact that we, as white people, tend not to focus on ethnicity should not prevent us from learning how ethnicity operates, in the office and out in the marketplace.

CONVERSATION STARTER: *Analyze ethnicity. How does it affect you? Your colleagues? Your customers?*

THINK

■ **28** ■

Uncover and reframe
racist assumptions.

Earlier we defined **race** as skin color and other physical traits which influence complex social meanings and practical knowledge. A simple definition of **racism**, then, is belief and behavior that discriminates against people of a different race. A *racist* is a person who believes in and lives out such discrimination.

There's a more complicated definition of racism championed by many in the black and academic communities. They reason that, since *only white people as a race* have instituted an advantageous system of power and privilege that discriminates against people of other races, racism (at least in America) is a white sin. By this systemic definition of racism, only whites are racist. Louis Farrakhan and his anti-white sidekicks are merely bigots.

Take my word here: there's no point arguing this, because every definition of racism visualizes white men. It's not that all white guys are racists. But when racists are portrayed, they look like us. Ouch.

If a black person discriminates against me because I am white, it doesn't matter whether such behavior fits into some definition of racism or not. It's hurtful and counterproductive, and it may be illegal. It's also pretty rare.

Perversely, since expectations of white men who lead are so low, we have everything to gain when we seize the initiative, by uncovering and reframing racist assumptions, in us and around us. Few believe we care enough to do so.

I trust that you will not violate the trust I'm placing in you with this essay. Among diversity professionals, it is a common caution to avoid explicating stereotypes, saying prejudices out loud, and naming racist assumptions. Why? Because giving voice to the words of discrimination can re-wound victims who deserve better. In this instance, I am choosing to take a different approach, because I am confident that

- you will use this material to help uncover and reframe racist assumptions;
- you will discuss this list with a black friend *only* if you are one hundred percent certain that the conversation will heal and not wound.

I am *not* assuming that you make or act on all or any of these assumptions. I *am* suggesting that

- you are responsible for checking your own mental messages about race;
- you are responsible for not behaving on the basis of racist assumptions;
- you are accountable for managing misbehavior by other white people who operate with assumptions such as these.

RACIST ASSUMPTION: WHENEVER TWO OR MORE
BLACK PEOPLE GATHER, THEY ARE SAYING BAD
THINGS ABOUT WHITE PEOPLE. WE SHOULD
FEEL THREATENED AND SEEK TO PREVENT
THEIR GATHERING.

REFRAME: *People who are alike like to be together. Chill, and consider that
the assumption itself presumes that whites have done something that could cause
such a threatening response. Food for thought.*

RACIST ASSUMPTION: THAT BLACK PEOPLE
ARE POOR AND CANNOT AFFORD TO LIVE
COMFORTABLY, SEND THEIR KIDS TO COLLEGE,
TRAVEL, AND BUY NICE THINGS.

REFRAME: *Wake up! One of America's great success stories is the development of
a black middle class that can afford what the white middle class can afford. Yes,
there are still too many black Americans struggling financially, and that needs
fixing. Just don't stereotype.*

RACIST ASSUMPTION: THAT BLACK PEOPLE
CAN'T SPEAK, WRITE, OR THINK ARTICULATELY,
SO WE'RE SURPRISED WHEN THEY DO.

REFRAME: *I wish we could dismiss such crap because this assumption is made
only by white people who don't actually know any black people. But no, even
white people who know better may be surprised by the brilliance of African-
Americans. What facts or acts from the actual black colleague or customer would*

cause you to assume this? Ironically, it is the person making such an assumption whose thinking isn't so sharp.

RACIST ASSUMPTION: THAT WHAT WHITE PEOPLE SAY IS PROBABLY TRUE, AND WHAT BLACK PEOPLE SAY SHOULD BE QUESTIONED.

REFRAME: *This can sneak up on you. Watch yourself carefully, and simply refuse to interrogate black people with your words, tone, or nonverbals. Drop any pigment-induced doubt. Grant each person credibility based on their behavior, and don't permit skin color to cause you to withhold respect.*

RACIST ASSUMPTION: THAT YOUR BLACK COLLEAGUES WERE HIRED OR PROMOTED BECAUSE THEY ARE BLACK, AND NOT BECAUSE THEY ARE QUALIFIED; OR THAT BLACKS CANNOT MEET STRETCH GOALS, BECAUSE THEY ARE GENERALLY LESS PREPARED FOR AND INTERESTED IN TOP PERFORMANCE.

REFRAME: *Such a thought will flee from your mind once you build a personal relationship with a productive black colleague. Review essay 25 on qualifications, and mentally delete skin color as a risk to excellence.*

Racist assumptions such as these (and there's a shamefully longer list) are a tangible part of the problem black people have with us. Uncovering and reframing racist assumptions is one way to become part of the solution. Here's a practical resource to help: *Uprooting Racism: How White People Can Work for Racial Justice*, by Paul Kivel.

CONVERSATION STARTER: *Are you making racist assumptions? If so, what will you do to reframe them for yourself? Be very cautious about discussing your answers to these questions with a black friend, to avoid re-wounding them.*

THINK

■ **29** ■

See past the illusion
of color blindness.

You may be many things, but if one of them is black,
that trumps the rest in terms of how the world sees you. Black is definitive.

LEONARD PITTS JR., SYNDICATED COLUMNIST

T he nation's founding documents speak to our commitment
to equality, and even though the Founders didn't mean that
blacks were equal, we believe that now. The rule of law in the
United States prohibits us as managers from discriminating
against any person on the basis of race, when we hire, assign work, promote,
or terminate employment. I'm proud to live and lead under such laws.

However, the ethic of equality and the obligation of the law have produced a uniquely American illusion: color blindness. We all have heard white people say (or said ourselves), "I don't see somebody's color. I just think about them as a person like everyone else."

These words offer the appearance of equality, normally delivered as they are with a tangible tinge of self-satisfaction in being so enlightened. But this talk of color blindness fuels conflict and ignorance. Why? Because denying that we see a person's color is delusional—we most certainly observe their utterly visible race—and because the language of color blindness may not be received as we mean it to be.

Let me illustrate this intent-impact risk. When you say, "I don't think of you as black; I treat you like anyone else," a black person may think you really mean something along the following lines:

- "I believe that we are similar as people, and your race isn't a problem for me." We mean this as a positive sentiment. But when blackness is an essential part of someone's identity, saying "I don't think of you as black" is like saying "I don't accept you in the way you value yourself." Or a black person may interpret "Your race isn't a problem" to mean that "Deep down, I see you as white."

- "I'm not going to hold your blackness against you by doing something to you that the law prohibits." If you're black, you're glad the law protects you, and it's good to know that white managers understand that law. But when I, as a white man who leads, use words of invalidation (see previous point) to imply to a black person that I won't hurt them, it can remind them that I have the power to do so; that people like me have hurt people like them in the past; and that the law is what motivates me, rather than morality or basic business acumen.

- "If I don't see you as black, I don't have to see me as white." Review the reasons we hide from our whiteness in essay 9. It is a perverse self-delusion to avoid our own whiteness by falsifying another's plainly visible blackness.

This issue of color blindness gets at the heart of the dream Dr. Martin Luther King Jr. made famous: that people will see "the content of a person's character rather than the color of their skin." It is a compelling idea, that character would trump pigment. The vision powerfully affirms that what matters is who we are and what we do. It hearkens to a time when race no longer divides.

I choose to believe that Dr. King did not literally mean that we should not see color at all. We need to see it for what it is and is not. We need to do the right things with racial differences, and stop doing the wrong things (the law helps with that).

Blindness to the color of a person is not a biological possibility for any except the blind. A person's race is right there to be seen, and it deserves to be taken into proper account. Race and ethnicity will persist as potent social and political realities through the lifetime of anyone reading this book.

See past the illusion of color blindness. Such mental fiction does not serve us well: everyone is hurt when we pretend not to see color that counts. Instead, we must learn to give racial difference the attention it deserves: no more, no less. That's what I call *due regard* (see the next essay).

CONVERSATION STARTER: *Have there been times when you suffered from the illusion of color blindness? If so, how will you recover?*

THINK

■ **30** ■

Invest heavily
in due regard.

One of the key practices in this book is **due regard**, the ability to distinguish among the attributes and cultures of your employees, peers, superiors, and customers, so that you encourage their contributions. This is a method to individualize your leadership, by attending appropriately to differences. You must make your own informed judgment about the degree to which dimensions of diversity are operative.

Due regard is an approach through which you learn to give the right weight to diversity in your leadership work: not too little weight, in which a person's relevant traits are denied or ignored; and not too much weight, so that the race or gender "cards" are constantly in play.

Ignorance	Due Regard	Exaggeration

| Without regard for differences at work | With *warranted concern* for differences at work | With *excessive attention* to differences at work |

Figure 30

Here's an illustration from a retail company with a large presence in the South. James, a high-performing black department manager from Atlanta, was promoted into an assistant manager position in a Tennessee store. Ted, his new store manager (a white man with a great reputation in the company), was really excited about the promotion. James knew the operation inside out, related to customers beautifully, and handled employees with directness and humor.

On James' first day on the job (I'm not making this up), Ted took him out to raise the store's flags, a daily ritual of pride. Ted passed James the American flag, which he raised up the middle, tallest pole. Then James was given the State of Tennessee standard, which he also raised. And then Ted handed James the banner of the Confederacy. Oops.

James unfurled this symbol of slavery (this is how black Americans interpret the Confederate flag), and wondered what he'd gotten himself into with this promotion. His hesitation spoke volumes as he looked down at the flag. When he looked up, he could see that Ted understood the poignant moment.

So Ted got to provide us with this case study in due regard. Here are the options for Ted's path to action as they flashed through his mind.

Ignorance: Ted could try to ignore the painful and unspoken meaning in the moment, and mess up the start of a promising partnership. Ted could call the corporate legal department, hoping to validate his decision to handle the situation "without regard" for James' "over-sensitivity."

Exaggeration: Ted could make a fool of himself by blushing, stammering out a lame-ass excuse for the practice of flying the offensive symbol, and not raise the Confederate flag (do you suppose employees and customers might have noticed its absence?).

Due Regard: Ted, with remarkable poise, acknowledged the surprise and awkwardness of the moment, took the banner from James, and raised it himself. Then they returned to the office for their first substantive heart-to-heart talk (one of many, I'm glad to say).

Lead with due regard for human differences. This incident led to a long conversation in the store, the corporation, and the community. In the end, store leaders decided to stop flying the Confederate flag, out of respect for black customers and employees. This was not a minor matter, as a small and vocal number of white employees and customers felt their traditions were now disrespected. Some of these customers quit shopping at the store, although the loss in sales revenue was more than offset by new business from the black community.

STICK AND CARROT

The stick is the law, which motivates us to avoid discriminatory behavior and the lawsuits which discrimination engenders. Make no mistake: avoiding the stick is good.

But we lead to achieve results with our employees; we do not lead merely to avoid discrimination and litigation. If your natural approach to diversity is "I just don't take those differences into account, because I don't want to discriminate," you miss diversity's power when you focus on avoiding the pain. The stick can never deliver what only the carrot can provide.

Due regard is the carrot: take into account the uniqueness of colleagues and customers. The risks of ignorance and exaggeration will diminish. Then your leadership will evoke their full contribution, and your results will demonstrate your ability to lead a high-performing business.

CONVERSATION STARTER: *How could the practice of due regard equip you to lead with more confidence among diverse colleagues and customers?*

Learn

˅

I n essay 16, I defined transformation as dramatic growth in an individual or an organization's character and performance. Your commitment to work successfully with black colleagues and customers now presents you with an unparalleled chance for personal and professional development.

Learning is the method to this madness.

This section explores the remaining four stages of the Transformation Curve, launching beyond Pre-Awareness. This strategy helps you know what to expect from your diversity learning. That will keep your progress on track. An understanding of all five stages—Pre-Awareness, Interest and Necessity,

Careful Skill Progress, Adventurous Competence, and Relative Expertise—will drive diversity's contribution to your results.

The section closes with another key topic. Essay 36 focuses on self-monitoring, the skill by which we watch ourselves during our interactions, and make effective choices about how we think, feel, and act. It's a decisive daily discipline.

Diversity is proving to be an opportunity for transformation among white men who lead. And we thought it was only trouble.

As you focus on learning to lead as a white man, remember the words of Harold Geneen, former CEO at IT&T: "Leadership cannot really be taught. It can only be learned."

Transformation through Interest and Necessity:

Enlighten your self-interest and leverage your necessity.

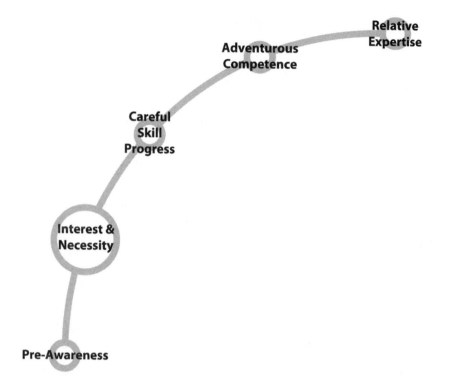

Figure 31-1

In essay 16 on Pre-Awareness, we looked at the natural order for learning within the five stages of the Transformation Curve:

Relationships When you explore differences with specific, diverse colleagues and customers ...

Knowledge you are motivated to learn what you need to know, and ...

Skills then you apply your knowledge to achieve results through your relationships.

Let's look at the way relationships, knowledge, and skill function in the stages.

Transformative Stage	Relationships	Knowledge	Skills
Pre-Awareness	Few	Little	Minimal
Interest & Necessity	Starting	Emerging	Tenuous
Careful Skill Progress	Growing	Building	Practicing
Adventurous Competence	Deepening	Testing	Strong
Relative Expertise	Widening	Refining	Mentoring

Figure 31-2

The Interest and Necessity stage signifies your new motivation to learn about diversity. You want to learn, you need to learn, or both. Deploying awareness (see essay 18) at this stage informs fresh and energetic inquiry, as you move from not knowing what you don't know (Pre-Awareness) to discovering avenues for learning about human differences.

Interest indicates your values and intellect have notified you that some sort of personal gain may be available by exploring a dimension of diversity such as race or gender. *Necessity* suggests that, in the case of many white men who lead, circumstances with colleagues or customers now compel you to invest in your diversity learning.

To illustrate how Interest and Necessity can develop, consider David's story. He was a vice president with a New York consumer products company. David had an Ivy League pedigree, a positive reputation, and a problem he didn't see coming. He was the point person for a new policy intended to boost morale and improve productivity (drum roll, please): a new business casual dress code. Intent: to encourage the troops by loosening up the tradition of dressing business formal (and maybe help with recruiting younger talent!). Impact: things hit the fan. Women muttered that whoever prohibited denim had no fashion sense; younger employees thought anything but jeans was still too uptight; and the policy pushed a perceived "Ivy League look" that ticked off employees with lower incomes. Even worse, the few black employees willing to speak up declared they would not dress down to the new standards, because they had to dress formally to be taken seriously.

David was not having fun with this. Fortunately, he had started what was growing into a very positive relationship with Cheryl, the only black manager reporting to him. So we pick up the story when David's *necessity* has momentum, using the relationships/knowledge/skills approach.

Relationships (starting): Sometimes one teacher can be enough. David wanted Cheryl's insight, and he had the good sense to protect her from getting dragged into the debacle. She decided to trust David enough to find out what his questions were. It was a chance to help her manager, even though it might shine a spotlight on her in a way she would prefer to avoid (white people seem to need black people to teach them about race).

Knowledge (emerging): His best query: What do I need to know that I don't even know to ask about? That is a world-class question to transition from Pre-Awareness to awareness. She helped him think through gender and class issues that the executives had not considered. When he asked about the surprising response from black employees, she explained her community's emphasis on professional appearance as a means for securing opportunity. He was shocked to find that level of intention; he got up each morning, walked into the closet, and put on whatever suit he saw first.

Skills (tenuous): The critical skill in this stage is teachability: the capacity and commitment to learn. David was willing to learn from a subordinate, he was able to simplify the policy to meet the needs of diverse stakeholders, and he grew intrigued with how practical diversity learning could prove. Cheryl built a stronger relationship with a prospective mentor, by adding *interest* to his *necessity*.

Learning doesn't always produce results as positive as David's. In each stage, watch for the undertow, a situation that can knock you off balance. When that happens, the best course of action is to return to your relationships and, like David, ask: "What am I missing? Why did I miss it? How can I see it coming next time? What could I do next?" This will rekindle your interest and reinform your necessity.

CONVERSATION STARTER: *In what ways do Interest and Necessity motivate you to learn about leading among diverse colleagues and customers?*

Transformation through *Careful Skill Progress*:

Practice and adapt; it's evolutionary.

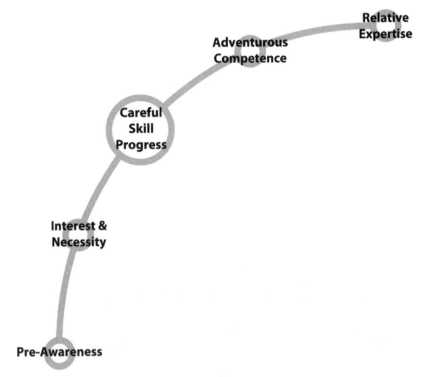

Figure 32

Congratulations, my friend! You have emerged from the risks of ignorance (Pre-Awareness) and made a stable, teachable start with your diversity learning (Interest and Necessity). Next up? Time to get in some mileage on the Transformation Curve.

Here's where you experiment cautiously and practice a lot. Your expanding relationships, knowledge, and skills can help you get new things done, win you respect, and yes, get you into trouble. You evolve your leadership skills through an unpredictable mix of awkward attempts and confident skill building.

The previous stage was more about learning and less about leading. For David, his relationship with Cheryl was key, and he needed to gather information. During Careful Skill Progress, you focus on skill development, stoked by your growing relationships and knowledge building.

Caution Is Advised

Why do you, as a white man who leads, need to be careful during skill progress? Here are four causes for caution.

First, pain avoidance. It's not much fun when your diversity learning hurts. We sense the risk inherent to growing our ability to lead with race and gender in mind. We probably over imagine potential pain from unknowable pitfalls, but clear-eyed caution is a useful companion at this stage.

Second, evading embarrassment. Our ego would prefer to avoid public blunders, and there's really no place to hide when you lead for a living. Courage will also be a constant friend.

Third, facing personal limits. Followers generally expect their managers to know more and to bring advanced skills to leadership. You highly value their expectations of your merit. In your diversity learning, though, you are exploring relationships, knowledge, and skills in areas some of your employees have known intimately for years. Hold humility as an ally.

Fourth, safety and validation. You have to feel safe enough to recover and move ahead. It takes careful attention and time to build ease and honesty into diverse relationships. Self-validation for your learning is also a priority; you should not expect to be showered with kudos for your hard-won progress.

Don't assume you're going to step on a landmine as you progress. It's just smart to be careful, so that you can sustain your skill building. Evolution develops its own safeguards.

Skill Progress

What skills are we talking about? Here are four skills to practice at this stage.

- *Listen to diverse stakeholders.* There are no shortcuts to an expertise with diversity. Respectful inquiry will cultivate your relationships and expand your knowledge base. Disciplined listening (during one-to-ones, interviews, focus groups, surveys, employee forums, team meetings) is the heart of inclusion. When a white male manager seeks diverse input, followers take note of his teachability.

- *Practice with quick wins.* David fixed the dress code. But that didn't mean he was going to lead the launch of a company-wide diversity initiative. Find opportunities at work where your skill practice will add value sooner rather than later (e.g., developing black employees on your team). Look for the quick wins.

- *Apply your learning to your unit's tasks.* Direct your diversity skill practice toward the actual work and results for which you and your unit are responsible. For example, if you lead a sales team, focus your skill development on improving the performance of women, people of color, and everyone else on your team to sell more effectively to diverse customers. Diversity works when it applies *to* work.

- *Track risk and opportunity.* We considered personal caution earlier. You also need to lead by calculating diversity's costs and benefits to the organization (see essays 76 and 98).

Your investment in learning pays off when you listen, earn some quick wins, and adapt your diversity learning to serve your unit. That's the careful progress that new diversity skills can produce.

CONVERSATION STARTER: *What specific diversity management skills do you need to practice, and how will you do so with appropriate caution?*

Transformation through *Adventurous Competence:*

Go for it; it's revolutionary.

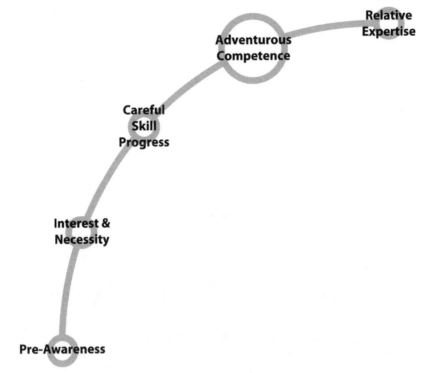

Figure 33-34

T his is the stage where your investment in leading among diverse colleagues and customers really starts to show results. You effectively diagnose differences at work, problem solve with sensitivity to diverse needs, and proactively manage multiple dimensions of diversity.

Adventure implies a higher level of risk and return. Your deepening competence propels you to recognize and seize opportunities you would have missed previously. You take risks before they take you. This isn't about being cocky; any day we lead with diversity in mind is a day we can be humbled. It is about the confidence that emerges from engaging diversity's Interest and Necessity, and carefully cultivating diversity skills.

Let's look at the three key areas for leading with Adventurous Competence. *Relationships* (deepening): During the previous stages, you've expanded relationships by listening to stakeholders and developing diverse employees. You've got to have strong people in your corner, and they have to know you also have their back. *If you don't have a black mentor already, find one.* They can be an elder or a peer, and they need to lead with their own power, and be willing to share it with you (see essay 83).

Knowledge (testing): Connect your diversity commitment to goals, gaps, and opportunities within your sphere of leadership. It's time to increase your diversity investment to yield a larger return. For instance: meet with leaders of the company's black employee network and find out how you can support their contribution; work with HR to ensure that all employees in your unit (black and otherwise) receive equal pay for equal work; identify and solve any race-related issues with customer service. Sit down with your manager and negotiate a diversity-related performance objective (see essay 76). Ask him/her to hold you accountable. You get the idea; it's time to step it up.

Skills (strong): Start sharing your diversity learning with other white men. Transparency is part of the adventure, and we strengthen our point of view when we teach it. By this time, your black colleagues have invested in you, and you can offer them some return on their investment by assisting more white men through the Transformation Curve.

Now let's check back in on David as he develops Adventurous Competence for leading on diversity. It's eighteen months later, and he has diligently and carefully progressed in his relationships, knowledge, and skills, with race and gender differences in view.

David's reputation on diversity improved when he was seen by all to resolve the dress code fiasco. Since then, David and Cheryl helped the company win a large contract with a city whose mayor was African-American. As a result, David supported Cheryl for a promotion to assistant

VP for sales, where she reported to a different executive as the highest-ranking black person in the firm.

David aggressively pursued connections with his alma mater to help the company recruit high-potential black undergraduates. Micah was the top talent to join the firm as a result of those efforts; he had started four months earlier, on the front line in distribution (one of David's groups), which delivered product into the field.

Unfortunately, Micah had two white male peers, both company veterans, who appeared to resent his education and his connections. Everyone knew that David was in on Micah's selection. They rode him pretty hard, and Micah figured it was just what you go through sometimes at the start of a career.

That changed when their language took on racial overtones. They used words and phrases like "uppity," "your kind is not welcome here," and "you're just an affirmative action suck-up." Micah asked them to stop, and then tolerated it for awhile, because he wanted to prove his worth, and didn't want to be seen as a complainer. Nothing improved, so he talked quietly with Paul, his manager, a white man whose impulse was to confront the tormentors and put them on an action plan. Micah was getting concerned that this thing would blow up in his face.

Paul went to the HR director, who quietly conferred with Cheryl. She didn't hear any names; HR just wanted her view because she had advised on a similar situation previously. Cheryl's advice was generic because she could not speak to the specifics, but she deduced who was involved, because there weren't many new black employees. Cheryl privately shared her suspicions with David about the situation two weeks after Micah first spoke with Paul, his own manager.

If you were in David's place, what would Adventurous Competence lead you to do? (I'll tell you what David did in the next essay, but don't cheat yourself by jumping ahead!)

CONVERSATION STARTER: *Are you leading with Adventurous Competence on any dimension of diversity? Is such confidence transferable to leading on other human differences?*

Study

a case in
Adventurous Competence.

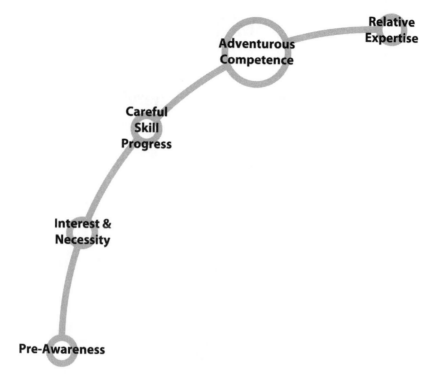

Figure 33-34

S o what *did* Adventurous Competence lead David to do? First, he privately expressed to Cheryl his anger at the way Micah was being treated. Next, HR calmed him down when he wanted to "cut to the chase" and speak directly to the two accused men. Cheryl served as a peer mentor, pushing him to think through the situation from a business perspective.

Here's an org chart for David's diversity adventure in this situation.

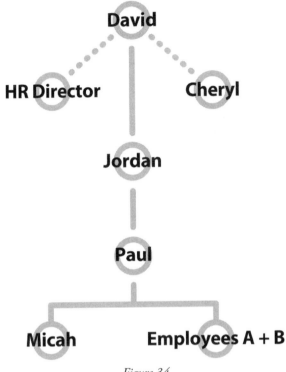

Figure 34

David:	Asked HR to remind all employees by e-mail broadcast about policies regarding inclusion, respect, and harassment
HR:	Declined; asked Paul (Micah's manager) to review the policy with his team
David:	Agreed with HR (learned to focus his solving on the actual problem, and not cause a wider wondering about the context for such a broadcast); told HR he planned to coach Jordan (the manager between Paul and David) on how to handle the circumstances
HR:	Asked David to wait so that Paul and HR could talk with Jordan, who had not heard about the situation
David:	Agreed to wait, asked HR/Paul to brief Jordan within two days; David recognized that his direct interest in Micah's

success must be balanced with this chance to coach Jordan and Paul as white men who lead, but time was critical

HR/Paul: Next day, he reviewed the situation with Jordan, including David's concern for the impact on Micah and handling this quickly

David: Did not wait to hear from Jordan: set next day appointments in order with Cheryl, then HR, then Jordan, then Jordan and Paul

David's Appointments:

With Cheryl: They refined David's intended course of action, and identified six preferred outcomes:

1) Coach Jordan and Paul to lead effectively

2) Equip Micah to be part of the solution, and retain him

3) Strengthen the partnership with HR (and Legal, if necessary)

4) Avoid damaging the productivity of Paul's team

5) Correct the behavior of the two accused, and retain their veteran contribution (or terminate if necessary)

6) Share the experience and business results with David's boss, the company president

With HR: Agreed on outcomes and a plan; HR would quietly investigate Micah's claims, securing available facts and the stories from the two alleged troublemakers

With Jordan: Jordan concurred with David's concerns for Micah and timely action, but also wanted to resolve this quietly if possible (reminder to David that Jordan and Paul needed safety, just like Micah; no one wants such a situation to blow up)

With Jordan and Paul: All three discussed HR's conclusions (Micah's story was basically confirmed) and the plan of action

Paul with his team: E-mailed related policies for next meeting agenda, then reviewed with verbal firmness (the accused understood the context due to HR's investigation, and Micah maintained a low profile)

With the troublemakers: Paul met with them individually. Employee A denied everything, maintained that Micah was making it up, and complained that "they always get away with stuff like this." Paul reminded him about company policy, and warned him that not following policy with regard to Micah or anyone else was grounds for corrective action and, if it continued, dismissal. Employee B was embarrassed, indicated he had already apologized to Micah, and assured Paul he never meant to get involved. Paul advised him to resist employee A's attempts to keep him involved.

Let's jump ahead in the drama. Paul and HR stayed on top of the situation. Micah became the team's top performer during the next quarter, and he stayed with the company. Employee B's performance improved, and the team's results did not suffer. David and Jordan also carefully monitored the situation.

Sadly, employee A continued to violate company policy (it just got more subtle). He was terminated, although it took seven months to build the case, during which Micah learned how to perform in spite of a colleague. When employee A's final day arrived, two things happened: first, Paul and HR covered the basics of ending employment with him; and then, one-to-one, David took the final five minutes to coach employee A on how continuing prejudice could affect his future success.

David and Cheryl learned a lot from this process, and they unpacked it for the company president. For all the participants in the situation (except employee A), David's Adventurous Competence revolutionized their confidence that the company was committed to attracting, growing, and retaining top talent with due regard for diversity.

CONVERSATION STARTER: *Have you observed Adventurous Competence like David's at work? If so, what impact did it have on you and the situation? If you haven't seen such competence, why do you think that is?*

LEARN

■ **35** ■

Transformation through *Relative Expertise:* *Lead with boldness and humility.*

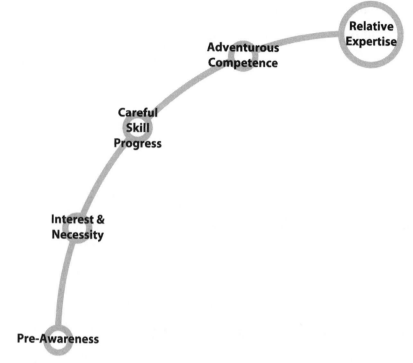

Figure 35

At this stage of your diversity learning, diverse stakeholders recognize you as an expert. You mentor others through the Transformation Curve. *Relative* means you hold your expertise with humility. You lead on differences from your side, always remembering your limits, so that you honor other's experiences and evoke their contribution. Being a relative expert means that

- colleagues recognize you as a high-value contributor when diversity issues arise, especially during conflict;

- stakeholders encounter you as a leader with integrity; a man who engages diversity with your mind, heart, and behavior;

- you remember that you're a man working to support women, a white person seeking to serve people of color, and a leader

influencing people so that they choose to follow; you know your
limitations, so your expertise is relative;

- other white men count on you to help them develop their own
Relative Expertise.

One of the white men I got to help was David. We worked together for
four years: he emerged quickly from Pre-Awareness and was seen as a go-
to-guy on diversity forty-eight months later. He invested in relationships;
learned fast, particularly from his mistakes; and always applied his emerging
diversity skills to add value.

Here's one more story with David, the tale of a time he demonstrated his
Relative Expertise by leading with boldness and humility.

The board of directors was exploring a strategic alliance with a large Hong
Kong manufacturer. There appeared to be a substantial mutual opportunity
in Asian and North American markets, if they could find a way to collaborate
on production (the Chinese firm's strength) and distribution (the particular
advantage which David's group delivered).

David was assigned a lead position to get the deal done, an exciting
opportunity because it offered the chance to profitably increase company
revenue by forty percent in the first three years. Cheryl was appointed to
the team as lead for ensuring that the manufactured products satisfied the
customers. They earned these roles, in part, because the president had observed
their success with diversity issues and opportunities. Ironically, neither Cheryl
nor David had much experience with Chinese people, culture, or business.
So while it was a moment to lead boldly, the occasion also whispered of the
need for humility (they hoped to avoid actual humiliation).

For David, the deal blew sideways after the first two-day meeting. In a
private session with David, Mr. Shen Zhang (his peer as the lead for the Hong

Kong company) expressed "discomfort with Ms. Jackson's role" (that would be Cheryl). He explained, without specifics, that "some of my less-progressive colleagues and customers would prefer to work with Mr. Jamieson" (Cheryl's boss). David was not able to pry any detailed feedback from the man. It was implied that they weren't "comfortable" with Cheryl's gender and race. They took no issue with her qualifications. And other leads on both sides shared her level in the management hierarchy, so it wasn't a "level equity" concern that required more involvement from Cheryl's manager. David told Mr. Shen that he would give appropriate consideration to the concern.

Initially David took this personally, as an attack on Cheryl. He then decided to set aside what he *wanted* to do (react) for what his leadership role *needed* from him. Here's what he did.

To evaluate options, David secured personal, cultural, and business information about Zhang (Mr. Shen's "first" name, in the Chinese order) and other people with whom they were negotiating. His research led him to suspect that Zhang's objection to Cheryl was a ploy to threaten a key interest and force concessions. If David dropped Cheryl, Zhang was one up in the negotiations. If he refused, Zhang could respond with "if you won't cooperate on the Ms. Jackson issue, then what about ...," naming a concession for which Zhang would give nothing in return. David wanted to play the game on his own terms.

David flew to Chicago to consult with William, a black VP in a financial services firm with deep Hong Kong interests whom David had befriended at a executive roundtable on diversity the previous year. William doubted that Cheryl's race was a problem. Her gender could be an issue, but he had never run across such prejudice among senior executives in Hong Kong, as they were used to doing business with women from Britain and the United States.

Based on this due diligence, David talked confidentially with his president and board chair about the situation, to confirm their approach and to gauge the courage of their diversity convictions. Not surprisingly, they wanted David to handle the situation so they would not be forced to choose between the company's growth and the company's diversity commitment. They were willing to do their part.

David then sat down with Cheryl for a humbling heart-to-heart, because he couldn't scurry around behind the scenes pulling strings like she was a performing puppet. The situation angered her: now her being a black woman was a problem for people halfway around the world! But they had a lot of experience with working diversity issues together, and she deeply appreciated how David and the company were handling the situation. She needed to focus on her job to the best of her abilities.

Meanwhile, the president and board chair called their peers in Hong Kong and indicated that Mr. Shen had raised an issue with David that could threaten the alliance. They further noted that they had instructed David to meet Zhang in LA to resolve the situation, which they were confident would occur. This forced Zhang to disclose the "Cheryl" issue to his side: if his senior execs didn't know about the ploy, this put Zhang in a bind with them; if Cheryl's presence was their concern, they now understood that David's company wasn't going to simply concede.

David built an LA agenda with Zhang that included the "leadership team change request." David opened the meeting by expressing his own (fabricated) concern about a member of Zhang's team (who just *happened* to be a sales AVP like Cheryl), who had strong ties to "socialist complications" in Beijing. David was signaling he could play this game. Zhang offered to drop this person of concern from his team, if David would drop Cheryl. David smiled and indicated that, "given the serious interest that my president and board chair have in Cheryl remaining on our team" (followed by a brief pause), he would be willing, after all, to work with the troubling member of Zhang's team.

This gave Zhang a way out of the corner into which David believed his counterpart had painted himself; during David's pause, he thought he saw Zhang's subtle reaction to the mention of the president and board chair. David's leadership notified all involved that this negotiation would be tough and culturally sensitive. From that point, Zhang and David built a positive (if adversarial) relationship.

Most important, six months later, Cheryl, David, *and* Zhang organized a ceremony at which the alliance deal was signed.

This situation tested David's Relative Expertise. He was confident in his relationships, knowledge, and skills (bold expertise), while the predicament forced him to remember his relative limits (humility). As a leader, he leveraged his competence with human differences to deliver powerful business results.

CONVERSATION STARTER: *Have you ever led with Relative Expertise on a dimension of diversity? If so, what did it produce? If not, what could such leadership evoke?*

Watch Yourself:

Build the critical skill of self-monitoring.

Insight doesn't set us free—it just lets us know where the fight is.
The question remains whether we are willing to fight it out—
not with others but with ourselves.

DAVID SCHNARCH, PHD

Passionate Marriage

In corporate life, the pressures of productivity often overwhelm thoughtful learning. "Get it done now" prevails over "Do it this time in a way that improves getting it done next time." Such an obsessive task orientation inhibits self-appraisal; we often fail to find time for deep personal reflection.

A growing competence with diversity requires the capacity to monitor your thoughts and behaviors while you lead. The ability to observe your mental messaging and consequent behavior pushes your progress through the stages of the Transformation Curve. Self-monitoring drives you to delve into your inner white guy, so you can lead from a place of purpose instead of Pre-Awareness.

In essay 4, I introduced the idea of groupism as the unthinking presumption that cultural connections determine individuality rather than shape individuality. As white people, many of us suffer from groupism when we encounter black strangers (that is, people we don't know). We judge the book by its cover, and we don't monitor our inner processing.

Let's imagine our internal conversation in the moment we encounter a black person we don't know. And note: this little drama of pre-judging (the root of prejudice) unfolds in a second or two, before a word is spoken.

Our Thought	Our Behavior
"Look, there's a black person."	No problem yet; noting skin color is unavoidable if your eyes can see.
"They're different from me."	Still no issue – the difference is a fact. But here comes the chance for trouble, and you make a choice, on purpose or not. A different range of behaviors emerges from each of these choices.

Choices

"I am threatened by this different, black person."	From threat comes car-door-locking, a hostile tone of voice, angry eyes, and other defensive and confrontational indicators. *The difference between us is bad.*
"I am uncomfortable with this different, black person."	From discomfort comes loss of eye contact, awkward speaking, arm-crossing. *I don't know how to handle the difference between us.*
"I am going to ignore this different, black person."	Ignoring is non-verbal avoidance (like looking right through them), rendering the black person invisible. *I try to deny that the different person is still there, or that they exist at all.*
"I am intrigued by this different, black person."	Intrigue manifests in positive eye contact, engaging tone of voice, genuine empathy, positive expectation, active listening. *The difference is an opportunity.*

Figure 36

Many of my black friends, colleagues, and clients are perversely expert at unpacking such momentary judgments from white people. I honestly wonder if they're making some of it up, misperceiving what's really going on. And as white people we don't all suffer from this malady of prejudice all the time.

But admit it. Some version of the little screenplay above has passed through your brain and appeared in your behavior a hundred times. That's the risk of prejudice in me and you, and it can seriously inhibit our ability to lead. The individuals we lead, black or otherwise, are shaped but not determined by the groups of which they are part.

Self-monitoring is the skill by which we watch ourselves during our interactions, and make effective choices about how we think, feel, and act toward the other.

The most brilliant demonstration of self-monitoring I've ever witnessed came from my daughter, Melinda. She played a lot of basketball from ages nine to eighteen. One day, when she was thirteen, we stopped after practice at a convenience store. As we climbed out of the car, two black men were getting out of their car next to us. We went in first and looked around for what we wanted; the men bought their snacks, left the store, and drove off.

When we came out to our vehicle, I got in, and Melinda went around the back of the car and bent down, looking at something. After she got in on the passenger side, I glanced over at her and saw an odd look on her face. I asked her, "What's up?" (Just two words can take you on an adventure with a thirteen-year-old girl.)

She looked at me and then half-shouted with dramatic exasperation. She was suddenly and seriously frustrated with something, and I had no clue. As it turned out, she had just humiliated herself, all by herself. Here's what she told me:

> "Dad, I noticed the black guys when we went into the store. They didn't do anything suspicious or threatening, but I still watched them when they paid. Then I couldn't see them once they went outside. So when I came out of the store, all of the sudden I'm

so stupid and I think 'what if they put a bomb under the back of our car?' So then, this is just so lame, I went around the back of the car to check for the bomb!"

Now she was truly angry with herself and almost in tears as she blurted out: "What is wrong with me! Just because they're black men doesn't mean they're bad!"

I had such mixed feelings in that moment. Like Melinda, I was sobered that she had been infected with such unconscious racist crap (as you can imagine, she didn't get that from home). Yet I was so proud of her self-perception. The elapsed time from the unwanted suspicion that these black guys were bombers to her stark self-confrontation was less than fifteen seconds. That was an awesome display of self-monitoring, even though she still gets slightly embarrassed when I tell this story.

So, like Melinda, watch yourself, my friend. There is no substitute for self-monitoring, and it is always hard earned. To lead and succeed among black colleagues and customers, your capacity for disciplined self-perception is crucial.

AN EXERCISE IN SELF-MONITORING

Set aside fifteen minutes each workday to assess how you think and feel about differences that could affect you at work. To generate fresh insight, ask yourself unusual questions like the following:

About me:

- How much pressure am I facing today?
- What does my manager expect of me today?
- What is my physical and emotional state right now?

About the people I'm working with today:

- Am I reminded of anyone else by this person? If so, who? How does this affect the way I feel about this person?

- How do I feel about their style of dress and grooming?
- How does the sound of their voice make me feel?
- Am I aware of their smell? Does it remind me of anything or anyone?
- Have I made assumptions about this person based on the region from which they came?
- What do I believe about the college they attended? Or does it matter to me if they don't have a college education?
- What assumptions have I made about this person's job history? About the job titles they've held? The companies they've worked for?
- Has the person shared personal details with me? Is that having an impact on the way I see them or view their work performance?

Try this exercise in self-insight for a few days. Many of our female colleagues and clients are highly skilled in self-assessment that takes angles of inquiry that rarely occur to us. I marvel at the advantages they gain by habitually taking personal responsibility to this level. They've convinced me that intuition is not only for women, and I am persuaded that it is healthy to think all the way around a situation. It's about accessing all the information available to me as I lead, sourced from cognition, emotion, and intuition. The most amazing talent known to me in developing such self-aware leadership is Nancy D. Solomon, based near Seattle. Take a look at www.nancydsolomon.com.

My own experience as a manager confirms that it is easier to tell my truth to others as I grow more honest with myself.

And that's what the skill of self-monitoring is all about.

CONVERSATION STARTER: *When you focus on self-monitoring, what do you learn that you can use to improve the way you lead?*

Manage Emotions

I assert that the emotional life of white men is every bit as rich and varied as the inner workings of people who are not white men.

Having feelings is a human trait. It's just that, as white men, we have ours in our own way. We're different, and different, as they say, does not mean bad. And there is a wide diversity of emotional experience and expression among us.

In many of us, emotions can operate in a steady state, burning less intensely than in other folks. We may express our feelings less frequently. Don't get me wrong, I love life with women, but I deeply enjoy being in the company of white men who don't need to talk much to still feel connected.

Apart from our noisy advocacy of the sports teams we love (competition apparently brings out our passion), our emotional style tends to be quieter (some say boring). If calm is our yang to women's chatty yin, so be it.

I have heard this quietude defined as an ethnic trait common to men of northern European descent. Wherever our emotional culture comes from, it is authentic and valid for us. And many white men hail from the more expressive cultures of southern Europe.

Our particular challenge? We sometimes lack a *fluency* with what we're feeling. It always irritates me when a woman will correctly interpret how I'm feeling—"You look tired today; everything OK?"—when I myself have not realized how tired I am. We know we're feeling something, but we're not always sure what it is. And once we gain a smidgen of emotional insight, we tend to rush into action, or on to the next thought.

This brings us to the purpose of this section. We contemplated the skill of self-monitoring in the previous essay. As white men who lead, one of our pivotal challenges is handling the emotions that arise when we "watch ourselves" during our diversity learning. The following essays seek to encourage in you a growing proficiency with facing and managing the emotions that accompany a commitment to diversity.

Our black colleagues and customers need to see just *how* we "have a heart." So this section explores transforming gut reaction to heart felt.

■ 37 ■

Deal
with denial.

D enial comes in two flavors.

The first tastes of refusal: noncompliant, contradictive, a repudiation of what is presented, as in "I deny that what you say is true."

The second carries the savor of Pre-Awareness, with denial as a more specific refusal to face reality, as in "I don't even want to think about it." Psychologists describe this sort of denial as an unconscious, common, and risky unwillingness to fully engage reality. Denial may be an effective short-term tactic for mental health, serving as a temporary defense mechanism to help us maintain our emotional balance, or permit a tough issue to infiltrate our minds at a pace we can handle. But a head-in-the-sand habit will lead to failure. And denial can degenerate into evil.

If you were in denial about leading with race and gender in mind, of course, you wouldn't have read this far. But it is not unusual for us as white men to miss the reality of our advantages, and not see the challenges that black people face.

So we should not be surprised when we find a profound denial of diversity's contribution in places where white men lead with position power. After my presentation on diversity as a business imperative to an executive team at a Fortune 500 company (where twenty-one of twenty-five leaders were white men), an EVP quietly snarled at me when no one else could hear: "Why the hell are you pushing this agenda; you're an educated white man!" His denial was fully operational, and I know for a fact that his organization suffered from his refusal to engage the reality of talented black colleagues and the needs of diverse customers.

Pre-Awareness or Malicious Neglect?

Women and people of color are knocking on the door to our denial. When we defend ourselves for some unintended mistake with a protest like, "How could I have known?" a black person may respond (or think) "Well, forty years after the Civil Rights movement, and 140 years after the end of slavery, you *should* know. So if you don't, one of three things is true: you aren't smart enough to figure it out, you've made sure you didn't learn, or you just don't care enough to find out."

From the white side that seems so unfair—hey, we just don't know what we don't know. But from the black side, when "death by a thousand nicks" seems your fate, the most recent nick may be just too much to take, even if it was unintended. A suggestion: replace the language of denial ("How could I know?") and miscommunication ("That's not what I meant!") with words of accountability ("I'm sorry that what I said—or did—affected you like that. It's not what I intended. Can I tell you what I did mean?").

I also recommend that you never mentally deny the current existence and impact of racism by believing that "racism isn't a problem anymore; we've taken care of that in the past forty years." No black colleague or customer wants to hear that sentiment emerge from your mouth or find expression in your behavior. Believing that the problem is solved prevents us as white people from becoming a continuous contributor to the solution. We are not done with this struggle ... not even close (see essay 45).

The horrific impact of denial can surprise in everyday life in corporate America. Here's an example. Lenora worked as an arbitrator for a major law firm. During a meeting with two white male attorneys, the discussion turned to the size of awards in wrongful-death claims. She listened, aghast, as they matter-of-factly discussed two settlements that typified an appalling practice: the cost to compensate for a little blond white boy's accidental death was three to four times the expense to settle the comparable death of a young black girl.

Suddenly Lenora did not feel safe. These two highly educated white men were utterly unaware of the effect their words were having on her; they appeared to simply accept that their sons were worth four times more than her daughter.

They weren't testing or teasing Lenora; clearly they did not respect her very presence. These experienced attorneys chatted about the formulas quantifying the difference between the two children's lifetime earning potential, as if the formulas were merely value-neutral calculations of the actuary tables. Lenora could not understand or address their denial of her and her daughter. Within a month she was gone from the firm. They never understood how they had squandered their investment in her: she had always been "such a good employee!"

For a leader, denying reality is like disavowing gravity; it will bring you down. Our moral and practical authority as leaders is grounded, in part, in our awareness that evil may grow from denying diversity's contribution.

CONVERSATION STARTER: *Do you find denial operating when you closely examine your relationships with those who are not white and male?*

MANAGE EMOTIONS
■ 38 ■

Face
the fear.

W hen a human perceives threat, we feel the spark of agitation, the pinch of anxiety, the impulse to fight or flee. Our word for this emotion is *fear*. And this feeling operates in us beyond the instant of danger. The fear of black people germinates in white Americans, and if left unchecked, it can bloom into misbehavior and violence. As English historian J. A. Froude noted, "Fear is the parent of cruelty."

As white men who lead, we may be afraid of diversity itself. Human differences place pitfalls and landmines in our path, and as leaders, there is little chance we will avoid the occasional crisis. Face the fear; it's better to take risks than to permit your risks to take you.

WHAT ARE WE AFRAID OF AS WHITE AMERICANS?

First and foremost, we fear the black Others, those beings whose existence is necessary so we can define our identity by who we are *not*. For 150 years before America became a nation, white people established a colonial economy largely built by black Others deemed subhuman.

For white American men, black people have always been the Other like no other. This is especially true of black men. They were a perceived threat to "our" women, so we used the law against them (Have you seen the film *A Time To Kill?*). Or we took the law into our own hands by lynching thousands of these black Others.

One modern and disturbing manifestation of white fear may be seen in our common reaction when we happen upon two or more black people gathered at work: in the hallways, elevators, conference rooms, lunchroom. Journalist Lena Williams observes that one legacy from the Jim Crow era—the prohibition of three or more black people gathering, because they may conspire to do harm to whites—is alive and well among us today. More than a dozen times I have heard white people in corporate America speak of their discomfort in encountering even a small cluster of black people. A number of black clients and friends have spoken openly to me about this, saying that black employees know to be careful about gathering, even by accident, because it makes white people uncomfortable.

Forgive me for suggesting that this gut reaction among whites signals something creepy and deeply bent. Such discomfiture with congregating black folk feels like some ancient, visceral fear of a slave rebellion, like the latent taint of our white racist ancestry. I hope we will call out and challenge such a fearful response, in ourselves and from others, because it says, "These people are a threat to us, and we feel at risk when they are together in our presence." That's no way to lead.

Here's a second fear: we may worry about our physical safety. That's healthy if you're in a neighborhood where you're an unwelcome stranger, or when a black person seeks to intimidate you. Manage the risk by moving out of harm's way; flight serves us better than fight almost every time. Remember to monitor your thoughts, as well. Have you ever caught yourself feeling threatened by a black person who intended you absolutely no harm? I have, many times, and it embarrasses me.

Third, many white men who lead fear being blamed for ignorance. We're so afraid to be called a racist that we lead without regard for race, when due regard (see essay 30) is the solution. When we lead authentically with diversity in mind, we won't fear a black person playing the "race card," because their criticism won't stick to us, and sometimes black allies will come to our defense.

English statesman Edmund Burke wrote: "No passion so effectually robs the mind of all its power to act and reason as fear." Try this: when you encounter a black man you do not know, look him in the eyes with a smile and a nod. Don't stare. And observe your own reaction. How does his response (or lack thereof) affect you? I first tried this small discipline in 1987, and it has become a healthy habit for me. I feel like I have a lot more positive experience with black men and women now, even though some of it comes only from these tiny encounters. This little practice has been an antidote to fear of the black Other for me, and maybe it will serve you.

To lead effectively as white men, we need to literally take fear at face value; when we engage the faces of black women and men, we can learn to account for fear operating in our hearts, minds, and behavior. We need to face our fear of the Other whom we identify by their black skin.

CONVERSATION STARTER: *Are you afraid of black people? Dig into when and why and what you can do about it.*

■ 39 ■

Get past the guilt,
and shed the shame.

My chief diversity mentor was Dr. William Pannell, a member of the faculty at Fuller Theological Seminary in Pasadena. I remember a time when I was really feeling guilty about being white, struggling with the burden of knowing how horribly some men of my race have behaved. Bill, who is black, was often surprising me, frequently with humor and sometimes with brutal candor. He let me moan for a bit and then delivered this tidbit: "I see that you're feeling bad … but I don't have time for your guilt."

The Gift That Keeps On Giving

Guilt is defined as being responsible for and feeling remorseful for wrongdoing. Bill described guilt as God's kick in the butt to wake us up to the choices we have, to set things right and make things better. He noted how nauseating it had become for him to see guilty white liberals spend so much time flogging others for the sins of the past that they were useless to the needs of the present. Racial reconciliation could not wait for another round of Caucasian dysfunction, so he would not permit me to wallow in my guilt.

I didn't expect getting past the past to be so hard. But guilt truly is a gift that keeps on giving. As soon as I feel like I'm not so haunted by the complicity of white men for slavery and lynching, another movie (like *Amistad*) or atrocity (like the killing of James Lee Byrd) shows up to indict me and my kind. And it's not just about history. When I open my mind and heart to the way many black Americans cope today, my face can grow hot with the complicity I feel for merrily pursuing my opportunity (see essays 23–26), while they would love to enjoy the advantages I have.

So let Bill's voice ring in your ear, too. Convert feeling bad about being a white man who leads into actual leadership. Climb out of your chair, listen to your coworkers and your conscience, and act on your best judgment. Wield the power you possess; don't deny possessing it, and don't apologize for it. Envision and actualize choices collaboratively. Travel the Transformation Curve to Relative Expertise. Life is too short, and there's too much effective leading ahead to squander time feeling guilty.

What a Shame

While we serve as judge and jury to our private sense of guilt, shame is a collective culpability roiling the soul of white folk. **Shame** is guilt publicized, a deserved or perceived disgrace for behavior that dishonors. White shame is metastasized guilt, the cancerous and silently shared suspicion that, even if we live as moral individuals, "our kind" deserves to be condemned.

Shame peels back the curtain on our vulnerability as white people, this raw and exposed place of identity from which we only want to escape. It is no mystery that being white is an unattractive point of meaning around which to organize one's identity. At Seattle's memorial service for Dr. King in 1968, there were 11,000 black people in attendance, but only 300 white people showed up, including my parents and me. At age thirteen, I was ashamed of my white community's dishonor toward Dr. King's leadership and sacrifice.

We may feel little guilt for how we have personally acted. But shame is a community-based illness that gnaws at our sense of social responsibility. When we are brave enough to diagnose this communal dis-ease, we come face-to-face with a love/hate ambivalence toward our own kind. It's hard to shake off the truth that our race brutalized the innocent, and that we still reap the benefits of our ancestors having done so.

Dr. Pannell's advice offers us a partial antidote to the dis-grace we may feel in being white: shed the shame. Acknowledge what you feel, but don't let it get in the way of productive leadership.

But putting our dishonor behind us will require some extra collective effort. First, we need conversation in the white community about shame, because it is a malady we share. This will require that we actually admit that the white community exists, which will not be easy (see essays 9 and 48). Next, it will require conciliation between individuals and communities—no small feat, as we can see in the sobering and amazing efforts in South Africa toward racial reconciliation. Finally, it will require that white people cease behaving in ways that bring us ongoing dishonor. I think we're doing better at that than our grandparents' generation. I also believe that our grandchildren will say the same thing.

One final Pannell story: at a luncheon in 1982, a white male executive named Bob held up a piece of watermelon on his fork, locked his gaze on Bill, and said "Hey, here's your favorite fruit!" Bob wasn't just teasing; the two of them were not real friendly with one another. I was appalled to see this application of a slavery-bound generalization (black people like watermelon) with bias (he said it to assert his assumed superiority) to stereotype one of the most remarkable men I will ever know. This racist motive apparently crawled from Bob's fruit salad right into his brain, and he had no mental monitors to control what happened once the message hit his mouth.

I wanted to hit his mouth. I was shamed by Bob's behavior. With immense presence and without one word, my mentor shut Bob down with a flat-faced stare. Bill then glanced at me with eyebrows raised, and silently communicated a very simple but profound message: "Are you watching? This jerk deserves not a word from me." Bill has paid a price for being black in the white academic world, and the restraint and grace he demonstrated that day (and every day) still astounds me.

Like Dr. William Pannell, our black colleagues and customers need us to get past the guilt and shed the shame. Then the lifelong challenge to forgive ourselves and our own kind will fuel effective leadership.

CONVERSATION STARTER: *How does guilt and shame operate in you? Which friends (white, black, and other) can help you leverage these feelings for motivation to learn and lead?*

■ **40** ■

Metabolize

anger constructively.

Anger is one of the sinews of the soul.

Thomas Fuller, English preacher

Anger is an emotion common to white and black men alike; a strong feeling of displeasure or hostility sparks in our gender. When we react in anger, people often get hurt. Anger may ignite in us knee-jerk behavior or ill-considered words. Unrestrained hostility in the workplace provokes all manner of grief, from unpleasant customer interactions to damaged relationships to lethal violence.

Yet I believe anger also has its positive purposes and results. We can mitigate anger's cruel impact by learning to metabolize anger constructively.

Metabolism has to do with the complex processes in a living organism necessary for the maintenance of life. Anger is such a process in us. It serves as the sharp end of the emotional stick, the impetus for fight or flight. Anger is necessary in the sense that it is inevitable: anger simply rises up in us, unbidden. And some of the best leaders I've followed used strong feelings of displeasure as an indispensable process tool:

- The football coach who channeled his anger at my mistakes to specifically redirect my contribution

- The manager who, upset by team conflict, confronted our misbehavior and spelled out the consequences

- The executive who, provoked by clumsy implementation, held us to public account for not keeping our promises

If denial is numbness and guilt is like anxiety, anger is heat. As a white man who leads, I try to metabolize anger constructively by controlling this burn in three steps:

1) Admit that my anger evidences a deeper cause, and uncover that cause

2) Respond to the cause and the target of my anger in a way that develops my competence with diversity

3) Follow up with the target and mend the relationship, if my anger damaged it

Consider what metabolizing anger constructively could look like at each learning stage of the Transformation Curve.

Pre-Awareness

Target I get angry at anyone who forces me to consider diversity, or makes me fear that I may be accused of discrimination or harassment.

Cause I want to avoid trouble, and I don't want to consider advantages and risks I haven't had to examine before.

Response Rather than react in fear and ignorance, I can "be a man" (as they say), and accept personal responsibility for leading with my eyes open.

Interest and Necessity

Target I get angry at myself as I learn about diversity and keep finding prejudice and ignorance I didn't know was in me.

Cause There is a lot going on around me and in me that I have not previously seen; this challenges my presumption of achievement, and embarrasses me when I realize that others see how little I know.

Response Find the courage to pursue my learning, while continuing to demonstrate my leadership gifts; trust my diverse colleagues to reward me with patience and reciprocal good faith.

Careful Skill Progress

Target I get angry at a black employee when he claims my behavior is motivated by racial differences, when the situation is really about his poor performance.

Cause	I'm not confident I can defend myself when the "race card" is played.
Response	Verify and document that I have managed the struggling employee consistently with the way I assign, coach, and evaluate work with all my direct reports. Validate this with a black colleague; confer with HR. I will focus on the facts of the performance problems, stay positive and behavior-oriented, and be open to input on issues from the employee. I might be missing something race related, such as issues with others on the team, but it's my job to help the employee accept that he needs to improve performance.

ADVENTUROUS COMPETENCE

Target	I get angry at my manager and my company when they talk about diversity but don't back it up with action and a true business case.
Cause	I'm unhappy with the integrity gap between what we say we believe and the way we act, and I suspect black employees feel this more than I do.
Response	I will not waver in my commitment to doing everything I can to support black colleagues and customers. I must also accept the organization's limitations, and look for ways to evoke in my manager and in the company a stronger capacity to walk the diversity talk.

RELATIVE EXPERTISE

Target	I get angry at other white men when they discriminate against black people and make me look bad by association.

Cause   I'm working hard to lead effectively with race and gender in mind, and I'm embarrassed when other white men behave stupidly.

Response I need to stop taking myself so seriously, and remember that black coworkers will prize me even more highly when other white men misbehave. More importantly, I should recognize that black colleagues and customers rely on me to help other white men move out of Pre-Awareness.

Approaching anger from another angle, I am deeply grateful when black Americans metabolize *their* anger constructively. If I had been born into a black family and was otherwise put together like I am, I would probably be dead or in prison by now, consumed by my anger for the disadvantages that accompanied my black skin. Instead of responding with fear and labels like "angry black man," here's another practical way to metabolize anger constructively. When we do encounter anger from black colleagues and customers, we can react with respect and validation rather than fear. And when anger runs through us, we can thoughtfully examine the causes, find compassion for the targets of our anger, and respond professionally.

CONVERSATION STARTER: *What and who makes you angry about diversity (causes and targets)? Where does such anger fit into the Transformation Curve? What responses can help you use your anger to improve your leadership?*

■ 41 ■

Redirect excuses
and whining.

O ne time I had the chance to sit in on a meeting of eleven black female managers at a financial services company in LA. They were part of a black employee network within the firm, and they met monthly to discuss career development, mentoring, and case studies on leadership issues. Once in awhile, they asked a guest in to discuss mutual interests. I was doing some onsite training with white male managers, and had interviewed three women from this group, so they honored me with an invitation.

The lively session started as a "What's up with white guys?" Q&A. When I protested that no one had ordained me to speak for white men who lead, they laughed and pointed out that they were continually expected to represent all things black ("Hey, Shondra, how could black people really think O.J. was not guilty?"), so now I got to answer for the views of all white men. They seemed to operate with a sense of humor, so I tried to retain mine.

The only acutely uncomfortable moment in the hour-long exchange followed this question: "Why do white male managers spend so much time whining and making excuses for not getting diversity?" My lame response went something like this: "Well, as a group, we don't know a lot about race and gender because our being white men works pretty well for us. So when we feel pushed to change, sometimes it's easier to blame others or complain, than it is to do the hard work you're used to doing." They got real quiet for a moment. (Trust me, that was the only moment they were quiet!) They were surprised that I'd said such a thing out loud; it was sobering to have some of their suspicions confirmed. Then they energetically unpacked the excuses and whining they heard from white male leaders.

Here are the four excuses and whines they disliked the most, distilled from my postsession notes. I've added my thoughts about our possible motivation for such outbursts, and how we, as white men, might lead by redirecting such excusing and whining to a more productive end.

WHITE GUY WHINE #4: *I am so sick of diversity and political correctness. We need to focus on people as individuals, and quit making everything about race and gender.* Sometimes we tire from toiling up diversity's learning curve. But how much sympathy can we expect from our black colleagues and customers, considering their labors on the same mountain? Openly admit your discomfort to yourself. And remember: while you may not expend a lot of calories thinking about how race and gender shape your individuality, exercising due regard for the diversity-related concerns of black people is essential to leading them individually.

WHITE GUY EXCUSE #3: *Hey, I'm just as sensitive as any other guy. But we're here to get the job done, not be all friendly all the time. It's not my job to babysit these people.* Sometimes those we lead bring their emotions into work with them (like we do with an excuse such as this). Sometimes they cannot find their motivation (just like us). The challenge is to "provide support without removing responsibility" (a maxim from Development Dimensions International). It's entirely appropriate to focus on getting the job done—and you will lead for results more effectively by attending to the emotional and motivational needs in your employees. Sure, they are responsible for themselves in a way that you are not. But making excuses to yourself about "babysitting" won't induce them to follow your lead.

WHITE Guy WHINE #2: *The company can push this diversity agenda all it wants, but it's really just about not getting sued. All that matters to me is not being accused of anything and staying out of court.* Litigation avoidance is a worthy goal for any employer and every manager, white male or otherwise. But when we distill diversity's business case down to staying out of court, we are trying to escape the risk that approaches on the horizon: the challenge to lead diverse humans more effectively. "I just won't get in trouble" is a mental gyration that allows us to run and hide from this prod to improve. A healthier message to self? "I'm going to avoid getting sued on diversity issues, *and* I'm going to figure out how diversity will help me succeed in my career."

AND the #1 White MalE EXCUSE THAT THESE FINE BLACK LEADERS FOUND MOST DISTURBING: *"She only got the job because she's black, not because she was qualified."* This is a profoundly insulting assertion. Maybe we're afraid we can't compete, or maybe we suspect the playing field has now tilted away from us to favor black people. It may simply be that we've never imagined losing a promotion to a black woman. Perhaps we just didn't expect to report to a black boss and we're uncertain about the risks involved.

Once in awhile, being black does provide an advantage in an employment decision. There is no excuse for that sort of discrimination, either. But even in such an instance, we still have choices: we can permit this upsetting disadvantage we feel in being white to fester, or we can name it as discrimination and move on. If we choose to stew, it may hamper how we live and lead among diverse people. We can also leverage such an experience to see, in a more personal light, the struggle for opportunity facing many black people.

When we slide into the lazy default of excuses and whining, we're probably tired of the diversity drumbeat. Perhaps some aspect of denial, fear, guilt, shame, or anger is surfacing. But advocating our alibis and complaining like a teenager doesn't strengthen our credibility as leaders.

Watch for the temptation to serve up a glass of white whine. There's no excuse for excuses. Redirect excuses and whining by figuring out what's really bugging you about human differences. Then you can solve the problem instead of resisting the pressure to grow.

Conversation Starter: *What whining and excuses come easy to you about diversity? What's behind this response in you, and how will you deal with these causes rather than carry on with the symptomatic excuse making?*

MANAGE EMOTIONS

■ 42 ■

Engage change
and risk.

Isn't it possible to improve your opinion of me
without my changing in any way whatsoever?©

ASHLEIGH BRILLIANT

Every contemporary leader learns to navigate through change
and risk.

Large-scale changes and risks confront our organizations:
international markets, profit and growth expectations,
technological innovation, outsourcing, agile competitors, environmental
concerns, relations with regulators. And people-related change tests our

leadership skill: winning the talent we need at a cost we can afford, developing employee capabilities, managing people remotely, retaining high performers.

Each one of these arenas for change offers opportunity when we get it right, and risk when we don't. Risk is how we assess the uncertainty and danger that could accompany change. Change is about life not staying the same, but becoming different.

It is therefore useful to recognize that change and diversity share a mutual meaning. They both pivot on the idea of difference. Change brings difference in situation; diversity delivers difference in people.

And leading as a white man necessitates change and risk in one more arena: our own hearts and minds, in our emotion and cognition.

I encourage you to engage the change and risk that diversity supplies to you. With the personal and business case for this work so clear (see essays 74 and 75), there's not much neutral territory here. You can step up and lead. Or you can keep your head down and try to sidestep differences in circumstance (change) and in the diverse humans you want to follow you. Such avoidance puts your standing as a leader at severe risk.

It is easier, then, to sustain our engagement with diversity-related change and risk when we mentally situate our diversity learning as a natural part of managing change. Here's a great tool to help: get yourself a copy of *Changing For Good*, by James Prochaska, John Norcross, and Carlo Diclemente. These three psychologists have developed a powerful program for overcoming problems like smoking, weight control, and emotional distress. While their approach focuses on building new behaviors to shed unwanted habits, and does not address diversity specifically, it explores the science and practice of personal change that you can apply to your diversity learning.

You'll notice an overlap between their six-stage method and my Transformation Curve, which is a paradigm for engaging diversity's change and risk. It's all about growing your competence for leading through difference.

A Unique Risk for White Men Who Lead

When it comes to leading with diversity in mind, we face a particular risk: forsaking our duty to provide corrective feedback, because we fear that an employee will claim racial or gender prejudice. The risks we juggle in such a moment are crucial to our confidence and credibility as leaders.

If we relinquish our responsibility to address a performance problem with an employee because he is black, for example, we surrender to our fear and ignorance. Such cowardice may register as a short-term win in our private calculus—"Man, I'm glad to avoid the race card getting played."

But consider the risks that bloom outward from that causal "rock in the pond":

- We abandon our obligation to provide this employee with the chance to improve.

- We set the stage for a legitimate complaint of prejudice: "You gave white people on the team the chance to get better; you never helped me figure out what to do."

- We allow the team to suffer from the black employee's unimproved performance.

- We reinforce our own sense of incompetence with managing human differences.

- Our team can see we are not managing a diverse employee effectively.

- We will likely end up trying to explain this mess to our own manager.

- We may get to wallow in these shortcomings if what we fear most comes to pass—when the attorneys get involved in resolving the conflict.

You get my point. It is advisable to prepare for the risks inherent to providing corrective feedback to *all* employees with candor and equity.

Get out ahead of the risks that diversity brings your way. As the winds of change sweep through, lean in and maintain your leadership pace. Sometimes such a wind blows at your back, and you are rewarded for managing risks.

CONVERSATION STARTER: *Audit the diversity-related risks and changes you face. How can you lead into them, rather than resist or hide from these changes?*

■ 43 ■

Accept
your losses.

This book equips you, as a white man who leads, to work successfully with black colleagues and customers. There are some surprising wins for you when you grow your way through the Transformation Curve.

But it's not all profit as you learn to lead with diversity in mind. You also need to account for and accept your losses. Let's name what you're likely to lose.

First and foremost, you lose being able to live and lead while *not knowing:* not knowing about the advantages your white skin and gender bring, not knowing how people see you because you lead in a white man's skin, not knowing how dimensions of diversity influence your leadership choices. Once you've awakened to awareness (see essay 18), you cannot go back to sleep.

This can be a rude awakening. Consider the experience of an MD I'll call Jonathan. He is a top medical administrator in a large urban hospital, and a nationally known physician in his specialty. He also leads with a keen sense of ethics and humor.

For two years we worked intensively on the hospital's diversity program. At the beginning he didn't really know what he'd gotten himself into, and at the end he had earned a reputation as a "diversity guy" (usually meant as a compliment).

One day I dropped into a chair across from Jonathan in his office, and noted his troubled look. A "what's going on?" query from me evoked a bit of a rant from him. He had been counting the cost of his diversity learning. Here's a paraphrase of our conversation:

Jonathan: "Sometimes I wish I could go back to when I wasn't factoring diversity into everything. Leading was a lot simpler when I didn't have to work so hard at it."

Chuck: "Kind of hard to get it out of your mind?"

Jonathan: "I don't really want to forget about it, because it matters so much to my leadership and the medical center's success. But sometimes it doesn't feel very productive when I'm wondering if something related to race or gender is going on, and I can't see what it is, or I don't know how to find out, or I can diagnose the diversity issue but don't know how to handle it."

Chuck: (as I raised my water bottle toward him) "To the good old days ... learning sucks."

Jonathan: (grin) "Yeah." (drink)

The loss of not knowing is an unavoidable result of growth. When we return from travel in a developing country, the poverty we saw stays with us. Our experience forces on us an unasked-for perspective, and we can't shake it. Going through the process of my father's dying changed me forever, and I felt diminished after learning some of those lessons.

We can't expect much sympathy for losing our ignorance. No one will hold a memorial service for the life we used to lead without due regard for race and gender, so we must validate our own sense of loss when we miss a life that was simpler and easier for not knowing. We could also talk through this loss with other white men who lead, although in my experience this rarely occurs until a man (like Jonathan) is well into Adventurous Competence.

Here's a second diminishment to accept: a loss of self-confidence as a leader. In our pre-aware ignorance, we not only didn't know what *we* didn't know; we didn't realize what our diverse colleagues *did* know. When a white male leader learns his way through the Transformation Curve, a loss of face materializes in a humbling progression:

1) I don't know what I don't know about diversity.

2) I start to learn, and begin to recognize that my diverse colleagues/ employees/clients know a hell of a lot more about what's going on with diversity than I do.

3) I worry how to lead by applying what I'm learning about diversity, when some of the people who are supposed to follow me know so much more than I do.

4) I am mortified to realize that, all along, they have understood how little I know about diversity, and how I'm only now learning to lead with it in mind.

These are unpreventable blows to our self-view when we seek to grow as white men who lead. Fortunately, they are only momentary jolts of painful awakening for us. And when I've admitted my humiliating limitations to colleagues I trust, their response has always been a mild and positive, "It's good to see you coming around. Keep going." It was great to discover that my standing as a leader was actually enhanced by my teachability and transparency. But it still stings to have lost my naive belief that I know at least as much about what was going on around me as do those I am supposed to be leading.

I have often heard people who are not white men observe that we, as white men, resist leading with human differences in view, because we fear the inescapable loss of power, position, and preference. That's not how I see it. While increased competition will challenge us, white men who lead will retain much of our opportunity because we work hard, we want to achieve like anyone else, and our privilege ain't gone yet. We don't have to lose for black people to win. The rising tide will lift all boats.

So welcome the wins your diversity learning delivers. And accept your losses. Acknowledge that leading on diversity serves up slices of humble pie: unexpected self-awareness, public mistakes, human complexity, new career competition, more temptations to whine, ad nauseam. Your courage will be tested in this struggle. You won't always be up to it, and that will hurt.

Since you can't expect sympathy about such loss from those who have suffered more, feel free to retreat into the easy fellowship of other white guys. It feels good to hang out with your "Like Some Others" group. And maybe someday we will even be able to talk about our diversity-related losses over a manly beer while we watch the game.

CONVERSATION STARTER: *What losses have you experienced as you've learned and led on diversity? What losses do you fear? Which white male friends will you discuss this with? (Remember the beer.)*

■ **44** ■

Celebrate
the courage of your convictions.

There are many, many good people around,
but very few who are good enough to disturb the peace of the devil.

WALTER RAUSCHENBUSCH *quoted in* Sojourners Magazine

I t is a rite of passage to master the emotional challenges of leading as a white man. Along this journey, there's another positive practice of the spirit: celebrate the courage of your convictions.

Courage is an attribute men generally aspire to and admire in others. **Courage** may be defined as facing fear and managing conflict with self-possession and resolve. Today is the time for you as a white man to courageously step up to diversity's challenges, and speak your peace: no more silence calling itself patience, no more fear of unintended offense, no more reticence to lead on diversity from the inside out. Our lethargy is weakness, our complacency is cowardice.

Now is the time for us to disturb this peace of the devil, the quietude around diversity among white men who lead.

If we define **convictions** as strong and convincing beliefs, then what could the "courage of your convictions" look like? And how could you celebrate that?

The Courage of Convictions

Return to the introduction and review my six convictions, my assumptions about leading on human differences as a white man. Then sit down and answer this question for yourself: *What are your convictions, your strong and convincing beliefs, your assumptions about leading with race and gender in mind?* It is only possible to lead with and celebrate the courage of your convictions when you are clear about what your convictions are.

I have introduced you to a number of white men who lead with the courage of their convictions:

- The VP in essay 5, who believed in leading people as individuals
- Max Depree in essay 7, who believed in inclusion as a leadership imperative
- Kevin Costner in essay 11, who believed in portraying men as good and connective and effective
- David, in essays 31 and 33–35, who believed in learning to lead through the Transformation Curve

- Jonathan, in the previous essay, who believed that counting the cost of diversity learning is a part of leading effectively

The past and present provide us with many more dramatic models of white men leading with courage and conviction:

- William Wilberforce, who led the fight to outlaw slavery in England (1807); see the movie *Amazing Grace*
- Theodore Weld, whose leadership at Lane Seminary in Cincinnati (1844) helped to ignite the abolitionist movement
- Dietrich Bonhoeffer, whose convictions courageously led him to oppose the Nazi menace (1938), an ideology built on the presumed superiority of white men
- Morris Dees, whose leadership (since 1971) has established the Southern Poverty Law Center as the most successful opponent to white supremacists across America
- Former president Bill Clinton, who used his bully pulpit to spark a national conversation on race. Mr. Clinton, popular with African-Americans, has worked from an office in Harlem.

CELEBRATING

Here are ten ways to celebrate your courage in leading on diversity with conviction. And you know how you like to celebrate, so you'll think of more.

1) Discuss your answer to the "What are my convictions?" question with a black friend, and kick it around together. Celebrate that you know what your convictions are! And learn about his or hers.

2) Privately observe why it is so much fun to hang out with other white guys, and congratulate yourself for noticing.

3)   Make sure your manager sees the impact of your leadership on diversity.

4)   Calculate your stage of learning about race and gender on the Transformation Curve. Acknowledge the specific lessons you've learned to get you where you are. Identify what you need to learn next.

5)   Send a donation to the Southern Poverty Law Center (see Resources). Invest in fighting racism as a way to honor your progress.

6)   Get tickets to the Oprah show, and take your wife, daughter, sister, or mother. Or take all four.

7)   Plan a ski trip for next January's Dr. Martin Luther King Jr. holiday.

8)   Take someone you love to hear gospel music.

9)   Participate in the campaign of a black political candidate.

10) Make a plan to get Tiger Woods' autograph. You know you want it.

Leading with diversity in your mind and heart requires courage and conviction, and offers the chance to party over your progress! This combination of resolute self-possession, convincing belief, and the willingness to celebrate will sustain you as you learn to manage emotional challenges as a white man who leads.

CONVERSATION STARTER: *What are your convictions, your strong and convincing beliefs, your assumptions about leading with race and gender in mind? How and when will you share these convictions with your manager, peers, and team? How will you invite them to hold you accountable for leading on the basis of these beliefs?*

Respond

*There is no way that a problem of difference
can involve just one group of people.*

ALLAN G. JOHNSON, PHD
Privilege, Power and Difference

When we interact with our black colleagues and customers, we need to dial directly into the exchange. Attention must be paid. These are the moments where we collaborate and apply our diversity learning. We demonstrate cultural knowledge and personal respect. We invite mutuality and conciliation. And those who are supposed to follow our lead decide if they actually will.

These ten essays hone in on developing, as white men who lead, the ability to respond; the response-ability to react appropriately and lead with wisdom. A white man knows he's leading effectively when there's a healthy give and take with his black colleagues.

It's all about reciprocation, the lifeblood of response-ability.

Identify progress,
but focus on joint achievement going forward.

Generally speaking, whites believe that our nation's problems with racism and civil rights were solved three decades ago, while blacks see racial discrimination as an ongoing and daily obstacle to opportunity and equality.

LEONARD STEINHORN AND BARBARA DIGGS-BROWN
By the Color of Our Skin: The Illusion of Integration and the Reality of Race

Every week in the news you can find another nauseating act in a dreadful drama, played out in black and white. Some opportunistic black activist seizes the media platform to castigate the nation for oppressing African-Americans, in response to the latest police brutality, racist verbal gaffe from an influential white guy, or most recent depressing statistic on urban poverty or crime or education or housing or health or … Switch the channel, turn the page, click onto another Web page, and you'll find the bow-tied white conservative commentator: defending the police, reinterpreting a politician's racist crap as free speech, skewing statistics to blame the poor, and generally waving the Red, White, and Blue at any black person who moves.

Is someone paying these people to spew their never-ending argument about whether America's racial glass is half empty or half full? I believe most of us are dead tired of this perverse fight no one is ever supposed to win.

So let me offer a productive proposal to put these pundits out of our misery. As white men, we should acknowledge progress, but we should lead by focusing on joint achievement going forward. That's a practical way to work successfully with black colleagues and customers.

WE'RE MAKING PROGRESS

The emergence of the black middle class in America since 1960 is an amazing American achievement. Educational and economic achievement among black Americans is at the highest level in our nation's history. Here are some of the facts:

- Civil rights legislation and enforcement has effectively ended most blatant forms of racial discrimination.
- More than eight thousand black Americans now hold public office.

- Fifty years ago, black America was largely illiterate; today, black students complete high school at the highest rate ever.

- The economic standing of the black middle class is a world-class success story. Median income among blacks is trending up.

- Black people represent America to the world: in politics, sports, music, higher education, religion, entertainment, and other fields. And Mr. Obama's ascendancy validates the American dream.

We should be proud that America has become a place where so many descendants of slaves have become the owners of their lives and dreams. I would personally like to hear more black leaders articulate this story line, as a celebration of America.

WE HAVE A LONG WAY TO GO

As far as we've journeyed as a society, there's still a long road ahead. There remains a profound gap between what we aspire to as a nation, and how we deliver on the promise of America. Here are some examples:

- One third of black Americans live in neighborhoods that are ninety percent or more black, and a large majority of all black people live in communities that are predominantly black. Seventy-six percent of white American adults own their own homes, while only forty-eight percent of their black counterparts do.

- A California study found that ninety-two percent of black men arrested on drug charges were subsequently released for lack of evidence or inadmissible evidence. "Driving while black" is one phrase African-Americans have coined to express their daily experience with white police officers.

- As we continue to invest in and hold K–12 education accountable for academic achievement, each year it is clearer that teachers, textbooks, and technology cannot resolve the challenges that only a student's family can solve. In particular, the health and coherence of many black American families is trending downward, as more children are raised by single mothers, and miss out on the distinctive parenting a father can provide. My point: education succeeds when families are strong, and strong families require living-wage jobs, stable marriages, and skilled parenting.

- The median net worth of black families is a small fraction of the asset base white families enjoy. In 2006, the annual median income among black men was twenty-six percent less than white men.

- *One in fifteen black American men are in jail.* This fact alone demonstrates how far we have to go to realize the promise of this nation.

As white male leaders from the middle and upper classes, it feels good when we see progress among black Americans. It means to us that they are "catching up"—we don't have to lose for them to win. We may suffer from the Most Recent Successful Black Person Syndrome, where the latest highly visible black person validates our heartfelt beliefs about opportunity. We view their success this way: "See, the system works; the American dream is available to all." The hypersuccessful black person becomes a walking affirmation of bootstrap-pulling, individual achievement, and getting ahead.

In contrast, black people commonly believe that they have to be twice as smart, work twice as hard, and look twice as good just to get a fair shot.

The most recent black success story may mean a lot less to them. When you or your parents have to work two jobs to get an education and support the family, then life can still feel like running a marathon. That's especially tough when white people seem to drive the same 26.2 miles in a new car.

We struggle with profoundly divergent experiences and interpretations of the same facts about how far we've come. Here's my solution: I believe that black citizens will focus more often on what we have achieved as a nation when we white Americans focus on what remains to be accomplished. And we need to get busy achieving it—together.

CONVERSATION STARTER: *Specifically, what evidence compels you to appreciate how far we've come as a nation on racial issues? Specifically, what evidence indicates how far we still have to go?*

Cultures at Work:
Affirm the power
of group identity.

D
r. George Koch, the pastor of a church in West Chicago, tells this story: "Several years ago my brother was staying in a small village in Ireland. He asked in the local pub about a similar small village a mere six miles away that he was considering visiting. He was told sharply that the village he was in had nothing to do with the other village, that they would not speak to anyone there, ever, and that they had no information about that village to share with him. The anger and distrust in their voices were obvious. The nearby village was the Other, the enemy.

"Nonplussed, he asked about the reason for the anger and distrust. They said, 'In 1066, when William the Conqueror came through Ireland, he attacked that village first. They didn't send anyone here to warn us that he was coming.'

"So 'they' couldn't be trusted. 'They' were a danger. And for nearly a thousand years, 'they' had remained the Other, the enemy."

If a visitor from another planet observed humanity for a year, the alien would surely report back that humans are tribal creatures. Our past and our present is a story of human groups: ethnic, national, racial, religious, economic, geographic. We fool ourselves if we fail to comprehend the power of group identity.

In essay 4, we considered the significance of cultural connection (Like Some Others). While our individuality is not determined by the groups we're part of, each one of us is profoundly shaped by the values and behaviors of people we are like. This cluster of essays (46–49) explores learning about and participating in black and white cultures. This is a critical skill set for the response-able leader.

Today there is a global shift in how cultural diversity adds value. For the first time in history, strategic leaders are developing human differences as a transformative asset to improve relationships and grow the enterprise. This growth may be viewed in terms of an historic paradigm that moves from *dependence* to *independence* to *interdependence*.

Intercultural relationships are moving beyond the power-over dynamic (dependence) where, for example, the black community depended on white culture for its basic resources. Cultural communities now transition toward operating with parity (independence), where each group evolves the capacity to stand on its own. Sometimes this brings more conflict, as we see with the Hispanic community in the U.S. immigration debate, or with Islamic societies struggling for new status. We can see early signs of global interdependence between national economies—Japan and the United States, for example—where collaboration becomes critical and conflict must be managed, because each partner depends on the other.

That's a view from 10,000 feet. Down at ground level, the power of group identity operates daily in human organizations. For instance, in many companies there are networks of affinity groups, organized by race/ethnicity, interest, gender, or other shared characteristic. To illustrate: the Blacks at Microsoft group is very active in career development, social connection, and recruiting.

Smart organizations encourage these affinity groups to pursue their distinctive needs and interests in a manner that explicitly strengthens the company. Identity groups can provide the space for people traditionally on the downside of power-over to recalibrate their professional aspirations, and to make choices informed by their own self-interests. These peer groups are a powerful transformative tactic, as long as the independence they foster pushes the organization toward an interdependence that builds on differences and similarities.

But when affinity groups compete with each other for attention and budget, or frame their agenda in blame-game language (us versus them; "diverse" people versus the white guys in charge), the resulting fragmentation casts diversity in the spoiler role. Some white male leaders are only too glad to interpret such division as further evidence that "'those people" can't get their act together. Everyone loses if distinctive-specific groups behave divisively.

So there are risks to leading in a manner that affirms our cultural connections. But it's the wiser choice to take those risks, thereby leveraging the power of group identity to strengthen relationships and grow the organization.

CONVERSATION STARTER: *What subcultures can you identify at work (for example, at the team or department levels)? How does such group identity drive or limit performance?*

RESPOND

■ **47** ■

Cultures at Work:
It's black culture, not a conspiracy. Inform yourself.

I admit it. Kwanzaa renders me clueless. Does it replace Christmas for some black people? No, that can't be right; many of the people celebrating Kwanzaa are Christians. Hmmm. Must be a cultural difference, so I won't understand it without some learning.

One of the premises of this book is that "different does not mean bad." This is particularly true when you're learning and leading across cultural lines. Approaching black culture with inquisitive intrigue will serve you beautifully. But criticizing the ways of black people without understanding them will not

216

position you to lead. Let's say it straight: white America has the nasty habit of assuming the worst about black America.

To illustrate, permit me to answer a question I have been asked at eighteen client sites:

Q: *Why do black people sit together in the lunchroom?*

A: Because they are "Like Some Others"; they like hanging out with one another. It's not a conspiracy, it's a culture. We often eat lunch with white people.

I'd like to ask a question in response: Why do we tend to get nervous whenever two or more black people congregate? Review essay 38 on facing our fear.

It's a Culture, Not a Conspiracy

Here's what to do if you wonder or worry about black people associating in the cafeteria, in the hallway, or on the street corner. R e l a x. When women get together, they spend less time talking about men than we think they do. It's the same when black folks congregate: somehow they find something worthy of conversation beyond white people. The world doesn't revolve around us, we do.

By definition, cultures cluster. Humans organize and survive with those with whom they hold important things in common. It's about safety, identity, comfort, and opportunity. And to some degree, culture involves excluding those who are different. These group boundaries only become a real problem when they are guarded with hostility and violence. For example, the identity of white supremacists is so tied into their whiteness that, to maintain their ideological selves, they must threaten black or Jewish Others.

Simply stated, you need to examine your basic attitude toward black culture. Are you intrigued by how black folks relate to one another? Or do you sit in judgment, focusing on what's different between us (with difference being bad)? Are you looking to find what's messed up in the black community? There's plenty in black America that needs fixing—too many children born without fathers in the home, the idea that academic achievement is a white thing, to name two—but it's their culture, and their job to fix it. Maybe we can help. We need to become sympathetic students of black culture, recognizing our limits, yet engaging the black experience with an open heart and an open mind.

LEARN BLACK CULTURE

A key resource in your cultural education is Thomas Kochman's *Black and White: Styles of Conflict*. Read this short classic on differences across the racial divide.

There are two ways to learn black culture: we can learn *about* it, and we can learn *in* it. Both are useful, but you have to go into a culture to really learn its lessons.

Learning about black culture

There are many ways to do this. Here are four.

- Search for black culture online. Go to Black Voices on AOL, or the websites for vital black organizations, including the NAACP, the National Urban League, and the Congressional Black Caucus.
- Subscribe to *Black Enterprise* magazine.
- Watch the Black Entertainment Television network.
- Read books written for and about black business professionals. One of my favorites: *Black Enterprise Titans of the Black Enterprise*

100s: Black CEOs Who Redefined and Conquered American Business, by Derek T. Dingle.

Learning in black culture

Put yourself in the presence of black people where they gather: church, music venues, sporting events, political functions, community events, the black affinity group in your company. Don't intrude, but go to them, and stop expecting them to come your way. They already live in a white world. And go anywhere black and white families interact (e.g., a multicultural church, daycare center, or community association). When our children are friends, a lot of goodness falls into place.

One clue for your learning in black culture: don't be surprised by the noise. In my experience, when black people get together, it usually gets loud. In a project with a bank, I mentioned this when we were planning a series of race-specific focus groups. My black client laughed (loudly), amused that I knew that tidbit, and because it was true. So they held the event off-site, so they could be authentically noisy without disturbing their coworkers and customers.

Do you know the official African-American national hymn? It's a powerful song called "Lift Ev'ry Voice and Sing," and has been sung by black Americans since 1900. You will understand something core to black culture if you learn the song, and study its meaning and history. Every celebration of the Dr. Martin Luther King Jr. holiday should feature a gospel choir blasting this anthem to black patriotism and pride.

In my experience, black people are surprised and mostly pleased when my understanding of their culture becomes evident. It opens doors in these relationships, and they remember me for it, particularly because I make sure to mention how aware I am of my limitations as a visitor to the black experience.

There is a wonderful personal result from learning and living across the white/black culture line: another facet of our Creator's character is revealed in the expression and experience of being black. So the energy and gifts and connectedness among black people is *for me, too,* because it all comes from the same God who made me a white man who leads.

CONVERSATION STARTER: *What are you doing (and what will you do) to become an openhearted student of black culture?*

Cultures at Work:
Grow the culture of white male managers.

*Years ago, manhood was an opportunity for achievement,
and now it is a problem to be overcome.*

GARRISON KEILLOR

O ur leadership as white men is influenced by our participation in one particular group: the culture of white men who lead.

One of the exercises in my training with white male managers brainstorms with participants a list of words

221

describing the attributes common to white men who lead. The list invariably looks something like this: White male managers are effective, smart, productive, organized, results-focused, task-oriented, and (upon prompting from the facilitator to list what others say about us) task-obsessed, usually listening with their motors running, arrogant, and incapable of not using sports references. The group usually knocks this exercise out of the park with more traits … oops, sorry. Here's my point: white men often lead with attributes that can be generalized to us as a culture.

You may doubt that such a culture exists. But just in case this is one time when the fish doesn't know it's wet, go to diverse colleagues you know well, and ask these two questions: "Do white male managers have a culture of their own? If so, how would you describe it?" This inquiry usually produces an introduction to the culture of white male managers as it is perceived by those who are not members of the group.

It is certain that, as white men, we lead from our own cultural context. This is a crucial area for insight, because you must be aware of the groups that influence your own identity and behavior as you seek to understand the cultures of others.

One value embedded in the culture of white men who lead requires special attention: the primacy of individualism. American culture and the culture of white male managers prize individualism over group identity. Talk to twenty white men who lead, and every man will be able to articulate why individuality is important. Very few of them are likely to be ready to speak sensibly about how we have been influenced personally by the culture of white men who lead. It would be a very different conversation with twenty black men or women (or white women, for that matter). Paradoxically, the more the culture of white male managers emphasizes individualism, the harder it becomes to discern the existence of the culture itself.

I encourage you to analyze the norms and behaviors of our culture. This process for me is a bit surreal; this group that nurtures me is like a forest ecosystem with an attitude. I can relate tree to tree, but no tree is inclined to recognize its interdependent need for water and soil and sun. In fact, the forest continues to grow its trees with the tacit agreement that no tree will admit it is part of the forest. Hopefully, I won't get cut down for saying this out loud, because I deeply admire the culture of white men who lead. Join me in seeing and growing this forest *and* its trees. I'll bring the organic fertilizer.

A SPECIAL CHALLENGE FOR THE CULTURE OF WHITE MEN WHO LEAD

To grow our culture, there is a challenge that involves a dimension of diversity beyond race and gender: sexual orientation. We need to take care of the diversity business *within* our culture, as we seek to relate successfully to people of color and white women. Inside the boundaries of race, gender, and occupation, our culture is also straight and gay. Here's an illustration of this test.

The top three executives of a publicly traded manufacturer in Texas were known to "get it." They established a clear business case for diversity, reinforced by the way they handled problems and opportunities facing diverse employees and customers. Litigation decreased, sales to corporate and public sector customers increased, and the company was competing effectively to hire diverse talent. Retention was up. These white men were leading successfully with regard to race and gender concerns.

Issues related to sexual orientation, however, had been carefully avoided. These straight executives, perhaps due to their shared conservative religious commitment, simply did not want to hear about workplace issues with homosexual staff, clients, and suppliers. They ignored the conflict at the all-company picnic when a few straight employees acted out toward a gay manager who brought his partner. They denied the request from gay and lesbian employees for an affinity group similar to what African-American employees enjoyed. These leaders stonewalled issues that related to differences in sexual orientation.

The marketplace interrupted their denial. The City of San Francisco passed a regulation that required all City suppliers to provide to gay and lesbian employees the same benefits it provided to straight employees. An $800K contract was at risk, and the City monitored compliance carefully.

The executive's initial reaction: "We walk away from the business. Customers don't tell us how to run our company." The real issue, however, wasn't control of the firm, but the integrity of their diversity agenda. After all, engaging gender and race issues was required by law, delivered a measurable return, and generated positive press. Creating opportunity for women and people of color was also the right thing to do.

But the prospect of providing benefits for domestic partners forced these executives into a very personal conflict. Their unspoken qualms about homosexuality squared off against the loss of a high-profile contract that would have to be explained to shareholders, the negligible cost of domestic partner coverage, and their shame in recognizing their bias against colleagues with whom they'd worked for years.

To their credit, they brought in help to facilitate a healthy dialogue with the diversity council and selected employees. These straight white male leaders learned to balance their private views with the need to lead congruently on diversity.

Domestic partner benefits were arranged at a small net cost, and an $800K contract was saved. Business expanded in San Francisco. And the executives learned a gainful lesson: it may seem right to avoid a diversity issue, but an honest commitment to engaging human differences requires consistency in the end.

So part of growing the culture of white men who lead involves managing differences *among* those of us in the culture. In this sense, the diversity challenge is bigger than we thought. To succeed, we need to lead effectively *within* our culture, and out among the diverse cultures of our colleagues and customers.

CONVERSATION STARTER: *How would you describe the culture of white men who lead, and how do you participate in this culture?*

Cultures at Work:
Anticipate and handle resistance from white people.

I learned how to persecute the Jews
by studying the manner in which you Americans persecute Negroes.

ADOLPH HITLER

I t would be a naive mistake for us to assume that all white Americans will welcome our leadership on diversity with open arms and minds and hearts. Many will, and their teachability and partnership will sustain us.

But I would be remiss if I failed to point out that the implied shadow of Hitler's quote lingers today. There still lurks in our white American culture some weird, ancient, and racist shit. This profanity is carefully chosen, as you may be confronted with some truly ugly stuff, coming from men who look like you but believe their white skin is a license to dominate. So let me say a word about handling resistance from our crazy cousins, the white supremacists.

Henry is a friend who worked as an HR leader in a large energy company with a growing diversity commitment. His firm decided that all employees would attend a day-long training session on the business case and fundamentals of diversity at work. This included a facility with about thirty employees in rural Idaho. It was common knowledge in HR that this office had a number of male employees who were involved in a white pride organization. Their on-the-job behavior did not violate any company policy, but they were well known in their community for their racist views, which were antithetical to the message of the upcoming diversity training.

When it came time to decide who would deliver the training to this problematic facility, no other facilitators were willing to go, because they were black or female or both. Henry decided to take on the assignment, as he was the only white guy in the trainer group. Ironically he is both Jewish and gay, but he figured out how to deliver the training without either attribute receiving attention. The racist employees gave him some minor grief during the training session, but they knew they had to behave if they wanted to stay employed with the utility. Here's the point: there may be moments when we must lead with courage, as Henry did. We have to step up and deal with the misfits in our own culture. No one else should be expected to put themselves at such risk.

Let's also come right out and admit that such courage can be hard to muster in the face of evil. It was really bothering me that Muslim leaders were not speaking out against the jihadists from their own community of faith. Then it occurred to me that these leaders are concerned with their personal safety if they oppose violent cultural peers, just like I don't go looking to confront white supremacists. This is tough stuff.

But you will more often encounter subtle resistance. As a white man who leads, you should expect pushback, especially if you manage in an organization that does not pursue diversity as a strategy for business success.

White colleagues may fear candor or hide behind "political correctness." They may squirm when you come right out and say what you think (as in "We need to reexamine this idea that our workforce should look like our customers. What does that actually mean when it comes to hiring? Does someone's race count as a job qualification?"). If a white male colleague doesn't feel safe when diversity issues are on the table, he may steer clear of you. But when he sees you lead on diversity effectively, perhaps his fear will dissipate, and he will step up, too.

Other white men may see you as a sellout when you build powerful relationships with diverse colleagues. So far, no one has called me a "race traitor" to my face. But I did have a participant in a course with white male managers chirp at me during a break: "You can't possibly be that interested in all this diversity crap. What are you really after here?" Resistance from other white men may deepen when your productive partnerships with diverse colleagues and customers help you win choice work assignments, promotions, and positive attention. Remember that the *sustainable collaborative advantage* you can achieve (see essay 8) is usually an advantage over less-responsive white men. The winner should anticipate unhappiness from the losers.

How are you handling white men who hinder diversity's business imperative? This is one of your most important opportunities, because people are watching to see whether the organization's diversity commitment is real enough to extend to how white men relate to one another. Communicate with candor and provide positive incentives for resisters to change their behavior. For example, show them how improving their performance on diversity issues could enhance their evaluations and open the door to new responsibility, better bonuses, and consideration for promotions. Exercise your enforcement options sparingly and for maximum effect. If it becomes necessary to demote or terminate for insubordination over diversity issues, make the hardball count. Find a way to respect confidentiality while making an example of the resister.

A dimension of diversity that can fuel resistance is *economic and social class*. As white men who lead, most of us reside in the middle or upper class, and our relative financial security makes us less likely to be threatened by economic progress among colleagues of color. But white coworkers with fewer resources may believe they are losing jobs or promotions to people of color. So they could view "diversity progress" as steps in the wrong direction for them and their children.

During the past two decades, my research has identified five basic reasons why white male managers avoid diversity's contribution. More than 800 respondents were asked to mark each answer with which they agreed. *When I resist diversity at work, it is because:*

  78% I'm not sure how it helps me do my job.

  57% I'm already too busy, and it seems like another trendy distraction.

  44% It is not clear that diversity includes me, except as the bad guy.

  41% It seems to divide people rather than bring them together.

  23% I don't see how diversity adds value if it isn't related to the customer.

So you can counter most of the resistance that comes your way with a clear business case for diversity, a lack of blame, diversity-related performance objectives (see essay 76), and a clear explanation about how getting better at handling differences will fuel a shared success.

CONVERSATION STARTER: *When you lead on diversity, what resistance from other white people do you expect? What are your options for dealing with it?*

Learn about
Living While Black
and cultural differences
between women and men.

Whites who never live through the inconvenience and degradation
of being black in America don't fully understand how profoundly different
the black daily experience is from theirs.

LEONARD STEINHORN AND BARBARA DIGGS-BROWN
By the Color of Our Skin: The Illusion of Integration and the Reality of Race

231

I t will help you respond as a leader when you become a student of contemporary issues related to race and gender. In this essay we will briefly consider how these differences matter, and I'll introduce you to more learning resources.

LIVING WHILE BLACK

As white men who lead, we need to grow our understanding of what black colleagues and customers experience in their daily context.

Freedom of mobility: If you drive from Seattle to other urban areas in the Pacific Northwest, you can drive south to Portland, east to Spokane, or north to Vancouver. I do it without a second thought. But I have heard from black friends that they either fly or service their car before setting out, so it doesn't break down going through the intervening white rural areas. It's not only the chance they'll run into skin-headed Aryan Nation racists; the odds of that are slim. Almost as bad, they worry about how they will be treated out among typical white rural fellow citizens in twenty-first-century America. It angers me that they face such limitation, but their perception is their reality.

Housing: The third of black Americans living in poverty are stuck with the housing and neighborhood they can afford. Another third live in the suburbs, but these tend to be black suburbs. When black people choose to live around one another, it may be an expression of "Like Some Others." But when black Americans with the means to live anywhere are prevented from doing so by white Americans, it is tragic. See the "real estate" section (pages 29–42) in *By the Color of Our Skin*; we need to appreciate the different reality in which our black colleagues and customers reside.

Personal safety with law enforcement: Driving while black is known as DWB; it's so prevalent there's an acronym for it. When officers (usually white) pull over black drivers (mostly men), it may be legitimate. But many black men know they are stopped simply because they're black men. Don't dismiss this dynamic just because you don't experience it. How would it affect you if you had to worry about your physical safety around the police? This issue will continue to play out until white men lead with due regard in municipal governments and police departments.

Shopping while black: In this oft-experienced corollary to DWB, black customers are scrutinized carefully from the time they enter a store. They may shop under a cloud of suspicion, wondering why a storeowner who wants their money still feels free to deem them prospective shoplifters, just by the color of their skin.

Walking into work while black: Being black can even prevent you from getting to your office in the morning. In a Denver medical center, a veteran black physician was stopped by a security guard, supposedly because the doc was not wearing the new ID badge. While he showed his old badge to the guard (he'd worked at this hospital for twenty-seven years!), he observed another guard letting white doctors without the new badge stroll right in. When he pointed this out, the guard got testy and barked, "Hey, we're talking about you, buddy!" This physician was a gentleman, so he pulled out his cell phone, called the CEO, and asked him to come down to the main entrance for a chat. Oops.

If a black associate of yours has an encounter with the police or security, talk with your colleague about it, and support them however they want to be supported: a quiet shared anger between friends, going with them to complain, a beer or two. However they decide to respond, they deserve to know you have their back.

Living While Female

If you want to lead well among female colleagues and customers, it is simply smart to discern how gender differences operate at work. Sadly, this is a topic far beyond this essay and this book. But permit me to climb out on a limb and offer three answers to the question that has haunted men for millennia: *What do women want?* (Remember the difference between generalizing and stereotyping from essay 19.)

Answer #1: Women want to be heard, because they are going to listen. As men we may not have as many words to offer as the women in our lives, but when we master our own authentic listening skills, we are much more likely to collaborate with, lead, and follow the women we work and live with.

Answer #2: Women want relationships to matter, because they are going to care. For a leader, empathy is nonnegotiable. If we attend to the personal needs of those we lead, the chances for professional success skyrocket. You don't have to be a therapist. Take personal responsibility for your own emotional life (see essays 37–44) and simply care for others the way they want to be cared for.

Answer #3: Women want us to try and keep up with them, because they're going to get the job done, and it would be easier if we participated. For most women, communication and relationships are how they get things done in life. While I freely confess that my brain is incapable of matching the multitasking I observe in many women, I generally look forward to the challenge of working alongside women who live with high expectations and lead with high performance.

Work and lead across the gender lines by learning from resources like these:

- Subscribe to *Ebony* or *Essence* for a year. You won't understand everything you read or see in these magazines, but you'll learn a lot. And imagine how much fun it will be to start out a conversation at the Club with, "I was just reading *Ebony*, and I saw …"

- Find five colleagues—two other men and three women, all with a durable sense of humor—and together read and discuss Deborah Tannen's *Talking from 9 to 5: How Women's and Men's Conversational Styles Affect Who Gets Heard, Who Gets Credit, and What Gets Done at Work.*

The response-ability of a white man who leads depends on his fluency with the gender and race issues that require his response. Learn about Living While Black and cultural differences between men and women.

CONVERSATION STARTER: *What have you learned and how will you learn more about the cultures of women and people of color? How will you apply this learning in your leadership?*

RESPOND
■ **51** ■

Validate.
Do not equate.

The more whites minimize discrimination,
and elevate 'reverse discrimination'
as the moral equivalent of the black experience in America,
the more blacks feel compelled to validate, defend, and amplify their grievances.

LEONARD STEINHORN AND BARBARA DIGGS-BROWN
By the Color of Our Skin: The Illusion of Integration and the Reality of Race

Here's my straightforward recommendation: as a white man who leads, never equate your experience to the experience of any black American.

When a black person tells you about an indignity they suffered due to their race, do not respond with an unthinking, "Yeah, that happened to me one time," or "I know just what you mean." While your positive intention is to identify with them, you may come across as negating their experience. The fact is this: something similar may have happened to you, but it was much less likely to be linked to you being white. Black people live with the consistent risk of race-derived affront; you don't. And they are force-fed this diet of slights by people who have white skin like you and me.

Instead, respond by validating their experience. Try this: "I'm so sorry that happened to you. Is there anything I can do to help you respond?" And then avoid the temptation to apologize for all white people. While it may be a heartfelt sentiment, you can no more speak for your race than they can for theirs.

Another arena for validation may first appear to us as paranoia among black people; sometimes they seem to believe white folks are out to get them. But a black person is not paranoid when people who look like us *are* out to get them, and there are still white people who try to keep black people at a disadvantage. So don't make blacks defend their view that racial difference is working against them. They may be right, and they may not. But they are not likely to graciously receive your white doubt about their experience. Rather, respond with something like this: "That has never happened to me, and I can see how much the situation bothers you. Is there anything I can do?"

It will help us to validate but not equate when we truly hear a black person describe their knowledge of the world. We may, in fact, have very similar experience (Like All Others). But because race is a key cultural differentiator between us (Like Some Others), it is wise to avoid the premature conclusion that your experiences are identical.

When you're in the early stages of building a relationship with a black colleague, validate and don't equate. Once you build a relationship of mutual trust, once the two of you become friends, you'll have the chance to discuss these incidents of injury with them in a way that does not provoke their defensiveness. They will trust you, in part, because you have demonstrated your respectful response-ability.

CONVERSATION STARTER: *With a friend, practice what you could specifically say to empathize effectively when a black colleague mentions a race-related slight.*

■ **52** ■

Respond with intellect
and care to the crosscurrents in your interracial learning.

A s you develop your response-ability as a white man who leads, you will encounter crosscurrents with black colleagues and customers. The flow of your education may take unexpected and confusing turns. Apply your intellect and empathy to navigate through these twists and turns in your diversity learning.

CROSSCURRENT #1: GROUP IDENTITY VERSUS SPEAKING FOR BLACK PEOPLE

You may be confronted with this paradox: sometimes a black person strongly identifies with being part of the black community ("Let me tell you what it's like to be black ..."), and at other times the same black person will bristle if asked by a white person to speak from a generalizable black viewpoint ("So, Gerald, why do African-Americans always vote for Democrats?"). This crosscurrent can confuse us; we want them to make up their minds so we know what the "rules" are for communicating across the color line. My advice: be gracious in the way you receive their representation of blackness, and from your side, avoid asking them to speak for their whole group.

CROSSCURRENT #2: KEEP AN EYE ON GENERATIONAL DIFFERENCES

Younger black coworkers in your organization may experience the workplace quite differently from older black colleagues. This is likely evidence of progress. It may be due to the fact that the younger crowd has less life experience; it may be that bias is now more subtle than it was twenty years ago. When I asked one fast-rising young black manager about diversity in his organization, he said, "Diversity is the word your generation uses to fight about race." Accept each person's portrayal of their own story, and watch for impactful differences in age and generational experience.

Crosscurrent #3: Understand the Dynamics between Black People and Other People of Color

Don't make the mistake of assuming "people of color" consider themselves similar. To my limited knowledge, black and Native Americans tend to recognize a similarity between their particular experience in American life. But some black people resist and resent it when white people equate black experience with that of American-born Hispanics and Asians, or nonwhite immigrants. It's a very confusing ethnic muddle.

Nationality can also pop up here. The daily reality of black people born in America, for example, may differ from Haitian immigrants. A black person born in America is also likely to hold a very different worldview than an immigrant from an African nation. What you don't know about these cultural crosscurrents can bite you: at a graduate school where I worked, there was a serious conflict when an unknowing white male leader invited a South African immigrant to speak about racial reconciliation. Some of the black American leaders felt their voice would not be heard, because an African's experience with racism and black-white issues is generally different from that of black Americans. You see why intellect and empathy are useful here?

Crosscurrent #4: Remove the Stigma of Presumed Preference

Many highly qualified black people are put in the position of defending their selection into a university or a good job. Their merit may be attacked by white people who feel threatened. We must exercise caution here: a white male manager who questions the achievements of a black person needs to remember the architecture of privilege and opportunity (see essays 24 and 26) undergirding his own achievements.

CROSSCURRENT #5: DISCUSS A CULTURE'S WORK ETHIC WITH HONESTY

Black Americans commonly believe they have to work harder than white Americans just to get a shot at success. This idea of a strong work ethic in black American culture is substantiated by 240 years of slave labor, generations of antebellum sharecropping, and the past century of hard-working black parents sacrificing to help their kids go to college. So black people do not respond positively when a white person perpetuates the stereotype of black people as lazy ("welfare queens"), and then proceeds to claim that everything white people have comes from talent and achievement, without regard for white privilege and opportunity.

These are just a few of the crosscurrents we must weather. Leading with diversity in mind will demand all the smarts and care we can muster.

CONVERSATION STARTER: *Since there will always be confusing crosscurrents as you learn to lead on diversity, how can you get your questions answered?*

RESPOND

■ 53 ■

The 55% Rule:
Differentiate for reciprocity.

I n this section we have examined leading response-ably as white men. You know you are responding effectively when diverse stakeholders reciprocate. With a healthy give and take across the color divide, you can lead a diverse team wherever the organization needs you to go.

Let's look at a leadership boundary tool that elicits steady reciprocity from your black colleagues and customers. It's called the *55% Rule*.

Suzanne, my wife, and I have been married for more than thirty years. I've turned into a leadership and diversity guy, and she is a clinical psychologist with a successful practice near Microsoft. We live in a kind of "relationship lab"; there's so much to learn about building a marriage and a family and a life full of love, and it's a joy that the two of us get to figure it out together.

243

To help us, fifteen years ago we came up with the **55% Rule**: each person is responsible for fully holding up their 50% (no easy thing), and each person can expect the other to extend an extra 5% for the sake of the relationship.

This rule holds us accountable to delivering on our commitments, and going some extra distance for one another. It is daunting just to fully hold up my part of the relationship! The rule sets a boundary; if Suzanne is responsible for too much of my stuff, it's not fair to her and we need to recalibrate. Of course, we cannot precisely quantify what the 55% entails. But you can see how the rule provides us with a way to show full responsibility for ourselves, and equalize our reciprocity.

Every effective leader is familiar with the challenge to hold up their end and delegate well so that team members will perform. Leadership cannot be sustained when a manager crosses the line and handles an employee's responsibilities. To overstep like this is to rob those who report to us of their chance to perform. And such boundary mistakes divert us from doing what we're supposed to do as a leader.

This is especially true for white men who lead, because we inevitably face situations when the only way forward requires our black colleagues to contribute at least their 50%. There's no presumption here that they don't want to step up. But to lead means that we not only expect black colleagues to perform, we must be prepared to require it from them, just like we would anyone else. The 55% Rule gives us a way to talk with them about performance and boundaries without shining a spotlight on race or gender.

In his book *Passionate Marriage*, Dr. David Schnarch comes at this idea of equitable reciprocity by using the term "differentiation," which he defines this way:

> Differentiation involves balancing two basic life forces—the drive for individuality and the drive for togetherness. Individuality propels us to follow our own directives, to be on our own, to

create a unique identity. Togetherness pushes us to follow the directives of others, to be part of the group. When these two life forces for individuality and togetherness are expressed in balanced, healthy ways, the result is a meaningful relationship that doesn't deteriorate.

For the white man who leads

- the 55% Rule helps you take response-ability for performance, while managing boundaries;
- the practice of differentiation helps you balance individual and team needs;
- reciprocity provides a measuring stick for collaboration—when there's active give and take with black employees, that's a good sign they are choosing to follow you. And it signals that you are open to their lead.

Here's the key challenge for response-ability: how to lead unique individuals (Like No Other) to achieve results as a team (Like Some Others). It all starts with our personal capacity to pursue our own goals in a way that helps others reach theirs.

Think long and hard about how to lead as a white man in a way that invites a return on your investment in diversity. Reciprocity is core to that ROI, so look to build relationships with black colleagues and customers who show you *their* response-ability. When such collaboration takes off, it becomes less about being black and white, and more about the human-to-human connection. Amazing things emerge from the mutual commitment to respond to each other's best contribution.

CONVERSATION STARTER: *How can you apply the 55% Rule to your relationships, and how will you know reciprocity when you see it?*

Talk

When you are a white man leading in a diverse world, you want to be known for saying what needs to be said in a way people can hear it. You're motivated to avoid remarks that offend. Sometimes you stay quiet for fear of hurting others or sounding stupid.

Words are the crucial leadership tool you wield with your mouth.

In these five essays, I want to share with you how you can lead by giving the gift of words to black colleagues and customers.

No one appointed me the Talk Tutor. It's a free country, as they say. May you choose the words that literally serve a good purpose.

It's as simple—and as complicated—as that.

Constantly calibrate
intent and impact.

I don't really want to communicate—I just want to be understood.

ASHLEIGH BRILLIANT

"Why don't people understand exactly what I say? It's clear enough to me."

"Why do my employees misconstrue my words? Don't they know I'm the boss?"

"Why does my wife misunderstand some of the most obvious stuff I tell her?"

Uh oh. I feel a whine coming on.

Leaders must attend to this gap between what we mean (intent) and how people receive what we say (impact). And we have to close the breach in the other direction, too, by discovering what the other person means, not what we "heard them say." This gap-closing skill has been called *listening*; you might have heard of it. To communicate effectively, constantly calibrate intent and impact. Here's how, in six steps:

- *Monitor your internal diversity messages.* In essay 36 we considered the art of self-perception. Take this art to heart; your words and nonverbals may find a way to communicate more or less than you intend.

- *In your own mind, clarify what you intend to communicate.* When you are clear about what you're trying to say, you will likely decrease the gap between intent and impact.

- *Consider your audience.* It is a powerful internal discipline to actually care about the impact of your words. What do you know about how your receivers receive?

- *Communicate.* Practice beforehand if you have a tricky message to deliver. This is leadership in action—saying what needs to be said in a way people will comprehend and choose to follow.

- *Identify impact.* Stop talking. Ask an open-ended question. Watch for nonverbal responses (furrowed eyebrows, crossed arms). Say point-blank, "I want to make sure I'm communicating clearly. How would you paraphrase what I just said?"

- *Clarify intent.* Say what you mean another way. Send your message until the meaning they receive is what you want to convey.

It's always difficult to dig into how communication actually operates, because it happens at the speed of mind and mouth between us. And that's precisely why you need to constantly calibrate intent and impact. The faster that the meaning sent is the meaning received, the more efficiently you move individuals and your team ahead. And when differences in race and gender are present in communication, a high-speed intent-impact mistake can force you off track into a real train wreck.

As a white man who leads, you want to communicate effectively. But black colleagues and customers may still interpret your words or actions in a manner that you did not intend. Such situations tend to go in one of three directions, with each party shaping the outcome. Let's play this out.

Imagine you lead a sales group of fourteen, four of whom are black. In a team meeting, you announced the following: "Next quarter we're going to roll out the new product to markets in Munich, Singapore, and Africa. Let's talk about scheduling the marketing mix and where we are with current customers and prospects." The team had a productive discussion, but Jason, who is black and normally one of the most vocal team members, was quiet and looked unhappy.

You need him on board for this launch (particularly in Africa), so you seek him out for a private chat. As soon as you mention his response in the meeting, he blurts out, "I am so sick and tired of Western and Asian cities getting named right, but you can sum up a whole continent of black people with just one word: 'Africa'!"

SCENARIO ONE: You say, "I'm sorry that what I said had that impact on you. Can I tell you what I intended?" If Jason shows an openness, clarify what you meant in new words. For example, you might tell him that you're aware that there are world-class cities in Africa, but the choice between Johannesburg and Nairobi has not been finalized. So you unfortunately used the word *Africa* to summarize. Once you calibrate the impact with intent, you can talk with Jason about his participation in the rollout.

SCENARIO TWO: You say, "I'm sorry that what I said had that impact on you. Can I tell you what I intended?" If Jason says no, perhaps there's more going on in him, or between you, than he is willing to address right then. There are times when people would rather assume they know what you *really* meant than give you the chance to clarify. In such moments there's not much room to move ahead, so it's time to disengage respectfully. When you anger someone unintentionally, and they are so offended that they refuse you the chance to make it right, then communication on that point is done for the moment. It may be possible to check in with Jason later and try to clarify and move ahead. If you are not allowed to try again, then the relationship will be limited, partly because of your ineffective communication, but largely due, in this illustration, to Jason's choice.

SCENARIO THREE: You are embarrassed for miscommunicating with Jason, or you are angry at his being "too sensitive." You clam up and stop caring about impact, which may confirm his interpretation of the disrespect in your intent. This will damage your ability to secure Jason's contribution to the project.

The challenge here is to communicate (creating shared meaning by correlating intent and impact) interracially (between people whose culture and skin color has influenced how they send and receive meaning). Work to ensure that the impact of your words is what you intended, to achieve mutual understanding.

CONVERSATION STARTER: *What precisely can you do to monitor the match between what you intend to say and how it is received?*

TALK

■ **55** ■

Words that Wound, One:
Make your mouth obey your values.

Words are the most useful tools of adult life. The way you talk is a powerful leadership choice, so use language respectfully to engender trust.

As a white man who leads, your talk can be both constructive and dangerous. Every manager has observed the heartening impact of an encouraging word to an employee. And we have let escape from our lips mortifying comments we would dearly love to pluck from the air before they reached anyone's ears. Our fingers may also betray us: one time I was writing an email to a client, and in attempting to type "Dr. Chin," I typed "Dr. Chink." Proofreading pays.

The point of communication is to create shared meaning, not to merely transmit one way. Since dimensions of diversity influence the way we send and receive messages, follow the cardinal rule of trustworthy communication: *Use the words people want you to use to refer to them.* People are more likely to hear you that way.

If a person prefers *gay and lesbian*, then don't say *homosexual*. If a younger woman wants you to refer to her as a *woman*, and not as a *lady*, respect her choice. An older coworker may prefer *lady* for herself, which is fine. If you don't know, don't guess. You might ask: "Laquisha, I want to make sure I use words you're comfortable with. Do your prefer the term 'black' or 'African-American,' or are both okay?"

Listen to the way people describe themselves or others like them. Overcome your fear of saying the wrong thing by admitting your discomfort to yourself. Then get busy discovering the words that work.

Finally, avoid giving black people the following two pieces of "advice":

- *Don't be so sensitive.* As white men who lead, we are in no position to counsel black Americans on excessive sensitivity to their diet of race-related slights, which have been described as "death by a thousand nicks," "microaggressions," and "indignities du jour."

- *You need to get over it.* If you were a black person, constantly wondering if the color of your skin was a problem, you might not appreciate hearing "suck it up and get over it" from a white man who has barely considered what it means to be white. As we take personal responsibility for the challenges our white skin brings to us, black people will be freer to live without the constant calculation of race at work. That's how they'll "get over it!"

Show people you're striving to communicate respectfully, and don't permit a fear of offending to tie up your tongue. Accept the awkwardness of a changing language by identifying and avoiding words that wound. Maintain a sense of humor, and make your mouth obey your values. Your black colleagues and customers will reward you with their patience and trust.

CONVERSATION STARTER: *Think back to a time you offended a person of color or a white woman inadvertently. Remember a time when you spoke from anger, not caring if you wounded the other person. In those situations, what was going on in your mind that permitted those words to escape? What can you do to avoid such miscommunication?*

Words That Wound, Two:

Never let the "n-word" leave your lips,

and quit using the Exclusion Code.

THE "N-WORD"

I n an insightful article in the February 2007 issue, *Ebony* magazine described the "n-word" this way: "Six simple letters that convey centuries of pain, evil, and contempt." True, some young black men call one another "n——." They claim that using the word on their own terms steals its sting. As a white man, I am in no position to judge their experience, or their opinions about free speech.

But since you're not a young black man, either, I beg you to accept this simple advice: never allow the n-word to escape from your white lips. I don't even permit myself to say or write the word when I'm counseling my white brothers and sisters never to use the term. This isn't about freedom of speech. It's about being able to look in the mirror and see a decent person. This is about being the kind of man and the kind of leader who avoids words that wound.

A sign at the city limits of Siloam Springs, Arkansas, read: "N——, don't let the sun set on you in Siloam Springs." This sign was removed in 1990. Eight years later, when I consulted with a company there, local white folks stated that their town "has no racial problems; that's down in the southern part of the state." Minutes later, however, they were complaining about how many Spanish-speaking people were moving in to work at the poultry plants.

In localities across America, the n-word has evolved into the ultimate national obscenity, a two-syllable code word for four hundred years of black pain and white shame. Even today, white people use the n-word to vomit up their contempt for people with black skin.

Recently the New York City Council passed a resolution (49–0) to urge all citizens to stop using the slur. *JET* magazine reported that Councilman Leroy Comrie, a sponsor, said: "The resolution sends the message that as a community we are no longer going to stand by and watch our children wallow in cultural ignorance."

Whatever the black community says to itself about use of the word, *never utter the n-word if you have white skin.* That includes younger white men and women who are into the rap and hip-hop scenes.

THE EXCLUSION CODE: GUARD YOUR TONGUE

White America has evolved what I call the Exclusion Code. These are seemingly innocuous words (beyond the n-word) and meanings that we as white people implicitly use to exclude or demean black people. My advice: stop using the Code. And we should wince and speak up when we hear other white people using common Code words like the following:

- *Intelligent*, as in "Wow, Gloria, you're really intelligent."

    More often than not, lurking in such a comment is the racist stereotype of the poor, uneducated Negro who wouldn't really be expected to contribute with a true intellect. When you recognize in yourself surprise at how smart a black person is, don't mention it. And contemplate just how smart this thought makes you.

- *Qualified* and *quotas,* as in "Louis, I'm sure *you're* qualified to do the job, but you have to wonder about people with all these quotas in place."

    Louis already doubts that you think he is qualified. Be careful about operating with the white man's default opinion about hiring or promoting: "Of course, we want the most qualified person." Black colleagues may assume that the unspoken whole sentence runs like this: "Of course, we want the most qualified person, *who will turn out to be a white person as often as possible.*"

    Implicit in the use of "quotas" is that black people tend to get hired and promoted for merely being black, but it is presumed that white people earn our achievements. This is profoundly insulting, and directly reinforces the powerfully racist assumption that white people are qualified and black people are not.

    The solution here: engage in substantive discussion of preference and qualification (see essay 25), and beware of how Code words can exclude.

- *Articulate,* as in "Michael, you're so articulate. "(with surprise in your voice)

   Even when you intend it positively, the use of the word alludes to the racist expectation that black people are not as well spoken as white people. Or they don't use the idioms we prefer. Instead, just say: "I like the way you said that." I have never heard one white person describe another as "articulate" with surprise in their voice. We expect white people to be articulate. What is behind our surprise when black people speak well?

- *Fit* and *team player,* as in "I don't think we should hire Michelle. I'm not really sure she would fit, and she doesn't strike me as a team player."

   Journalist Lena Williams describes this idea of *team player* as "white speak for someone who plays by the (white) rules." In language that conceals the relevance of race, *fit* can be an instinctive exclusion, by which we as white people justify refusing opportunity to black (or other) people, with the implication that they would be uncooperative or unlikable members of the team.

Watch for words that wound or reject. In particular, never say the n-word, and quit using the lexicon of the Exclusion Code. Develop the reputation for leading as a white man who guards his tongue, not from fear, but out of openhearted respect for his black colleagues and customers.

CONVERSATION STARTER: *Where do you stand on use of the n-word and the Exclusion Code? What will you do when other white people use such language?*

TALK

■ 57 ■

Conversing in White and Black:

Keep four things in mind.

FIRST: WHAT'S IN A NAME? SCORE POINTS BY GETTING NAMES RIGHT AND SHOWING RESPECT

Because black people suffer at the hands of some white folks who think and behave as if "all black people look alike,", it can be particularly offensive to use the wrong name, or mispronounce the name of a black person. Every effective leader learns how to address people with respect. If you're unsure about how to say a name, don't mutter "I just can't pronounce those African names,", or communicate in any other manner that their unusual name doesn't merit your respectful effort. Instead, ask "How would you like me to pronounce your name? I want to make sure I get it right." This shows an intentional respect. Or don't use their name until you can ask someone who knows them how you should say it. It is sad that this is still an issue among leaders in twenty-first-century America.

Early in my career I worked extensively with people from Southeast Asia. I found that they at least appreciated my effort at getting their name right. Even my haywire attempts earned a good smile from them, because they knew I'd get it right eventually. Have you noticed how National Public Radio asks listeners who write in or email to advise on pronouncing their name? That's what respect sounds like in our multicultural age.

Err on the side of formality when addressing a black person, especially when they are in an older generation. Use their last name and the appropriate honorific: Mr., Ms., Dr., Rev. Be cautious about using their first name. Until you know them personally, premature familiarity or informality may be seen as an attempt to establish superior standing. If you tend to informality yourself, like I do, this may be a challenge. And don't take liberties with a black person's name by shortening it or using nicknames. Unless told otherwise, Robert is not Bob, Charles is not Chuck, William is not Bill.

SECOND: HONEST INQUIRY? YES. IGNORANT INQUISITION? NO.

It can be enlightening to ask a black person an honest, practical question. Don't hesitate to do so. I've encouraged you to engage black people many times in this book.

Meanwhile, keep in mind that God probably did not put black people on Earth to be the sole source of information on all things race related for white people. So make sure your inquiries are not investigations. It can feel like an awkward inquisition when a white person, with excessive energy or naivete, asks a black person

- about their background and qualifications for a job;
- to interpret black cultural expressions like rap or R&B;
- to explain the behavior of O.J. Simpson or any other misbehaving black person;
- to speak for "what black people think" on any topic.

Match your race-related queries to how well you know the person. A close black friend provides a relationship in which you can ask anything, because they will value your teachability, forgive your Pre-Awareness, and learn from you, too.

THIRD: BUILD RELATIONSHIPS BY DISCLOSING YOUR LIMITATIONS EARLY

When entering a conversation involving race and gender differences, pre-empt unspoken concerns about your credibility to participate. I will say something like this: "As a white man, my life experience is very different from yours. I know that limits my perspective, because I'll never see some things from the same view you have. But I'm teachable, and I hope we can really speak our minds here, so we can move forward together. How's that sound?" Sometimes, if we don't acknowledge our limits in a way that invites collaboration, the conversation is stifled from the outset. This is about admitting the relative aspect of Relative Expertise; humility comes in handy.

FOURTH: HANDLE PUSHBACK, ANGER, AND INTIMIDATION WITH GRACE

In a situation where blame is on the loose, a white man who leads may be seen as the nail that sticks up on diversity. And you know what happens then: the nail gets pounded down by people of color or white women. Even a white man who confidently engages diversity and seeks to lead on it (as a *relative expert*) may not be well received.

There are many possible causes for such resistance: you remind them of someone who treated them poorly; they're fed up with disrespect, and the crap they got from the cabbie on the way over was the last straw; you unintentionally said or did something that offended them; there are organizational issues you don't know about; their spouse just chewed them out in a voice-mail message; or maybe they're just in a mean and nasty mood today. Coming face-to-face with a white man who doesn't have the good sense to take whatever blame they want to dish out just makes their fire burn hotter.

A white man who leads on diversity may be so counterintuitive, so unexpected, so previously unencountered, that a black person's reaction may be simple disbelief. I have been criticized for acting with "typical white male arrogance" for my good-faith efforts to lead on diversity with confidence. I guess I didn't know my place.

When you're unfairly under fire, you must not cave in or fight back. It is an important opportunity for honest self-reflection. It is a time for compassion and grace toward your "opponent." Remember that people are watching:

- White men are concerned about safety, so they're looking to see if you run, fight, or stand by the courage of your convictions.
- A few women and people of color may be cheering on your detractor, and they need to learn that bullying won't work.

- Some people of color and women will come to your defense if they see that you are holding on to a positive approach, and if they can find their own courage.

Respond with controlled integrity, stay openhearted, and speak your truth as directly and calmly as you can. Take a look at *Crucial Conversations*, by Kerry Patterson, Joseph Grenny, Ron MacMillan, and Al Switzer. This is a very effective approach to conversations where emotion and stakes run high, and opinions clash. Sometimes conflict, handled with grace, can turn a foe into a friend. Afterward, process the experience carefully with friends and associates, so you can learn your lessons in preparation for the next adventure. Leading on diversity is not for the faint of heart, the weak of mind, or the careless of mouth.

CONVERSATION STARTER: *What conversational habits will you deploy to strengthen your communication with black colleagues and customers?*

Our exemption from respectful talk has expired:

do not presume immunity and impunity.

Back in essay 20, we considered our normativity. White men have been our nation's norm (a standard or model) for leadership. This means that as white men who lead—a group made up of just two percent of all Americans—we exercise an influence far beyond our percentage of the population. But that is changing.

Normativity includes the presumption that "what I intend counts for more than whatever the impact may be." Being the norm carries with it the prerogative to restate "what I really meant." The lower-status person is then expected to honor my intention, or at the very least, they must accept my apology. I escape any culpability for my impact on them.

Historically, as white men who lead, we have been able to say pretty much whatever we please, to black people and about black people, without much consequence. It's a free country, we like to say. Such verbal freedom for us may be summarized as *immunity* (exempt from liability) and *impunity* (exempt from punishment).

In other words, some higher-status white men (leaders, that is) have granted to themselves an exemption from respectful talk. They expect that whatever comes out of their mouths will be understood for what they mean, even if they speak from ignorance.

And if they mess up and say something naughty, well then, boys will be boys. Watch carefully for the dynamics when another white man complains about "political correctness" (see essay 22): does he want to speak with disrespect and not be held accountable for it?

I am sorry I get to be the official harbinger of an historic shift: as white men who lead, our exemption from respectful talk has expired. We presume immunity and impunity at our professional peril.

Actually, we should welcome this change. A nation whose Founding Fathers were all white men can become more than they envisioned. Holding white men to account for disrespectful speech does not prevent us from saying whatever we want. Free speech still means we get to speak our minds. But it no longer means that our normativity renders us free from the consequences of speaking disrespectfully.

During the time I've been writing this section of the book, three white men of influence have earned public disgrace by speaking disrespectfully of black people. These men presumed their immunity and impunity:

- Actor Michael Richards's racist rant at customers in a comedy club was laced with the n-word.

- Joseph Biden, a U.S. senator, blithely indicated that a black presidential candidate could be distinguished from previous black contenders because this candidate was "articulate" and "clean." (Remember the Exclusion Code?)

- Don Imus, a nationally syndicated talk radio host, was thumped off the pinnacle of success for describing an outstanding women's college basketball team as "nappy-headed hos." His popular show had produced $15 million in revenues for CBS the previous month; then the line of business had to be written off the books. He has returned to the airwaves, chastened and stained.

And these men talk for a living!

Mr. Imus provides a near-perfect name to this cautionary tale: Imus = I'm Us. So we'll call this dysfunction the *Imus Syndrome:* When a white male leader disrespectfully talks to or about black people, he risks his position of influence.

By the time this book arrives in your hands, there will undoubtedly be more white men suffering from the Imus Syndrome, marching themselves right off the stage. For some time to come, we will watch these white-guy-flameouts, because they don't understand that their exemption from disrespectful talk has expired.

Avoid sharing their fate inside the world in which you lead. Watch your words. Guard your tongue using these two guidelines:

1. You don't get to decide for black people what should offend them or does offend them.

2. *Impact* trumps *intent*. The odds are increasing that you will pay a price for speaking to or about black people with disrespect. Mr. Imus was free to say what he wanted, but he was no longer free from the consequences.

You're cooked if you test your immunity and impunity without diverse friends to defend you. Don Imus built his reputation on insults, and no black friends stood by his side.

Let's summarize with a limerick for leaders:

> *A white man who leads may attempt*
> *Post-offense to reframe what he meant.*
> *But he cannot impugn*
> *Since he's now not immune*
> *So he talks and he leads nonexempt.*

Conversation Starter: *How will you balance saying what you want with speaking with respect?*

Act

So far we have studied ways to think, feel, and respond as white men who lead. We have considered the fundamentals of leading on diversity from the inside out.

We will explore *behavior* for the rest of the book, identifying choices for acting as a leader committed to working successfully with black colleagues and customers. Leading involves getting results. The remainder of the essays will help you translate your insight and intention into action.

And take a look at *Leading in Black and White: Working Across the Racial Divide in Corporate America*, by Ancella B. Livers and Keith A. Carver, from the Center for Creative Leadership in Greensboro. In chapter nine they list eighteen good actions for leading as a white man. Their book will help you walk a mile or two in the shoes of black managers.

It's about doing right and doing well.

Character counts:
Demonstrate your being in your doing.

Sports do not build character; they reveal it.

HEYWOOD HALE BROUN, CBS SPORTS COMMENTATOR

To this point in the book, we've focused on the thinking, values, and qualities that pilot your effective leadership as a white man. Now we're shifting gears into leadership action. Our starting point is a consideration of character and its expression in behavior; how what you do emerges from who you are.

269

Character may be defined as the intrinsic values, qualities, and gifts that find expression in a person or organization's behavior. The potency of character materializes in action. A leader's real influence derives from his ability to present his values, qualities, and gifts in ways that cause people to follow him.

Your reputation is largely built on the unique ways you exhibit your distinctive characteristics. And the depth of influence you wield as a leader flows directly from the way you display a positive ethical core. A leader may possess world-class leadership skills or a lofty job title, but character flaws will damage his opportunity to lead.

Character is

- the inner made known by word and deed;
- the life lab that forges the congruence between who you are and what you do;
- the pivot point where thought and feeling translate into behavior;
- you revealed.

In *The Soul's Code: In Search of Character and Calling*, James Hillman describes character as an "invisible source of personal consistency." This has to do with the *who* part of being a white man who leads. Character is vitally important to us because we seek to lead authentically so that diverse humans will choose to follow.

Character is the fuel that stokes the fire of leadership. Today, a white man's character can light the way, or it can burn down the house. Looking at leadership through this lens of character will equip you to do the following:

- Express the congruence between who you are and what you do, demonstrating your integrity.

- Distinguish your own personal brand as a leader, securing for you a sustainable collaborative advantage over less-intentional white male managers.

- Establish your reputation among women and people of color as a leader with deep human insight, and a bias to action.

Dr. Martin Luther King Jr. famously dreamed of the day when people will be judged "by the content of their character." You have the power to hasten that day by leading from the inside out as a white man.

I encourage you to purchase of copy of Shelby Steele's *The Content of Our Character*. In this award-winning book, he confronts the "received wisdom" about race, to challenge black and white Americans alike. And Dr. Steele attended to his own character as he wrote the book. Here's how he described the writing process: "I felt that if I could only stay with myself, I could get somewhere." There's an example of that "invisible source of personal consistency" at work in a Hoover Institution scholar who thoughtfully ruffles both black and white feathers.

Near the end of his tenure as chairman and CEO of Texaco, Alfred Decrane Jr. wrote the following:

> Real leaders are fair, honest, ethical, open, and trustworthy. These basic roots of character garner the respect that is needed in order for an individual to be called a leader. I've been in business long enough to see that short-term "wins" can be achieved without these qualities, but I've also seen that lasting leadership and success—at whatever level—is impossible without them.

What words would your black colleagues use to describe the basic roots of your character? Learn to lead through effective action as a white man, so that your black colleagues can answer this question with words that will make you proud.

CONVERSATION STARTER: *Ask your manager to describe your character, as it expresses your values, qualities, and gifts. Discuss with him or her how character affects leadership.*

ACT

■ **60** ■

Respect:
Give it. Get it. Keep it.

Respect is the art of showing deferential esteem. From A to Z, here are twenty-six ways you can cultivate respect as you lead among black colleagues and customers (and everyone else!).

Address black colleagues and customers more formally (with an honorific and last name), until you know them well enough to call them by their first name.

Be polite to black colleagues and customers by opening doors, saying "please" and "thank you," and simply caring (yes, respect has worked well since second grade).

Confess your limited perspective as a white man—it reinforces that you appreciate the differing viewpoints of others.

Do what works to make sure that black customers return.

Err on the side of inclusion. You'd rather have black coworkers tell you they didn't need to be in on the decision, than confront you for excluding them.

Find ways to support and fund organizations serving the black community, as a way to show your respect.

Give respect to get respect. Which of your specific behaviors express your respect for black colleagues and customers?

Handle conflict by listening to and validating the positions of all parties.

Involve people in key decisions, like setting goals and evaluating performance.

Jump into the conversations about preference and opportunity constructively, so a productive white male voice replaces white male silence.

Keep learning about black history and culture, to help you understand the views and concerns of black colleagues and customers.

Look for potential and merit in black employees, and move them into high performance development programs.

Maintain appropriate eye contact. Don't look away to avoid the encounter with another real human being.

Nail down a budget every year that invests in diversity, and then measure and market the ROI. This shows your commitment is real.

Offer corrective feedback to black employees in a timely manner, referring to specific behaviors, and seek their ideas for improvement (just like you do with every employee).

Protect employees' security needs. Remember that physical, financial, and emotional safety is paramount.

Quit calling on any black person to speak for all black people.

Recognize a black person's presence with words or nonverbally, and speak up if you see another white person look right through them (e.g., a maitre d').

Surprise black customers with special attention and respect. One bank branch trained all staff members to ask black customers: "Did our service meet your standards today?" (They ended up asking everyone.)

Take a stand against discrimination; when you see it, address it. Otherwise, your silence may be perceived as collusion by black colleagues, customers, and fellow citizens.

Underscore your personal diversity learning with other white employees, and make sure your black employees see you do it.

Vote with your feet by building a reputation for getting out in front of diversity issues, and leading with courage and transparency. When you respect black colleagues, you don't run and hide from their concerns—you initiate.

Watch for what motivates your black employees, and purposefully provide what is needed to induce their continuing excellence.

Xpect your black colleagues to contribute their best.

Yield to the best judgment of your black employees. If they're right, you've all benefited from their expertise. If they're wrong, they get to learn from their mistakes like everyone else.

Zero in on growth opportunities in the African-American market, and look to expand into African nations as well.

As you build this discipline of respect into the ways you lead as a white man, your black colleagues and customers will reciprocate by showing you the deferential esteem you have earned from them.

CONVERSATION STARTER: *Among the twenty-six, what three ways will you employ to give, get, and keep respect in your leadership work this week?*

Trust-Building:
Make promises, keep promises over time.

The most important single diversity skill for a white man who leads is the capacity for building trust with diverse stakeholders. Leaders and followers can deliver remarkable results when trust runs strong in the team and enterprise. Trust cannot be manufactured, it only can be crafted promise by promise. And it can be decimated in the breaking of a single commitment.

This definition of **trust** comes from ethicist Dr. Lewis Smedes of Fuller Theological Seminary: "the making and keeping of promises over time." In the next five essays, we will examine how a white male leader builds trust, by making and keeping promises to black (and all) colleagues and customers.

Make Promises, Keep Promises

Here's a true story about trust: Garrett, a senior executive, verbally promised Victoria, a black woman and a high-performing director, that the organization would provide the tuition support and release time she needed to earn a graduate degree. He assured her that, upon graduation, she would be promoted to a VP position on his team, even though a few of his peers weren't so sure. Early in her advanced study, however, Garrett died. His commitment, while known publicly, was not in writing, and the organization could easily have renounced the pledge. But they honored Garrett's promise and Victoria's hard work. She has now served as an effective senior leader for more than a decade. Due to her loyalty to the organization, she has refused several excellent offers from other companies.

Such is the power of trust. Garrett pledged to invest in Victoria, and his fellow executives, all men, kept his promise. The return on their investment in her talent is breathtaking:

- She has proven her promise as a leader in her division.
- Women and men in the organization expect to advance, like Victoria.
- Male managers actively mentor men and women.
- Her way of leading expanded acceptable styles of managing.
- Victoria is no token; four more women now lead in senior roles. Two black men are also top leaders, equaling seven women and people of color out of seventeen total executives.
- Female customers report that the company's demonstrated commitment to women motivates them to buy.

- Since the promise to Victoria was kept, retention of black employees is up sixty-seven percent, and their recruitment is up forty-seven percent.

While this ROI is attributable to more than one person's success, company veterans know that Victoria's story catalyzed many happy returns on what Garrett invested almost fifteen years ago.

When you make and keep promises with diverse stakeholders, you strengthen your standing and harness the power of diversity for the organization. Garrett achieved this even in death; today Victoria's leadership testifies to his trust-building.

THE HORSE IS OUT OF THE BARN

In most American organizations, key diversity promises were made long ago; the horse has been out of the barn for neigh on thirty years. This is true about two particular promises to women and people of color: recruitment and promotion.

Since the Civil Rights Act of 1964, American organizations have sought and secured new generations of diverse employees. For instance, in a 1995 study with twenty technology companies, I found thirteen distinct and highly productive diversity recruiting practices at Microsoft. The promise of hiring is the promise of inclusion: "Come and work here. We will compensate you fairly, and you will be able to contribute and serve our customers."

The promise of promotion is also an oath of opportunity, in which an organization affirms that, "as a valued employee, you will have the chance to develop your skills and advance into new positions based on your performance."

The mantra for Wal-Mart associates: "Our people make the difference." Does any American company not claim that their employees are their most valuable resource? Now that's a promise your people expect you to keep.

As a white man who leads you need to

- inventory the promises in play with those you manage;
- evaluate the way you make, keep, and sometimes break your promises.

And the promises intrinsic to selection and promotion are healthy promises to keep.

In the story of Victoria and Garrett, her leadership over the years delivers on his promise, and fulfills her own. Make and keep promises that show your character as a leader; promises are a place where we demonstrate who we are in what we do.

CONVERSATION STARTER: *What promises have you made and kept with your employees and customers?*

ACT

■ 62 ■

Trust-Building:
Renounce distrust, and don't break your promises.

T he familiar indictment of white men is that we "just don't get it." We are seldom trusted to lead by making and keeping diversity-related promises. If *trust* is making and keeping promises over time, then *distrust* is making and breaking promises, time after time. Houston, we have promise problems.

AN ORGANIZATION'S PROMISES

Distrust filtered through human differences can corrode our organization as a place where humans and earnings thrive. Failures of

281

trust squander a company's talent, market share, morale, and stock price; foment litigation and media fiascos; and suppress productivity. A short list of corporate diversity crises instructs us in broken promises to employees and customers. All these situations occurred during a two-year period in the United States:

- At Boeing, a class-action suit over discrimination against black people in hiring and promotion cost the corporation millions of dollars and untold embarrassment. The company's reputation (and their diversity program) suffered.

- At ARCO, female executives hit the roof when their company contributed to the legal defense fund of an accused harasser, U.S. senator Bob Packwood. Women customers talked boycott.

- At the Denny's restaurant chain, racist treatment of customers produced lawsuits that begat nightmarish media coverage, shaming the parent company into more active franchising with minority owners and multicultural advertising. Note: in 2006, Denny's was honored by *Black Enterprise* as the most improved company for diversity.

- At Texaco, a recording of a few prejudiced executives hit the public fan, resulting in humiliation and a $35 million diversity investment.

- At Mitsubishi, rampant sexual harassment and a bizarre public relations ploy (hundreds of employees were bussed to the courthouse to demonstrate against the harassment suit) maximized their mess. Costs related to replacing female employees skyrocketed.

Trust and distrust are not tame, trendy little management topics.

The Repercussions of Distrust

Broken promises recoil like the kick of a powerful rifle. For those white male managers who often break promises, relationships with black colleagues spark a hostile work environment, drive talent away, and fan the flame of litigation. High-performing employees

- will not follow a leader (for long) who does not keep the promises he makes (and you may have noticed it is difficult to lead without followers);

- will not stay in an organization that breaks its promises, and losing such talent damages competitiveness and is expensive to replace.

Customers watch to see if a company honors the promises implied in its advertising, through product quality, service, and community reputation. Breaking these good promises yields a distrust in customers that damages their loyalty.

Take a look at Frederick R. Lynch's *The Diversity Machine: The Drive to Change the "White Male" Workplace*. Dr. Lynch (this is a truly unfortunate last name for a white man writing on diversity) mistakes diversity management for a conspiracy against white men. But he rightly emphasizes one thing: diversity training itself has sometimes engendered distrust.

It is useful to emphasize valuing differences, and to teach us all that "different does not mean bad,", because such awareness is crucial, as we saw in essay 18. But diversity training adds no value as its own end, and such education often leaves white male (and other) participants asking, "What am I supposed to *do* with this?" Awareness training without skill building is knowledge without application. Unless you're leading in an educational institution, you don't go to work to learn for the sake of learning—you go to work to get things done. Awareness that does not lead to results is a broken promise.

The future will be full of conflict for the white man who leads among diverse stakeholders by making and breaking promises, time after time. Distrust bites back. Don't let it bite you. Don't break the promises made by you or your organization.

Build trust by making and delivering on six key promises with black colleagues and customers. That's what we will explore in the next two essays.

CONVERSATION STARTER: *Have you or your organization allowed distrust to grow among diverse stakeholders, by breaking promises? If so, what happened? How can you lead in a way to rebuild trust going forward?*

Trust-Building:
Deliver on Key Promises 1-3.

A t the heart of durable interracial relationships, we find promises – making, keeping, and yes, sometimes promise breaking. And at the center of every successful company dwells the demonstrated ability to deliver on its promises to customers and employees. Consequently, promise making and promise keeping are essential skills for a white man who wants to lead effectively.

A **promise** is a vow that creates expectation and accountability. You have experienced the power of promise making and keeping, in good times and bad. Do you remember when

- your manager believed in you enough to delegate more responsibility to you than you were sure you could handle?

- you received negative feedback based on performance objectives that you did not understand, accept, or even know about?

Delegation and performance evaluation are two management skills rightly seen as vows that create expectation and accountability. Promises are the building blocks of trust, vital to your leadership as a white man committed to working successfully among black colleagues and customers.

In this essay and the next, let's consider six priority promises you should make and keep.

PROMISE 1

I promise to be honest with myself and others regarding my concerns and fears about diversity.

Make the first promise to yourself. Fellow white male managers often share with me thoughts such as the following:

- Affirmative action and equal opportunity still seem to operate by lowering hiring and performance standards, but it isn't safe to raise the issue.

- I'm angry that managers get extra credit for mentoring a woman or person of color, and that certain jobs are preselected for "diverse" candidates. This is just reverse discrimination; some guys don't get mentored or promoted just because they're white.

For all the nerve white men are said to possess, many of us have grown timid when it comes to the candor that leading on diversity requires. There is a difference between reactionary whining about diversity (avoid it) or blurting out whatever pops into your head (don't go there), and finding the right way to express your honest concerns (work at it). Decide for yourself what is right. Trust yourself.

PROMISE 2

I will keep the promises required by law.

A law is a promise that creates expectation and accountability among a society's members. Under the rule of law, we elect lawmakers to frame these promises for us, we pay taxes to implement the law, and we hire lawyers, when necessary, to secure the promise of the law before the court as final arbiter. American democracy itself can be viewed as a spectacular test in trust: the making and breaking and keeping of promises over time, between the people of an intentionally diverse nation.

The law makes promises you must keep as a manager, in order to

- prohibit discrimination and harassment in hiring, promotion, and employee relations, and in treatment of customers;
- require accommodation of needs due to disability, health, and family circumstance;
- obligate employers to provide equitable compensation and a safe workplace.

You and your employer are both responsible for assuring that you manage legally. You deserve first-rate training in how to observe the promises required by law.

PROMISE 3

I will make promises about things that matter.

A manager makes many promises to employees, ranging from the expectations that accompany hiring, through the mutual accountability of a respectful end to employment. As a white man who leads, here's a promise about something that matters: build trust by focusing on how power works in your unit.

We've defined *power* as the opportunity and ability to see, make, and carry out choices. Foster trust among team members by emphasizing power-with rather than power-over. *Choose* collaboratively.

To assess how power functions with your team, evaluate how choices are identified, and how decisions are made and implemented. You can see the connection between the central behaviors of power (choices) and trust (promises).

Tell your employees you want to audit how power and trust operate in the team. Bring in a trained facilitator, and absent yourself so they will speak their minds. Responses must be aggregated and reported to protect confidentiality. Through interviews and/or focus groups, ask questions such as the following:

- Do you feel free to offer feedback to your manager and coworkers? Describe a situation when your input was well received, and a time when your feedback did not seem welcome. Is feedback provided to you in an effective way?

- Is the team identifying its most important opportunities and problems in a timely way? Describe an opportunity or problem the team handled well, and one it didn't. Are there opportunities or problems the team needs to address now?

- How do or should employees influence key decisions? Describe times when team participation helped or hurt such decision making.

- How does the team resolve conflict? What should it do to better handle differences?

- What could your manager do to improve team performance? Your own success?

It takes nerve to ask questions like these, partly because the very asking contains the implicit promise that you will respond substantively. That's risky, because you can rarely satisfy everyone, and many solutions exceed your authority or resources.

Intriguingly, such confident inclusion of team members motivates them to trust you more. They know it costs you to explore your promise-making and -keeping. When, as a white man who leads, you openly explore how power operates within the team, this notifies people of color, women, and other white men that you take trust seriously.

Make promises about things that matter. Trust is built when you exercise power—when you see, make, and carry out choices—*with* diverse team members.

CONVERSATION STARTER: *What are your priority promises as a white man who leads?*

ACT

■ **64** ■

Trust-Building:
Deliver on Key Promises 4-6.

PROMISE 4

I will make promises I can keep.

Make promises you can keep. Then do your damnedest to honor them.

Be realistic and honest, evaluating what it will take to implement a promise before you make it. For example, there is an implied promise to your black (and other) colleagues when they see you lead with diversity in mind; they expect you to continue doing so. Promise-making and promise-keeping sets high performance precedents.

Give yourself and your time to your people; you are your own promise as a leader. That's where character factors in. Joseph Olchefske, a former Seattle school superintendent, said it this way: "You need people to know who you are every day."

Effective delegation requires you to take time to know employees individually, and to be known by them. Delegation is a form of promise-making, where we trust others to get the job done.

Another method of promise-keeping: use the skills people know you already possess. In one training session, a sixty-year-old white male CEO blurted: "I don't need to learn about cross-cultural conflict resolution. I already have the skills. I just don't use them." As an executive and an elder, he was squandering his opportunity to model and mentor. Sadly, he failed to find new motivation after making this public statement, and he never experienced diversity as a sustainable collaborative advantage. His unwillingness to resolve conflict wounded the organization and the people he led.

Exercise due diligence in setting and evaluating performance objectives with those who report to you. These goals represent key promises between you, because they create expectation and accountability. Your employees should understand and accept the criteria by which their success will be measured. Deliver feedback constantly, and provide formal reviews quarterly; you can always choose to evaluate performance more often than your company requires. Praise, reward, and correct the performance of black (and all) employees, specifically and candidly.

Hold yourself utterly accountable for the promises you make. Then honor your commitments, and expect your employees to do the same.

PROMISE 5

I will make promises that evoke reciprocity.

By definition, trust is a two-way street. Your colleagues unleash the true power of collaboration when they make and keep promises with you.

To secure an employee's contribution, employers make the promises of hiring, compensation, development, and the possibility of promotion. When these promises are kept, it is right to expect an employee to invest their best in return. Can you remember a time when a manager entrusted you with challenging duties, and you delivered on that expectation with full accountability? Be that manager to your black employees.

Here are two more promises that invite reciprocity:

- Use the right words well (see essays 54–58). Then your diverse employees will speak well of you, and they will be patient with your mistakes.

- Establish and evaluate achievable goals *with* your employees. When they reciprocate by meeting their performance objectives, you also succeed.

Leaders are responsible for making and keeping promises. But the resulting expectations and accountabilities also oblige your coworkers to contribute their best in realizing a promise's potential. Your good-faith promise deserves their good-faith participation. Such give and take forges trust.

Promise 6

When I break a promise, I will spend relational capital wisely.

Relational capital is the goodwill you've accumulated through keeping prior promises. Such trust on account is crucial, because across your career as a leader, you will break enough promises to fuel many rounds of the blame game.

Sometimes we make promises we know we can't keep. Consider, for example, the challenge facing Alan, a bank manager in California. Many of his customers were recent immigrants, and preferred to do business in their native tongues (Spanish, Mandarin, or Korean), since they were still learning English. And some of these customers brought significant business into the bank.

Alan's staff spoke only English, and everyone suffered when language differences slowed service, and hampered the growth of accounts. Employees were enthusiastic when he promised that bilingual customer reps would be hired. Customers were glad to hear help was on the way.

Help wasn't. Alan suspected a hiring freeze was coming, but it was easier in the moment to promise bilingual new hires. When news of the hiring freeze went public, employees and customers were upset with Alan. Trust was being tested as they watched to see how he would handle his broken promise.

When a promise fails, you draw against the trust in your relationships with those affected. This is a time for candor, a time to admit directly that the promise will not be kept. Don't try to hide a broken promise, or revise a promise to match the brokenness. Look for ways to make it right.

Fortunately, Alan was liked and respected. He had delivered on previous pledges, and enjoyed a strong balance of relational capital. Know this: when attempting to recover from a broken promise, you may expend large amounts of this capital.

Alan discussed the freeze with his staff, acknowledged that no bilingual hires were arriving soon, and delegated the search for other solutions to several customer service reps. They secured the services of Spanish, Mandarin, and Korean interpreters. Alan also sat down with selected customers and explained how the branch was looking for answers to the language challenge.

There were three outcomes from Alan's broken promise:

- The customer service staff talked with English-learning customers. These interviews led employees to training and other resources for handling language differences in customer service. Alan could find budget to help current staff with language issues.

- Customers appreciated the improved service.
- The way Alan handled his broken promise actually strengthened his reputation!

When you make and keep your promises, employees follow you and customers return. When you handle your broken promises honestly and creatively, you will pay a lower price for your mistakes.

CONVERSATION STARTER: *Specifically, what leadership promises are you keeping with black colleagues and customers? Are they reciprocating? How are you handling broken promises?*

Trust-Building:
Assess team trust.

D o your employees trust you? You cannot answer this question without securing your team's input. Use the following survey to take trust's pulse in your organization, your unit, and your leadership.

- Download the following free survey from www. leadershipforwhitemen.com, and print copies.

- Arrange for a trained facilitator (HR, training staff, or external consultant) to receive and compile the results, review them with you, and then facilitate discussion of the results with you and your team.

- If there is sufficient race and gender diversity on the team to ensure confidentiality, code the survey forms so that the compiler can track differences in responses among men and women by race.

• When the survey is initially distributed, explain why trust is important to you, and promise that you will respond substantively.

Promises Made To You	As my manager you have:		This organization has:	
	Kept this promise to me	Broken this promise to me	Kept this promise to me	Broken this promise to me
Hiring You will be able to start in a good job that contributes to the lives of coworkers and customers.	○	○	○	○
Compensation You will be compensated fairly for the work you do.	○	○	○	○
Delegation You will be given increasing responsibilities as your skills improve.	○	○	○	○
Words of Respect When people talk with you, their words will show their respect for you.	○	○	○	○

Promises Kept?

Figure 65-1

Promises Made To You	As my manager you have:		This organization has:	
	Kept this promise to me	Broken this promise to me	Kept this promise to me	Broken this promise to me
Performance Management You will understand and accept your performance goals, and you will be evaluated regularly and fairly.	O	O	O	O
Conflict Resolution When you are party to a disagreement, it will be handled effectively.	O	O	O	O
Team Process The work teams you join will be healthy places to achieve common goals.	O	O	O	O
Promotion You will have opportunities to advance in your career.	O	O	O	O

Promises Kept?

Thank you for completing this survey – I promise to respond substantively.

Figure 65-2

Trust-building is an essential technique for you as a white male manager, and a core measure of your success. Modify this survey based on the lessons you learned from using it. Repeat this exercise annually as part of your performance evaluation with your boss.

A Closing Note on Trust

Trust, the making and keeping of promises over time, remains in short supply between black and white people. It is a precious asset precisely because it cannot be manufactured, only earned cumulatively. Distrust, however, intensifies with each broken promise. Establishing trust to bridge the racial divide will require focused effort across the remaining years in your career and beyond. Our own era, after all, is rooted in millennia of conflict between the genders, races, and nations.

Trust will serve you as a potent leadership resource when you make promises that matter, keep the promises you make, and, when necessary, break your promises with candor and creativity.

Trust is a powerful motivator for sustainable high-performing relationships among white and black people. When you habitually make and keep promises over time, black customers will return with their friends, and black employees will perform at higher levels and stay with the organization longer.

CONVERSATION STARTER: *Based on what you have learned from assessing the trust level with your team, how will you lead by making and keeping promises?*

ACT

■ 66 ■

A strong friendship
will change you forever.

"Some of my best friends are black." If this is true, you probably know enough not to defend yourself with such a cliché. When even one of your best friends is black, you're a changed man.

Find a copy of *Afraid of the Dark: What Whites and Blacks Need to Know About Each Other*, by Jim Myers. Chapter one focuses on interracial friendships: the opportunities they offer, and how friendships across the color line do not appear to drive social change like we might expect.

But the trend line on attitudes about white/black friendships is dramatic. In 1964, sixty percent of Americans polled indicated a belief that marriage between white and black people should be illegal. By 2006, a Gallup poll among people aged eighteen to twenty-nine found that more than ninety percent approved of interracial dating, and sixty percent had dated across the color line.

Friendships of every color enjoy the kind of connections listed below. How many of these statements describe your relationship with a person who has black skin?

- We have shared a meal in one another's home.
- We have stayed overnight in one another's home.
- We know one another's family.
- We participate in activities together outside of work.
- We've discovered what we may never agree on, and it's okay.
- We know one another's birthday.
- We have talked about race directly.
- We've stayed in touch when we don't live in the same area.
- We both feel the freedom and safety to ask the other a question that starts out "Why do (black/white) people …"
- We are so clear about what we have in common that our differences are intriguing rather than troubling.

For the white man who leads, an openhearted connection with a black friend is one of the most powerful sources for learning about race (and himself!). Such a friendship serves as a due regard lab, where two things clarify simultaneously: on the one hand, there's a lot more to being black than you ever imagined (Like Some Others), and conversely, we have so much in common as humans (Like All Others) that differences in culture and skin color become more intriguing and less troubling.

Black friends have proved transformative in my life. Here are five:

- *Ed King*

  First and foremost, Ed and I shared a love of skiing. He hired me to teach the sport, and he trained me so I could earn my certifications.

Three years later, I followed him as ski school director. Ed was my first black mentor, and we had a great time together in the mountains. We built a high-performance friendship.

- *William Pannell, DMin*

  Bill mentored me in graduate school and in life. His ability to combine truth telling with deep, infectious humor influenced me powerfully. I have always been in awe of Bill's giftedness, and his willingness to exercise those gifts as a leader, critical thinker, incisive scholar, and inspirational preacher. Being black is integral to him, but Bill's preeminent concern is who Christ is in him and through him.

- *Richard Gray, PhD*

  Rick, now a seminary professor himself, was a close colleague with me on work in the United States and internationally. I prize one lesson I learned with Rick in particular: while there's a lot of work to do across the black-white color line, we are still just part of the ethnic richness of humanity. Rick knew my heart, and we built bridges together.

- *Brenda Salter-McNeil, DMin*

  Brenda and I have had the chance to study and work together. Her commitment to racial reconciliation is a key motivator in my decision to write this book. Brenda's God-given energy and her hard-won wisdom stir me to action. She burns with a bright light, and illuminates the way of Jesus for so many. I treasure any chance I get to laugh with her. She is proudly and thoughtfully black, and she is so much more. (Go to www.saltermcneil.com)

- *Claudia White, PhD*

  Claudia is Jamaican-born and raised, and educated in the United States. We've had a great time learning and working together. I appreciate Claudia's international wisdom, and her take on race and gender as a woman with black skin who is from the Americas yet not culturally African-American. I find inspiration and focus in Claudia's dedication to what people need from leaders and want as customers. (Go to www.whitesandconsultants.com)

These friends have served as God's ambassadors to help me grow, changing me forever and for the good. I hope a black friend is proving such a transformative influence in your life.

One more stirring resource: look into viewing *An Unlikely Friendship*, a video that features an unexpected relationship between C. P. Ellis, a former leader of the Ku Klux Klan, and civil rights activist Ann Atwater (from producer Diane Bloom at www.dianebloom.com). You just never know where your next friend will come from.

CONVERSATION STARTER: *In the next month, what will you do to grow a deeper friendship with a black man or woman?*

ACT

■ 67 ■

Raise
white boys right.

When we hunt through the lessons of boyhood (see essay 21), we invariably uncover the influence of the white men who raised us: our dads and grandfathers, coaches, teachers, spiritual leaders, the fathers of our friends.

Now *we* are the white men who lead. Our leadership should extend with intention to our own boys: sons, nephews, grandsons, team members, students. They look to us. White boys need white men as fathers and friends: for protection, love, fun, and the confidence to achieve in life.

Obviously, women (and perhaps elders of color) have also loved us and shaped who we have become. Equally obvious, we will seek to do the same for our daughters and other young people.

But I'm focusing here on an intracultural, intergenerational challenge: it's a "Like Some Others" thing. We are, as white men, singularly obliged to raise white boys right.

This task requires us to lead so they will choose to follow in three areas.

CHARACTER

In essay 59, we explored **character** as the intrinsic values, qualities and gifts that find expression in a person's behavior. My son, Patrick, is a fine young singer and performer. But as much as I love to hear him sing and watch him act and dance, what I find really thrilling is the way he makes good decisions for himself, works long and hard to grow, cares for other people, and leads among other performers.

The positive formation of our own character is the most fundamental inheritance that we have received from the men and women who raised us. Now we have the chance to partner with younger white men and boys as they establish their values, test their qualities, and exercise their gifts.

I believe the generation of our white sons will lead effectively among diverse people, beyond what we can achieve. That's a legacy we can forge in their character.

HUMAN DIFFERENCES

As white men, it is our duty to shape our boys' opinions about human differences. The 1999 Columbine killings by two white boys marked the birthday of Adolph Hitler, the prototypical twisted white man. Take your son to the U.S. Holocaust Museum in Washington DC when he's old enough. Face the evils of prejudice together.

As white men, we are answerable like no other for thwarting the hateful ideology of racism. Presumed superiority is a not-so-little white lie fueling discrimination and even violence in some of our young men. The white male antidote: equip our sons to engage diversity with candor and compassion.

Such honesty and empathy about race and gender will spring from loving your son and befriending his buddies with disciplined intention. Listen to them without your motor running; talk with them, not at them; help them avoid school clique conflicts; learn a video game, fix the car, or take a hike together. If you are a dad at a distance, email constantly, subscribe to a telephone service with unlimited national calling (like Comcast), go crazy on texting, install a videophone or a webcam.

If we allow others to blame and shame our boys for being young white men, we permit the erosion of their self-esteem and the ambition that every young man needs. So we need to unmask "political correctness" (see essay 22), and help our young men to explore what the Advantage Complex (essays 23–26) may mean for them.

ACHIEVEMENT

It is indisputably true that, to succeed as men themselves, white boys need white men. We must continue to serve as models and mentors, because times are changing. Males are now the minority in undergraduate education, and white men now compose less than forty percent of the enrollment in professional schools in medicine, business, and education.

As the playing field levels out, young white men must truly compete to succeed. The advantage accruing to them because of their skin color and gender will only decrease. For their sake, we need to cultivate in them the courage to evaluate opportunity with utter honesty (see essay 26).

White men who lead, lead your sons well. Befriend the boys around you. It is our duty and our joy is to raise white boys right.

CONVERSATION STARTER: *Which specific white boys are you investing in? What are you doing to lead their development? How do you know it is working?*

ACT
■ **68** ■

Influence
with courteous nonverbals.

We—blacks, that is—have all felt the sting of being ignored in public by whites
we work with or attend school with. Some of us have developed a sixth
sense about such matters. We'd rather cross the street or avert eye
contact than be dissed in public by whites
we consider colleagues, classmates, even friends.

LENA WILLIAMS
It's the Little Things: Everyday Interactions That Anger,
Annoy and Divide the Races

D oes Ms. Williams' commentary embarrass you as much as it does me?

We often communicate and lead *without* words. We need to bring a new level of consideration and grace to our momentary encounters with black colleagues and customers. This nonverbal solicitude across the color line may be summarized in a word: we can influence by behaving like *gentlemen*.

Moments for Courtesy

The Golden Rule, treat others as you want to be treated, has now been augmented with the Platinum Rule: treat others the way they want to be treated. Perhaps we can use both guidelines to renew the practice of civility in the way we lead and live. Here are six ways to succeed by leading nonverbally among black colleagues and customers.

Acknowledgment

Lena Williams quotes Dr. Ted Manley, a professor at DePaul University: "White people do not maintain eye contact with black people, even if they know you. So they give you this white eye treatment."

Show your respect for your black colleagues and customers by catching their eye and holding eye contact, with a friendly expression. No more deadeye, expressionless stares, where we look right through them.

Acknowledge proactively with the technique of *triangling*. Here's what you do:

1)   When you're in a conversation with a black person and another white person;

2) And you notice that the white person is looking at you, but not looking much at the black person;

3) You continue to glance at the black person, especially when the white person is looking at you.

This will subtly redirect the other white person to visually include the black person.

Personal Safety and Comfort

Discipline your response to close proximity with a black man. As white men, we have been known to lock our car doors and call our children close when a black man comes near. Some of us have moved rather than sit next to a black person in a park or on a bus. Do not step off the elevator rather than ride with a black person; you wouldn't believe the stories I've heard over the years about white men acting inappropriately on elevators toward people of color and white women.

You are only unsafe around a black person who means to do you harm. So every black person who is not a threat (and that's almost all of them) deserves nonverbals from you that show friendliness, not fear.

Association

Another version of the "white eye treatment" imparts our discomfort in associating with black people. It is the look of doubtful scrutiny that silently wonders "what are you doing here?" perhaps accompanied by actual words of investigation. The implicit message: "This particular location is a zone for white people, and black people need to stay on the plantation." Ouch. Exclusion stings. One of the most common behaviors of *diss*-association: asking a black person to show their ID as a way to prove they are "supposed" to be there.

Turn-Taking

Don't cut in front of a black person in line. Don't allow another white person to move you ahead of a black person, like a white maitre d' seating you before a black person who arrived at the restaurant first. Each time you handle one of these small encounters with common courtesy, you prevent one of the microwounds in a black person's daily existence.

Deference

In hallways, on sidewalks, and at doorways, some black people are not inclined to give an inch when passing white people. For them, moving out of your way is a reminder of the days of Jim Crow, when black people were always expected to defer to whites. My advice: watch their nonverbals (body position, eye contact, speed of movement, set of mouth). Then simply make room for the black person determined to maintain their space and pace. The moment is just not worth a perceived slight.

As a simple signal of thoughtfulness, make it a point to hold the door open for black people (and everyone else, for that matter). Your mother would love to see that she raised a polite son.

And take a look at a resource to this end: Bruce Jacobs's *Race Manners in the 21st Century: Navigating the Minefield Between Black and White Americans in an Age of Fear.*

Watch Your Eyes

When you are facing a woman, black or otherwise, show your respect by looking into her eyes. Control your heterosexuality (if that's your operating system). Don't check out her physical appearance when you should be communicating respectfully and professionally. Women always notice when your eyes wander south, and they are often put off by it. Such discipline is especially important for you in your leadership role.

Good manners open a door to relationship. But if your nonverbals communicate disrespect, you simply will not lead effectively. Can we agree together, right here and now, to purposely extend every courtesy to our black colleagues and customers?

And go buy Lena Williams's book. It's a practical resource on race that every white guy should have.

CONVERSATION STARTER: *How does your nonverbal behavior demonstrate your savvy among diverse colleagues and customers?*

ACT

■ **69** ■

Evolve

the discipline
of daily reminders.

I've been accused of taking this "racial stuff" too far: "Really, Chuck, why should I have to think about diversity all the time? It just doesn't matter to me that much. You're a little obsessed." That's possible. But you won't become a better leader by just reading this book and hoping something you learned turns up in your behavior. You invest attention in what matters most to you. If you want to improve the way you lead as a white man, a new degree of determination is required.

When you train for a triathlon, you build into your days the time to run and swim and cycle. To prepare for the race ahead, intention is necessary.

When you want to work successfully with black colleagues and customers, you grow habits and reminders to reinforce that commitment. I recommend that you evolve a daily discipline of positive engagement with race, because it takes intention to develop the capacity to lead with diversity in mind. Here are ten ideas:

BEHAVIORS

Translate your learning into action.

- When you see a black person, *unlock* your car doors (when they can't hear you do it) as a mental exercise of openness and to disequate *black* with *dangerous*.
- Run a book group during Black History Month (that would be February), and study one of the following: Studs Terkel's *Race: How Blacks & Whites Think & Feel About the American Obsession*; or a book from journalists at the *New York Times, How Race is Lived in America*.
- Volunteer as a homework tutor in a local program helping black students.
- Practice the following phrase, so you're ready to say it the next time someone tells a racist joke or makes a prejudicial comment: "I'm not comfortable with that remark, and I'd appreciate it if you wouldn't say such things around me again. Thanks."
- Attend and donate generously at an event sponsored by the National Urban League, the NAACP, or another organization that primarily serves black constituents.

POSITIVE BLACK IMAGES

Expose yourself, your employees, family, and friends to images of black people as good and gifted human beings.

- Many banks have personal checks portraying black family life. My checks feature pictures of Dr. King.
- Decorate your office and home with photos and artwork depicting black culture.
- Check out "black" movies (*Barbershop* is great), or hold your own Samuel L. Jackson film festival (his movies have grossed more than any other actor).
- Find a great photo of Dr. Martin Luther King Jr., frame it beautifully, and put in on your desk at work.
- Attend theater or music performances that celebrate black culture and talent (a must-see in Seattle: "Black Nativity").

Weave reinforcements such as these into your day-to-day life. Find your own reminders. Craft a personal environment that *brings* to mind your commitment to lead with diversity in mind.

CONVERSATION STARTER: *What simple ways can you devise to remind yourself about your growing commitment to lead on diversity?*

ACT
■ **70** ■

Pay close attention
to race-related circumstances,
and be prepared to act.

The vast majority of unmet needs that bring sadness, heartache,
loneliness, and despair into human lives are merely ... good deeds left undone.

BILL HYBELS, PASTOR OF WILLOW CREEK COMMUNITY CHURCH
Making Life Work

One of the worst epitaphs I can imagine them scribing on my tombstone is "He left many good deeds undone."

In essay 43, we considered the loss of not knowing; how we are changed by the very act of learning as white men who lead. We are compelled to act in response, as an inevitable result from traveling diversity's Transformation Curve. We're men, so that generally means a bias to action. Among our kind, learning without doing is generally considered a waste of time.

So you need to watch for circumstances in which race and gender differences are operating. God knows, these situations will find you. And then be prepared to translate your learning into response-ability.

Here's a time when I paid attention and was at least partially prepared to act.

In 1985 I was managing a California staff of thirty employees from five nations. On contract with the Department of State, each month we helped 160 refugees from troubled regions around the world to start over in America. One of our lead caseworkers, Thanh, had worked for ARCO in Vietnam for twenty years, and spoke four languages fluently. He was proud to be a new citizen of the United States, and he worked with families emigrating from many countries.

Early in the outflow of refugees from eastern Africa, Thanh worked with a highly educated, upper-class man from Ethiopia named Jonas. One day Thanh accompanied Jonas to the local Social Security office to complete some paperwork. They went to meet with a case manager by the name of William, who was black.

Jonas walked into the office, took one look at William, spun on his heel and heatedly informed Thanh that he "certainly wasn't going to work with any n——." Jonas's skin was darker than William's.

Thanh, a new American himself, was floored; he had no clue about what had just occurred. But William was crushed, and his stricken look at Jonas's words shamed Thanh for bringing Jonas in. Thanh left when William put his head down on his desk.

We confronted an utterly unrepentant Jonas, and sent a letter of apology to William. I was ashamed to explain to Thanh that his new country had so thoroughly portrayed black men negatively that we unknowingly exported the stereotype around the world, even to men of Africa.

From that day on, William was never willing to work with anyone from our office.

So Jonas was unteachable, and there was no reconciling with William. But I was prepared enough to diagnose the situation and coach my own employee. We can only play the hand we're dealt, with as much skill as we can muster.

When you pay attention and proactively lead as a white man, your behavior signals that you have moved into Adventurous Competence. You fluently size up the situation, and act with all the response-ability you can bring to bear. You don't miss the race related dynamics, and you don't run from the challenge.

Here are six situations in which you can practice such courage and skill. Look for more.

- If you see that no cab will stop for a black person, ask them if you can help. If they agree, then they step back, you hail the cab, and they get in.
- If you see that a black couple (who came into the restaurant before you) was seated at a table by the kitchen, while you are shown to a nicer spot, offer to switch with them.

- If you see another white person cut in front of a black person in line, approach the white person and point out that they should be standing behind the black person.

- If you see a sales clerk treat a black customer with disrespect, make it clear to the employee that such behavior will cause you to stop shopping there.

- If your child's team is playing a team mostly composed of black children, monitor the way the white parents behave, to ensure respect (or at least discourage their disrespect).

- Intervene if you observe white men dominating in an interracial setting (e.g., when one or more white men speak over a lone black employee). I once was brought into an organization because several white guys were pushing to join the black men's employee group. There wasn't a chartered group for whites. Once the company indicated it would charter a group for the white men, they dropped it.

There are thousands of such circumstances in a career and a lifetime. Diagnose diversity dynamics at work and out in the community, and stand ready to step up and act. *That's* how white men lead.

CONVERSATION STARTER: *Think of a time when you failed to respond to a sensitive race-related situation. Bring to mind a time when you did step up with diversity on the line. How do you explain the difference in your willingness to act?*

ACT

■ **71** ■

Find
the fun.

Sometimes it's too much of an effort even to retreat in wild disorder. ©

ASHLEIGH BRILLIANT

Whoever designed this experiment called "human beings" somehow knew that a sense of humor would turn out to be a survival skill. This is especially true for white men in leadership jobs. In a diverse work setting, it's likely that folks will be laughing at me, because I can be such a bonehead. Apparently employees genuinely enjoy watching a foolish manager in full and fruitless bloom.

319

For some reason, I'm not always inclined to laugh at myself as loudly as others do. But I might as well join the snickering. Along the way, perhaps I will help my employees discover their own unique contributions to the idiocy of the moment.

Find the fun that crosses the color line. Mine the mirth to be found wherever men and women gather. Cheer on the Dilbertization of the office, where Scott Adams's skewering of management hurts so good.

Wonderfully, the need and ability to laugh is a universal trait. We share a capacity for high spirits with "All Others." Some of the chortling is at the expense of others, and we all need to be careful about that. It's always better to laugh *with* people than *at* them. Here are a few black-white moments that sustained my spirit:

- In the pretty-much-all-white suburb in which I grew up, our experience with black people was limited. After a hot spring weekend during high school, several of us on the high school track team were complaining about our sunburns. Our very black coach, Al Roberts (now coaching in the NFL), joined in, groaning about his crispy skin. There was a pregnant pause, and then we all cracked up; we students because Al's sunburn was invisible (a possibility previously unknown to us, because sunburn equaled pink and red skin). Coach Roberts laughed because he was in the presence of a pack of young cross-cultural morons.

- The first time I flew first class I was twenty-five. I was the only occupant in the sixteen-seat section. Before we took off from Burbank for Portland, the very attractive black flight attendant approached and asked me one of my all-time favorite questions: "What can I get you to take off before we drink?" You can work out what she meant to say.

As soon as the words escaped her lips, her face flashed an exquisite look of horror. I don't know how, but I could actually see she was blushing, even though her face did not redden. She met my eyes, and I'm telling you she was psychically begging me to be a nice man. I *am* a nice man, so I smiled and said: "Some orange juice would be nice." She looked profoundly relieved.

Racial difference was visible but irrelevant. Our gender and sexual orientation was in play.

I stayed on for the next leg to Seattle, still the only one in first class. When we were ready to lift off, she approached with a huge smile and asked with a verbal precision previously unheard from a human: "What can I get you to *drink* before we *depart?*" I knew the script: "Some orange juice would be nice!" My juice was delicious, and she sat down across the aisle from me for a great fifteen-minute chat about not much. It was just about being human together. Jo, wherever you are, thanks for a great flight.

- By happenstance, I once spent an hour over lunch with eight black women. We had about thirty minutes of Chamber of Commerce business to discuss. The rest of our time was filled with words such as (I'm not making this up; I took notes.) braids, weaves, kinky, extensions, frizz, highlights, choppy, layered, face-framing, fade, two-strand twists, hand-tossed, finger-shaped, curl, detangling, plumped-up volume and separation, hydrating, and 'fro. We just got our hair on, girl. They laughed at me ... a lot.

- Watch black comedians on BET or the Comedy Channel. Get your hands on a copy of Steve Harvey's *Don't Trip* DVD for laugh-out-loud funny. And maybe you can solve a mystery for me. I'm still trying to figure out what's so funny about references to black mothers smacking their sons around.

I once heard Will Smith, the black actor and rapper, define the perfect humor this way: "When I've got the white people and the black people all laughing hard, for different reasons, and they don't know that."

Finally, it can pay to be so proactively fun that you're laughing at yourself before anyone else does. Fine-tune your sense of what's funny about your own limitations. As Ashleigh Brilliant observed in another gem: "There are parts of me so private that I myself have no personal knowledge of them."©

CONVERSATION STARTER: *What's the funniest diversity-related thing you've ever seen (when you were laughing with folks more than at them)?*

ACT

■ **72** ■

Do what's right
in "only one" situations.

For generations, black people have experienced "only one" status: the only black person on the team or in the store, the only one in class or at church. If you stand out because you're different from everyone else, there is a price to pay.

Listen again to Lena Williams: "Few people I know of like being 'the only one.' Men don't like being the only one of their gender at a party overflowing with women, although you wonder why they wouldn't. Whites say they feel uncomfortable being the only one at predominantly black parties or clubs or schools. Young adults feel uncomfortable being the only one in the presence of older adults. It's human nature, not just a black thang." We are reminded of how powerful group identity can be (see essay 46): we're not content when we are surrounded by people who are not like us.

I have a black friend I'll call Robert. He was the only African-American manager in a large nonprofit, and he led effectively from his level. Things began to change the day the agency's president encountered a wealthy prospective donor who was black. Suddenly the organization needed a black face to be involved in cultivating this prospect's generosity. At first Robert was pleased to be lunching and traveling with the president. But then he realized it had only to do with Robert and the prospect's common skin color. Robert could not in good conscience represent the nonprofit as being truly progressive, because he was the only black American in leadership. The hot spotlight was on him as the "only one." Fortunately he was able to participate in securing the donor's support in a way that did not threaten his integrity or cause him to lose his job for telling the truth about his employer. But he worried that white leaders in the organization would not see his outstanding performance, believing he was getting opportunities and exposure just because he was an "only one." The experience left a bad taste in his mouth, and he didn't stay long.

In the '90s I consulted with a number of companies whose diversity recruiting strategy could be summarized as: "We've got to go out and get us some black employees." That level of thinking usually got them one or two. Diversification at the leadership level almost always begins with that first woman in management, that first black sales executive, that first foreign-born IT vice president. The simplest way to solve the challenges they face as the "only one" is to select, develop, and retain more people like them. They will stop coping with being the "only one" when they *aren't* the only one; when the firm actually commits to employing and promoting diverse people.

Black people grow weary of the majority white expectation that they should always come our way, and accommodate themselves to our style and location. I have an idea! Why don't we go toward them, with open hearts? We might learn something valuable when we become the "only one" in some situations.

With a black friend at your side, go to a black club, attend a black church, join a community organization in a black part of town, attend an event at a black college, travel to the Caribbean or nations of black Africa. Grant yourself the chance to be an "only one." Stay open-minded and teachable, and you'll return with newfound black acquaintances and friends in place. The black friend who accompanies you in these adventures can help you sort through your learning. They can also discourage any temptation among other black folks to misbehave out of resentment for a white person coming into "their" space.

And sometimes being the "only one" can exhilarate as well as stupefy. Remember the eight black ladies who permitted my participation in their hair-a-thon? Being in the minority earned me an awesome education; they were gracious and got me laughing about geri curl mishaps I didn't even understand.

Here's one of my favorite illustrations of how to do what's right in an "only one" situation. I worked in an office with an employee who was gifted at drawing cartoons of fellow employees, portraying them with humor and honor. When she decided to sketch the only black member of the team, she faced a dilemma: what color of crayon should she use to depict the skin of her colleague? She remembered from diversity training the idea of the Platinum Rule, where you treat people the way they want to be treated. So she went to her black coworker, and they selected the crayon color together. Such intention spoke loudly of the respect this black employee experienced in that professional setting. And there was a picture to prove it.

Do what's right in "only one" situations by hiring enough diverse people, so that no one *is* the only one. Avoid the temptation to spotlight people (like Robert) with "only one" status. Deepen your personal "only one" experience among black people. Finally, treat *each and every one* the way they want to be treated – with respect.

CONVERSATION STARTER: *How are you supporting colleagues and customers who find themselves in an "only one" situation? When will you seek "only one" experiences?*

ACT

■ **73** ■

Take care of yourself
so you can
keep up the good work.

*When power leads man toward arrogance, poetry reminds him of his
limitations. When power narrows the areas of man's concern,
poetry reminds him of the richness and diversity of his existence.
When power corrupts, poetry cleanses. For art establishes the basic human
truths, which must serve as the touchstone of our judgment.*

PRESIDENT JOHN F. KENNEDY

The New York Times, *October 27, 1963*

Learning to lead effectively as a white man is one of the most significant challenges you will ever encounter. It is no small accomplishment to manage human differences from the inside out, and deliver business results by developing people through work. Counting the cost for achieving such Relative Expertise with diversity forces on us an urgent realization: you're only good to others if you're good to yourself.

I still have a lot to learn about self-care so that I can run the long race. If that's true for you, too, perhaps you will find renewal in resources like the following.

YOUR SPIRIT

If you are part of a faith tradition, study what your religion and its organizations teach about human differences. If your spirituality is more individually derived, weave diversity into your personal values and commitments.

And look to the solace and reassurance that faith provides. As a leader, the lessons of humility teach me about my limits. When my experience slides over into humiliation, however, I try to remember God's good intentions for my life.

For Christians, I recommend two resources that equip white men to sustain their leadership on diversity:

- *Prayer*, by O. Hallesby. This simple classic fuels the practice of "letting Jesus come into our hearts." I can only lead as I am led by the Author of my life.

- *The Heart of Racial Justice: How Soul Change Leads to Social Change*, by Brenda Salter McNeil and Rick Richardson. The writers offer a compelling approach to internal change and community transformation, with a welcome focus on leading from the heart to produce results.

In my experience, personal renewal can come in accepting a spiritual dare. For white men in leadership roles who are also Christian and American, the words of Matthew 25:35 issue just such a challenge. Jesus promises an eternal inheritance to those who welcome the Stranger. I believe God is confronting white American Christians with this verse—black Americans are the Strangers to be welcomed by us. Do I encounter black people as if I am encountering Christ? Spiritual opportunity may be found when we answer yes to that question, by the way we live and lead. Try this: find fellowship with black brothers and sisters. You will never be, or lead, the same. And that will be good.

YOUR RELATIONSHIPS

Find renewal in your relationships—that's what they are for.

The Promise Keepers organization teaches that "success is when the people who know you the best love you the most." A potent tactic for taking care of yourself is to take care of your family, and relax into the ways they take care of you. I heartily recommend that you pick up *The Measure of a Man: Becoming the Father You Wish Your Father Had Been*, by Jerrold Lee Shapiro. This powerful resource will equip you to grow and lead as a good and connective man (see essay 11), whether or not you are a father.

There was a time in my management career where it seemed like all I ever did with my colleagues and employees was obsess on the work before us. We didn't really connect as human beings; it was just about getting things done. So I granted myself a secret sabbatical: for one week, I attended only to the tasks that I could not put off. Otherwise, I concentrated on my relationships with my boss, reports, peers, and customers. In my own head, I asked and answered questions like: What are their priorities? What do they like and dislike about the way we are working together? What moves them to motivate themselves? How am I treating them differently—am I listening effectively to colleagues I like, and interrupting people I don't get along with so well? How can I have more fun with them? You get the idea: it was a relationship renewal audit. I came out of the week with a new appreciation for the people I worked with, and I had some useful ideas for improving the relationships.

YOUR BODY

This is "Like All Others" territory. If you are operating in a human body, your physical reality influences your mind, spirit, and soul. White men who lead need exercise, nutrition, and sleep, just like everyone else. No one can give you these gifts; you have to give them to yourself.

If you neglect the care and feeding of your own body, the odds are strong that you won't stay in the game. You have to lead yourself to lead others.

Two restful pastimes for white men who lead include the following:

- *Literature.* President Kennedy's quote above, from just a month before he died, pairs power and poetry. The written word evokes in us a contemplative space we should not sacrifice to the tyranny of the urgent. For more thought-provoking words, see the Resource section at the back of the book.

- *Music.* Maybe it's the Beach Boys or Beastie Boys, maybe it's gospel, maybe it's Mozart. Musical interests are diverse, too. Whatever your taste in sound, use it to step back from the leadership fray. A five-minute break with your MP3 player can keep you on track.

In 1844, Theodore Weld facilitated an eleven-night debate over slavery at Lane Seminary in Cincinnati. With patience and intellect, facts and good faith, Mr. Weld and his antislavery colleagues persuaded all involved that slavery must be abolished. That pivotal event produced many agents of the emergent American Anti-Slavery Society, and the debates injected the entire abolitionist movement with the energy of faith. The story of Mr. Weld's leadership was largely unknown until the twentieth century, when a trunk of personal letters was discovered. I relate this story to honor his leadership, and also because the letters report that Mr. Weld died in Massachusetts at age 91, an embittered, lonely, and faithless man.

Mr. Weld led on diversity and generated great good. But along the way he was apparently unable to sustain himself. My prayer for you is this: may you find, with joy and discipline, all the resources you require to make you strong.

CONVERSATION STARTER: *How will you care for yourself so you can stay in the fight?*

Lead

I n every diversity course I've ever taught, a white man invariably asks some version of this question: "So now what? What can I *do* with all this awareness and new information?" This is where our masculine orientation to action and results serves us well. To lead with diversity in mind, we seek to make a difference with difference.

This section explores twenty-five leadership behaviors.

LEADING AMONG COLLEAGUES

#74   Navigate diversity's five business trends.

#75   Ground the diversity imperative in seven business motives.

#76   Establish accountability with diversity-related performance objectives.

#77   Attract, interview, and win diverse talent.

#78   Individualize the way you lead.

#79   Prevent inequity.

#80   Motivate with differences in view.

#81   Make decisions inclusively.

#82   Coach performance improvement.

#83   Be a mentor, find a mentor.

#84   Provide performance-based development opportunities.

#85   Develop a diverse team.

#86   Resolve conflict.

#87   Recognize and reward performance.

#88   Ensure that diversity training drives success.

#89   Prepare high potential employees for advancement.

#90   Promote high performers.

#91   Terminate with equity.

#92   Avoid litigation, and lead beyond the law.

LEADING AMONG CUSTOMERS

#93   Pursue the black marketplace.

#94   Develop products and services for black customers.

#95   Handle issues and opportunities in sales and marketing.

#96   Serve black customers effectively.

#97   Manage relationships with diverse suppliers.

While we focus on how white men can lead successfully among black colleagues and customers, many of these ideas simply work with all humans.

Learn to lead in a way that employees across all dimensions of diversity will choose to follow.

Here are two excellent leadership resources that cover many of these leadership topics in more current detail:

- Every white man who leads will benefit by subscribing to www. diversityinc.com and the related magazine, DiversityInc. These are comprehensive and accessible sources, and, interestingly enough, were founded and are now led by two white men.

- www.leadershipforwhitemen.com is the brother website to this book. There you will find much more on how to lead effectively as a white man.

To reach this point in the book, you have invested time and energy in the fundamentals of leading on diversity from the inside out. Now it's time to expand the return on that investment, by exploring specific leadership behaviors.

■ 74 ■

Navigate
diversity's five business trends.

L eaders look ahead. We watch for rapids downstream, we evaluate prospective threats, we probe for potential innovations, we scan for unreached markets. In short, we lead into and through trends.

Consider five diversity trends as a current in which we must swim.

These trends flow through your organization's future, with energy swirling up from the dimensions of diversity. You need to lead in a way that helps your people and your company to survive the whitewater.

TREND ONE: DEMOGRAPHICS

Recently the U.S. population reached 300 million, and fully one third of Americans are people of color—that's 100 million prospective customers and employees right now. Let's look at our demographic reality and destiny:

- In 1987, the Hudson Institute forecast that by the year 2000, only fifteen percent of new entrants into the labor force would be white and male. That is now true.

- Do you do business in California, Hawaii, New Mexico, Washington DC, or any of the top metro areas in the United States? These populations have diversified, with no ethnic majority. You can see the implications for attracting talent and winning customers in these markets.

- White Americans have an older median age and are not bearing as many children. By 2050, Americans of color will account for nearly ninety percent of total population growth.

- Before 2050, America will have no ethnic majority. At that point, the word *minority* won't mean much. When children born in 2010 are halfway through their lives, being American will no longer be associated with being white.

TREND TWO: EDUCATION

The achievements and inequities of American education are well publicized: while students from all over the world seek entrance to our colleges and universities, many black and Hispanic K–12 students receive a substandard education. Here's what's on the horizon:

- The percentage of people of color finishing high school and earning college or graduate degrees is growing faster that their growth in the population. The number of black women earning master's degrees increased 150% from 1991 to 2001, compared to a 10% increase among white men.

- White students rarely constitute more than fifteen percent of the students in our nation's urban districts. Academic success (in literacy, grades, test scores, and writing skills) among black students lags behind white students.

- Research shows that many teachers and parents have higher performance expectations for white students than for black students, beginning in elementary school.

- Black students often come from families with less money; thirty-three percent of black households live below the poverty line, compared to twelve percent of white households.

- In thirty-five states, K–12 funding per white student exceeds funding per minority student by more than thirty percent.

- We are a facing a critical situation, as middle school girls steer away from competency in math and science. While their interest and performance in these key subjects matches the boys in elementary years, we are permitting half of our population, around age twelve, to disconnect from math and science, two essential fields of endeavor in the twenty-first-century economy.

TREND THREE: OPPORTUNITY

After forty years of affirmative action policies and enforcement of equal opportunity laws, we've made some progress. White women, in particular, have benefited from affirmative action. Employers understand that the power of law and policy can drive inclusion and punish exclusionary practices. It is also clear that opportunity will expand only when organizations exceed the law's requirements, by vigorously responding to the trends and business motives for diversity. Here's what that looks like:

- There is a new architecture of accountability. For example, to ensure opportunities for women and people of color, Charles Schwab & Company carefully tracks hiring, retention, turnover, time in grade, and participation rates in leadership development.

- There is a new attention to affinity networking. IBM, for instance, supports "Like Some Others" groups for women, men, gays and lesbians, disabled employees, and people of Asian, Black, Hispanic, and Native American origin. These task forces meet quarterly as a council, with a senior leader. And the networks for women, gays and lesbians, and disabled employees extend globally, so they're not just a resource for opportunity in the United States.

- After a decade of diversity training for employees, Fannie Mae repackaged its diversity education, and released a training product to its customers (lenders). These resources equip mortgage lenders to pursue business with the high-potential market of lower income families and Americans of color.

TREND FOUR: PARTICIPATION AND ECONOMIC CLOUT OF AMERICAN WOMEN

Almost forty percent of all American managers are women, although parity still may be a generation away. Women compose at least half of many graduate programs, and they are fifty-eight percent of all undergraduate students. With women making more than eighty percent of all purchasing decisions and controlling more than $5 trillion in buying power, it makes sense for you to factor this trend into the way you lead.

More food for thought:

- A study with male and female business owners (by the Society for Human Resource Management) found that men and women shared similar traits and management styles. But women owners were better at hiring women, and employees of both genders preferred working for the female owners. Younger and better-educated men, in particular, reported that they enjoyed reporting to a woman manager.

- In 2002, 8.5 million black women composed almost six percent of the workforce. By 2010, they will be more than eight percent of the labor pool (over 10 million women).

- Women born since 1970 are significantly more educated, technologically literate, and global in perspective. They have more multicultural experience and less traditional prejudice, and they expect respect at work. They do not expect to build a career by staying with one employer.

TREND FIVE: GLOBALIZATION

Buy Thomas Friedman's *The World is Flat*. Read chapter one, on the emergent global economy, and chapter six, on the necessity of developing your personal brand as an employee. You must learn to lead your organization effectively in the intercultural economy, and you must do it in a way that demonstrates your unique personal contribution every day. Managing human differences with empathy and expertise will help you do both.

As Americans, we are uniquely positioned to collaborate and compete globally. When we actualize our best cultural values—individual freedom and happiness grounded in "out of many, one" (the community of *E Pluribus Unum*)—we can build partnerships and compete successfully. Our values beautifully prepare us for globalization, whether your business model is more Ben & Jerry's (do good and do well) or Wal-Mart (lower prices and great product choice because capitalism rocks).

We must deepen this powerful American advantage by growing our capacity to go global: expanding the momentum of our middle class through education and employment, improving our competence in other languages, leveraging the economic advantages from our immigrant populations, and pursuing political and diplomatic policies that open doors to American people, values, and business.

As the world gets smaller, Americans can provide something important and unique: the idea of *inclusive nationality*, where human differences are tolerated and accepted, and even, when our best selves step up, celebrated. In *The Accidental Asian*, Eric Liu speaks to this opportunity: "It is precisely in an age of globalization that America becomes the most necessary place on earth. That is why we owe it our undivided loyalty."

A useful tool to help you navigate these five trends is the SWOT analysis (Strengths, Weaknesses, Opportunities, Threats). Such an exercise can provide a snapshot of how these trends are operating among your customers, employees, and other stakeholders, and how your competitors are responding. For example, a SWOT analysis I facilitated with one technology client showed that they moved across national and cultural boundaries very effectively to grow the business, but female managers were leaving twice as often as male managers, and their top two competitors were hiring, growing, and retaining women leaders much more effectively.

Leaders influence people to follow them into the future. These five business trends are powerful currents in the river that is your organization. A trend is not to be avoided; go with the diversity flow. Build a reputation as a forward-focused leader.

CONVERSATION STARTER: *How will you lead differently in response to these trends? Are there other diversity-related trends impacting your business?*

Ground the diversity imperative

in seven business motives.

You cannot speak about growth and innovation and being a market-segment leader without speaking about diversity and inclusion.

RONALD PARKER, PEPSICO NORTH AMERICA

I n response to the five trends in the previous essay, diversity has emerged as a competitive advantage for many organizations. DiversityInc's *Top 50 Companies* shows the bottom-line contribution of leading with human differences in view. Diversity is no longer a "nice to have" business strategy. Here are seven reasons why inclusion is a twenty-first-century imperative.

COMPETE IN THE DIVERSE MARKETPLACE

Demographic changes and globalization guarantee that your customers are a diverse population. Very few white men lead enterprises that seek only other white men as customers.

Does diversity contribute to corporate performance?

- Former CEO Steve Reinemund attributes twenty percent of Pepsico's business growth to diversity and inclusion.
- Wells Fargo CEO Richard Kovacevich says most of the bank's business growth comes from new immigrants.
- William Weldon, chairman and CEO at Johnson & Johnson, notes that diversity drives innovation, growth, and the delivery of quality health care.

Go to www.diversityinc.com and click on CEO Commitment. You'll find resources that articulate how senior business leaders view diversity as a competitive advantage. For more on utilizing diversity in the marketplace, see essays 93–97.

SELECT, GROW, AND RETAIN TALENT

We've all heard employers say "employees are our most valuable asset." Sometimes that strikes us as a nauseating platitude, but it is literally true. Research from business consulting firm Accenture indicates that intangibles like employee engagement, creativity, and networked relationships account for seventy-five percent of the market cap in S&P 500 companies, as compared to twenty percent in 1980. Combine this growing value of human capital with projections of flatlined growth in the labor force by 2025, and you're faced with the challenge to find and keep the employees you need to succeed. Simply put, every leader must position their organization to attract and develop women and men of many ethnicities, languages, nationalities, and other dimensions of diversity.

There is currently a lively competition for talent. The National Association of Colleges and Employers notes that companies, for the fourth year in a row, expect a double-digit increase in hiring college grads. And employees across age groups are asking about the diversity commitment of prospective employers as they decide whether to sign on.

Some companies have built competitive momentum through such workforce development over time. More than a decade ago, Lou Gerstner, then IBM chairman, noted that "Our commitment to build a workforce as broad and diversified as the customer base we serve in more than 160 countries isn't an option; it's a business imperative as fundamental as delivering superior technologies to the marketplace."

IMPROVE BUSINESS PROCESSES

Evoking the best from diverse people helps a leader improve and monitor key business processes, such as product development, quality, marketing, performance management, and planning.

For example, Bank of America uses the proven methodology of Six Sigma to build its diversity management capability, including recruitment. Looks like its working: in 2006, fifty-five percent of BoA's new hires were people of color.

And in a recent DiversityInc article, KeyCorp CEO Henry Meyer II observed that the best business decisions come from decision influencers with diverse experiences and viewpoints. Process improvement requires an honest focus on effective metrics, and differences of opinion fuel such continuous learning and measurable progress.

LEVERAGE TEAM RESULTS

Dimensions of diversity and differences of opinion can cause conflict. Where humans tread, conflict appears. The particular challenge for every team leader is to manage such conflicts in a way that improves team results.

Research shows that high-performing teams benefit from diversity, as long as goals are clear and trust is established. Leading with due regard (see essay 30) is essential: team performance will be hampered if we ignore or overemphasize operative dimensions of diversity.

In a 1995 study with twenty technology companies (designed by my firm, commissioned by Microsoft), we found that collaboration and interdependence proved especially critical for teams working internationally. One manager noted: "We are located globally, and conduct our business (including technical and design projects) through the use of teams composed of culturally diverse individuals which function across our numerous worldwide locations."

For more on conflict and teams, see essays 85 and 86.

STRENGTHEN RELATIONS WITH SUPPLIERS AND OTHER STAKEHOLDERS

Your supplier base is evolving. With increases in the number of businesses owned by women and people of color, your organization has the opportunity to support diversity through contracts with vendors. This includes not only those from whom you purchase equipment and operating supplies, but also all types of consulting and other support services, and even as strategic business partners. Companies like Marriott use their capacity to work with local and diverse small businesses to help them win contracts for new hotels. In 2003, Chrysler's contracts with minority-owned suppliers hit $3 billion, or eleven percent of total vendor costs. In the 1980s, that figure was $25 million. For more on supplier diversity, see essay 97.

Corporations also use their resources to invest philanthropically in community needs. MGM Mirage, for example, reports annually on charitable support for needs in diverse localities. Employee affinity groups rooted in the local community identify product and service needs, and open the door to recruiting.

Your organization's capacity to manage diversity effectively also strengthens relationships with other stakeholders, including investors, regulators, the media, and organized labor. Some mutual funds and accountability groups evaluate a company's engagement with diversity, and government regulators like the Department of Labor have been known to target employers with poor reputations for working with women and people of color. The media is generally more than happy to investigate and report on diversity-related misdeeds of businesses large and small. While labor unions face their own diversity challenges, since many of their members are people of color, the unions can serve as key partners in developing and retaining a diverse workforce.

SUCCEED INTERNATIONALLY

Globalization opens the door to competing for customers, employees, and suppliers across cultural lines. Tom Solso, Cummins chairman and CEO, observes that his company's sales in foreign markets are growing at 1.5 times the rate of U.S. sales. There are tremendous opportunities in the expansion of business globally. Customers? There are now more than 400 million cell phone users in China. Labor? Noncore processes are commonly outsourced halfway around the world, where technology, language, and economics make it more cost-effective. Investors? Capital flows to any locale (in Bangalore just as likely as Boston) with political stability, profit potential, and favorable growth prospects.

Many organizations must learn to secure, conduct, and retain business across national boundaries, or they simply will not be able to compete.

AVOID LITIGATION

Any manager who has been involved in employment-related litigation can testify to how distracting and demoralizing it is. Sure, there may be times when the employer handles a situation well and still finds it necessary to defend itself in court. And I'm all for an employee's right to seek redress from an employer through the law (after all, I want that recourse myself). But from a leader's point of view, such proceedings render no winners in the end.

There is also the cost to consider. The three most expensive discrimination lawsuits in the past fifteen years—against Denny's, Texaco, and Coca-Cola—totaled $414 million in plaintiff payments, and may exceed $1 billion with legal costs added. The average settlement and legal fee expenses for a major discrimination suit: $4 million. Could you find a better way to spend that kind of cash?

For more on avoiding litigation, see essay 92.

The business case for diversity is solid, unassailable, inevitable. The white man who fails to lead by ignoring diversity's contribution jeopardizes his professional success. Worse, he imperils his organization's future. Don't let that be you.

Instead, navigate diversity's five trends. Ground your leadership in diversity's seven business motives.

CONVERSATION STARTER: *Are you prepared to articulate the precise reasons for a diversity strategy in your business?*

■ 76 ■

Establish
diversity-related performance objectives.

I n essay 13, we considered the particular contribution of white men who lead: *measurable results*. Diversity-related performance objectives (DRPOs) are a way for you to establish such accountability with your manager. Here's how.

First, participate in measuring diversity performance across the organization, in your line of business, and with your own team. Companies like SC Johnson, Sodexho, and Chrysler use manager scorecards for enterprise metrics such as recruitment, promotion, training, and market share. See essay 98 for a Diversity ROI Scorecard.

Second, ask partners in sales research and HR to provide you with demographic statistics on your target markets and labor pool. Seek company-wide data on sales and service (if your unit faces the market), hiring, promotion, and retention. Compare your unit's performance to corporate metrics; this will help you focus on any gaps you need to close and find successes you need to tell your boss about. You should also solve specific diversity issues in your unit, such as a challenging relationship that needs fixing (for example, the situation with Jason in essay 54), or challenges to team success (identified through the team trust tool in essay 65).

Third, select a specific area for improving your performance. It needs to be in your sphere of control so that success is within reach. Draft a DRPO and negotiate it with your manager, so s/he can support you and hold you accountable. Staying with Jason's situation (essay 54), here's what a DRPO looks like:

> *By the end of the month, I will restore my relationship with Jason by uncovering and resolving issues related to my communication style and race in our unit, and I will secure his participation as a team lead for the product rollout in the selected African city. At the end of the quarter, he will present the launch plan to my manager, and I will report on my progress with this DRPO to my manager.*

Fourth, document your learning and progress, and discuss it with your boss.

Fifth, move onto the next diversity-related performance objective.

In management work, we measure what matters. If it doesn't get measured, it's a "nice to have," not a "gotta do it." It's time for a DRPO that delivers.

CONVERSATION STARTER: *What ambitious diversity-related performance objective will you negotiate with your manager this week?*

■ **77** ■

Attract, interview, *and select diverse talent.*

L eadership literature often states that hiring the right talent is one of a manager's most important duties. You can only lead and learn from black employees that your organization successfully brings in the door.

Here are some of the twenty-first-century's saddest words: "We wanted to hire some black people, but we couldn't find any." Yes, friends, it's time to push the BS buzzer, because now you're in *Jeopardy,* by jeopardizing your company: "I'll take 'Couldn't Find Any Talented Black People' for 20, Alex." If you can't find black people with talent, consider these possibilities:

1) There may not be many black prospects where you're recruiting.

You're not to blame for labor pool demographics. But have you simply accepted your inability to compete for the talent that *is* there? And what does that portend for your future?

2)   You don't know where to look, or how to find black candidates.

3)   Black prospects are there to be found, but your company's approach or reputation does not attract them.

4)   Black people apply for your jobs, but they are not selected.

5)   Black candidates receive job offers, but they decide not to join your firm.

Don't accept anything less than success. A case in point: *Black Enterprise* recently recognized United Parcel Service as one of the 40 Best Companies for Diversity. *BE* noted: "With a domestic workforce that includes nearly 70,000 African-Americans, and with minorities accounting for 50% of its new hires last year, UPS has proven its dedication to cultivating a multicultural environment indicative of the company's global reach." I don't know about you, but I find the fact that UPS has 70,000 black employees immensely impressive. Clearly, they have learned how to attract talent because they are committed to doing so.

As a hiring manager, you may not be responsible for finding candidates. But you are the client for your HR partners and search consultants. Hold them accountable for finding and delivering talented candidates of color for you to interview. Participate with them in developing sources in black professional associations, local colleges, and community organizations. And make sure they keep the following in mind: a University of Chicago/MIT study showed that resumes with white-sounding names (Neil, Brett, Greg, Emily, Anne, Jill) received 50% more responses than identical resumes with black-sounding names (Tamika, Ebony, Aisha, Rasheed, Kareem, Tyrone). Discuss this issue in your business or unit, and ensure that staffing specialists and hiring managers avoid racial bias. [Note: the spell-checker built into my word processing software recognized all six of these "white" names, but recognized only half of the "black" names. Room for improvement at Microsoft …]

Once black candidates are in the selection mix, you have the chance to explore the critical questions around qualifications (see essay 25). Sort through issues around preference and affirmative action as you evaluate job match. Make sure you ask all prospects the same questions; don't modify the questions on the basis of the candidate's race. Monitor any Exclusion Code messages in the selection process that question a person's "fit" with the team. Another matter to watch for: a University of Georgia study found that skin tone *between* black candidates could affect their selection. The darker a prospect's skin, and more African his or her features (e.g., shape of nose and lips), the less likely they were to be hired, *even if their resume showed them to be more qualified*. Discriminatory treatment based on skin tone (called colorism by some) led to more than 1,400 cases with the Equal Employment Opportunity Commission in 2003.

Conduct your hiring process with due regard. In what ways and to what degree does a candidate's race actually matter?

If the position is responsible for reaching black customers, or extending business into a market where black people will be a significant share of the customer base, then the prospect's ability to succeed with such customers is relevant. Of course, there are white people with the cultural knowledge and experience to reach black customers, and some black candidates may not be comfortable in the black marketplace.

Usually there are no race-related factors in a job description: candidates of any color could succeed in the position. Your selection decision should use factors like the following: a rigorous analysis of qualifications (through the resume, references, testing, and interviewing), clear thinking about how you intend to evaluate *qualified* and *most qualified*, consideration of how each candidate could help the team improve its performance, and potential for advancement.

Finally, track the answers to these questions:

- In proportion to their percentage in the resume pool, are black candidates being interviewed?
- In proportion to their percentage in the interview pool, are black candidates winning offers?
- In proportion to their percentage in the "offers issued" pool, are black candidates accepting the offers of employment?

In 2006, about sixteen percent of all new hires were black, and seven percent of full-time MBA students were black. If you want to attract and keep black employees, you and your organization should be prepared to compete for their services, and build a work environment where they can succeed.

To help you do this, take a look at Joe Watson's book *Without Excuses: Unleash the Power of Diversity to Build Your Business.*

CONVERSATION STARTER: *What specifically will you do to add diverse talent to your team?*

Individualize
the way you lead.

Let's assume that each person has an equal opportunity, not to become equal,
but to become different. To realize whatever unique potential
of body, mind, and spirit he or she possesses.

JOHN FISCHER, MUSICIAN AND AUTHOR

H ere's a hard truth about leading: people choose to follow you one at a time. You may supervise many units and people according to the organizational chart, but you must also manage individually.

To individualize the way you lead as a white man means that you learn how race and gender shape the individuality of each person reporting to you. This is not easy, so let me offer four suggestions.

Lead authentically. People need to know *you* personally if you want to relate to them as unique contributors. Express and demonstrate how your leadership is influenced by your race and gender (as a white man, that is). In doing so, you cultivate a reciprocating due regard *from them toward you.* You help them take into account how your being a white man does and does not influence your leadership. That way, they will be less inclined to misattribute your motivations, and they will be more open to being authentic with you.

Get to know each follower as an individual. Respect the reality of uniqueness; this is the power of "Like No Other." Exercise special caution in "only one" situations. If, for example, only one black person reports to you, it's critical that you get to know them individually, to help you and others avoid seeing them as racial representatives.

Discovering family information over time is an excellent way to become acquainted. Without being intrusive, and while respecting each colleague's willingness to share, find out about the families of your employees, peers, and manager. This is tough and sensitive: in a recent study, seventy-five percent of black women indicated that, at work, they limit disclosure about their personal lives. If black employees are willing to let you get to know them as individuals, it means you're having some success at creating safety and trust in the workplace.

Let them know about your family, and that you would like to know about theirs. Make sure you *don't judge* what they share ("Wow, why would you want to go to family reunions every year like you do?"). Instead, use such information as a powerful tool for individualizing, because our families are our individual context. Make sure you take their family commitments into account when scheduling meetings, project work, and development assignments.

Remember the difference between "Like No Other" and "Like Some Others." While individuality is an organizing principle for many of us as white men, cultural identity often figures in differently for our black colleagues. Being white and male in America confers on me (and you) the personal freedom to identify myself first and foremost as an individual, and to underestimate the meaning of my race and gender. A black colleague or customer may not enjoy the same liberty; she is an individual as am I, but she is more aware of how being a black woman shapes her than I am conscious of how being a white man influences me.

The risk here is that we may be perceived by our black colleagues to be grasping individualism as a way to maintain the distance between us: "If I, as a white man, can see you, as a black person, only as an individual (like I see myself), then I don't have to consider that my white racial identity might mean something, and I can avoid dealing with you over the history between our peoples." So remember this: individual black Americans tend to remember they are part of a group.

Define "fair treatment" with your team. Lead your colleagues in a discussion of the concept of *fair treatment* as "consistent, individualized treatment,", rather than "the exact same treatment for each individual." Square such a definition with your mutual understanding of discrimination; this will be a lively discussion about individualizing.

Your experience as a leader has surely taught you that each follower cannot be managed in precisely the same fashion, nor do they want to be. Provide what people need individually to succeed as you consistently implement standards, policies, and procedures with everyone.

High-performing employees thrive with confidence when their manager understands, respects, and knows how to unlock their unique competence. That's what we evoke when we individualize the way we lead.

CONVERSATION STARTER: *How would you lead differently, if you sat down and planned out how to lead each employee as the individual you know him or her to be?*

Prevent inequity.

I'm no lawyer, and this book does not provide legal counsel. That being said, prevent inequity by learning to handle two concepts: *disparate treatment* and *adverse impact*. Here's my advice up front: don't make these mistakes yourself, and confront any person, practice, or policy that discriminates against black candidates or employees (or anyone else). Protect yourself, protect your company, and protect your diverse colleagues.

DISPARATE TREATMENT

Generally speaking, disparate treatment involves employer behavior with discriminatory intent. Such discrimination may be expressed through disparities like the following:

Recruitment: This includes discrimination at any step in the hiring process, such as women not interviewed and offered jobs because, on the basis of gender, they are viewed as unqualified; or qualified candidates with disabilities not interviewed or hired; or qualified candidates not offered jobs because they speak English as a second language.

Compensation: Equal pay for equal work is a critical concern. Research shows that black men with professional degrees earn only seventy-nine percent of what their similarly educated white counterparts make. If you want to retain your talent, such a statistic must not hold true in your organization. Comparable worth is an issue through which you, as a white man who leads, can challenge the way that unfair advantage may be built into a company's culture. Securing such equity for all requires your attention; every employee needs to know that people will be paid for performance, not undercompensated because of a dimension of diversity. The outcomes for attending to comparable worth? The improvement of performance, the retention of talent, and the forestalling of litigation and bad press.

Promotion: Preventing disparate treatment will benefit career opportunities for all employees. So we return to the qualifications issue raised in essay 25, on preference and affirmative action. In 2005, the journal *Government Executive* reported "a continuing tension across the federal government between the ideal of a meritocracy on the one hand, and the ideal of a diverse workplace on another. Federal managers are encouraged to make hiring and promotion decisions based on qualifications and performance, but they are also encouraged to *consider* [emphasis added] an applicant's or employee's race." This is the crux of the matter: when is such "consideration" good leadership on diversity, and when is it discrimination? I urge you to join your organization's dialogue to resolve this question.

Adverse Impact

The common meaning of adverse impact has to do with a disproportionate pattern of inequity in employment decisions. It typically refers to workplace actions in which people of color and women are hired, developed, and promoted below their proportion in the labor pool and workforce, or terminated beyond their proportion. Such measures may be the quantification of disparate treatment (intended discrimination), but they may also tell the story of discriminatory results from unintended bias. Here are several examples:

Employee Relations: Disadvantage may accrue on the basis of religion when requests for time off for religious observance are denied; with regard to shift scheduling, when employees believe that others aren't closing or working weekends because of favoritism based on age, family circumstance, gender, or race; or a gap in training security personnel to understand that black employees must be treated with due regard, just like white employees.

Advancement and Retention: A bias in retention may indicate that promotions are not equitable between the genders and races (e.g., a smaller percentage of qualified women or people of color are internally advanced to senior management jobs). Adverse impact in times of layoffs or terminations may demonstrate that more people of color are leaving than their proportion in the employee population.

How do we solve for these dysfunctions of disparate treatment and adverse impact? First, you can watch for symptoms in areas such as recruitment, compensation, promotion, employee relations, and retention. Second, recognize that these systemic problems require many leaders in the organization to get involved with the fix. Finally, build a reputation as a leader who secures equity, by joining the effort to eradicate disparate treatment and adverse impact in your sphere of influence and beyond.

For excellent resources on leading within the law, go to www.eliinc.com, the website for Employment Learning Innovations.

CONVERSATION STARTER: *What will you do to prevent disparate treatment and adverse impact? When will you share with your team what you've learned and done in this regard?*

Motivate
with differences in view.

To **motivate** is to impel to action. Is there a more important skill for a leader? Research on human motivation shows that, to be precise, leaders influence the followers to impel *themselves* to action. Employees move forward to produce and perform because they want to, not because the leader forces them. The work of motivation is to impel, not compel.

We influence the context in which our employees and other associates choose to contribute. We've been considering how the dimensions of diversity shape our colleague's character and performance. So it makes sense, as a white man, to motivate with differences like race and gender in mind. Here's what such a view entails.

- *Recognition:* Make sure that all your employees, including the black ones, receive all the credit and attention they deserve and want for their contributions. Remember that preferences for recognition are highly individualized; some employees want public attention, some want a quiet "thanks, that was a job well done."

- *Delegate for Employee Engagement:* Build an environment in which employees motivate themselves to step up to and exceed your expectations. Delegate supportively to set your employees up for success. When people have a growing stake in outcomes, they are more likely to act in a way that furthers the organization's interests. An engaged employee is a person who is fully involved in, and enthusiastic about, his or her work. In this respect, black employees are "Like All Others"; when humans are engaged, we look to bring our best every day. That's what motivation looks like!

- *Achievement and Visibility:* Assign work that suits the skills of your black employees, and then challenge them to stretch their performance. Make sure their success is observed by your manager, your peers, and members of your team.

- *Motivate Employees to Learn about Diversity:* At Pepco Holdings, a Washington DC–based energy holding company, they created a contest. A poster with diversity facts was hung in company offices, and when employees answered twenty-five multiple-choice questions correctly online from the posted facts, their name went into a pool from which the winner of a $5,000 trip was selected.

Finally, grow your understanding of motivation and influence. Three key resources:

- Review Maslow's Hierarchy, which frames human motivation in five ascending levels of need: physiological, safety, social, esteem, and self-actualization.

- Buy a copy of *12: The Elements of Great Managing*, by Rodd Wagner and James Harter from the Gallup organization. Study their "12 questions" formula for measuring the strength of a workplace. Highly motivated employees will answer yes to all these questions. Managers at Safeco Insurance use this tool to evoke employee engagement.

- A key part of motivational leadership is building your influence skills. Excellent training on influence skills is offered by Situation Management Systems, Inc. at www.smsinc.com. Their Positive Power & Influence course has equipped more than half a million professionals to pursue their objectives while building relationships. This is a truly powerful approach.

One of the most motivated black professionals I've ever met was Cheryl, the colleague of David in essays 31 and 33–35. She was impelled to action for three reasons: David learned from her and mentored her effectively, they became personal friends, and their achievements were tested through pressure and conflict.

Do you enjoy such a relationship with a black colleague? You have to motivate yourself to build one.

CONVERSATION STARTER: *Give the 12-question quiz in The Elements of Great Managing to your team, and discuss responses with each employee individually. Use the feedback to strengthen the motivational climate in your unit.*

■ 81 ■

Make decisions inclusively.

To build trust as you lead, make decisions inclusively. As much as possible, involve those who will be affected. Diverse colleagues in particular will scrutinize your decision making: how you make decisions, how you involve those affected, and the results of your decisions. Why? Because decision making is a function of leadership where your character is revealed and your use of power is interpreted.

Are you clear with your manager, peers, and direct reports about how and when decisions get made? For key decisions, make sure the stakeholders to the decision understand and accept the method for decision making.

Here are six ways to make decisions, in descending order of their potential for inclusion:

- *Self-directed team decisions:* With high-performing individuals and teams, there are times when you can delegate the decision and implementation of work. You are informed of their decision and their progress, but they are responsible for getting the work done and achieving results.

- *Team decides by consensus:* Here's where the group decides. It's a useful approach when the decision will affect everyone, when relevant information is available, and when each person on the team (including you as the manager) can openheartedly agree to an "I can live with that" outcome.

- *Stakeholders vote:* When the stakes are not too high and time is short, voting can be an efficient way to get a decision made. Just make sure that those who "lose" the vote are still on board for implementation.

- *You seek input and you decide:* Stakeholders need to know upfront that you value the best information and opinions they can provide, and then it is your responsibility as the leader to make the decision. Their job? To advise you, and follow your decision.

- *Leaders above us decide:* Many decisions are made above us in the organization, and given to us to implement. So we provide insight about *why* the decision was made, and then include our team in figuring out *how* to get it done.

- *You decide privately:* There are times in leadership work (with corrective action or termination, for instance) where you must make the decision, but there may be limits on what you can share. This puts people in the position of following on the basis of whatever trust you've established with them, so it's advisable to make this decision-making method a rarity.

As leaders, the decisions we deliver—"This is our team's direction." "Here's our budget for next year." "I've decided to promote Jamal."—quantify the promises we make to our manager, peers, and employees. Consequently, inclusion generates trust in the process of deciding, and the decision is more likely to be implemented successfully.

CONVERSATION STARTER: *Clarify how decisions get made in your sphere of influence, by discussing these six methods with your manager, peers, and employees.*

■ 82 ■

Coach

for performance improvement.

A ll sorts of coaches have appeared on the business scene: executive coaches, life coaches, performance coaches. It's the latter kind of coaching I'm focusing on here. How do you provide your employees with the behavioral perspective and resources they need to improve?

A coach in any sport is responsible for evoking optimal performance from the athletes. As an employee performance coach, you equip your people to succeed, but you don't play in their game. It's their job to improve their own performance.

In a recent study with HR managers, ninety-five percent indicated that the emphasis on coaching has increased significantly in the past five years. One key way for you to lead as a white man: fearlessly and effectively coach black (and all) employees to improve their performance. That's how you position them to succeed, even when that means that you help them learn from their mistakes.

The Courage to Deliver Feedback

Are you providing corrective feedback to the women and people of color who report to you, without fearing they could bring up gender or race issues? You absolutely must offer performance feedback consistently and fairly across your unit, or you aren't doing your job. To withhold correction from a person of color or a woman (out of fear they will play the race or gender card) is to deny them an equal opportunity to improve, and to abandon your responsibility as their manager. Establish sufficient trust with your employees so that you do not fear that anyone will claim harassment or discrimination, even when they don't agree with your opinion or decision.

Coach to Behavior

Always focus on performance: "When you failed to follow up with the client by the 30th, we lost an order worth $40,000." Be specific and provide information that is actionable. What can the employee *do* next to learn and move ahead? As you deliver behavioral feedback, remember that you're coaching an employee to help him or her improve performance, not judging who they are as a person. Coach to behavior, with due regard for dimensions of diversity.

Lead Generously with Praise

In my experience, the most underused tool in a manager's tool kit is authentic and specific praise for excellent performance. Maybe we work so hard to coach for improvement that we take our employee's success for granted. But that's a major blunder. It costs us so little to authentically come alongside an employee and be specific in our encouragement: "Mary, when you so effectively resolved that customer's complaint at the counter this morning, you not only saved that customer for us, but everyone in the store was impressed at your skill in handling conflict. That was outstanding!"

TAILOR YOUR COACHING STYLE

Research shows that the communication style of black Americans is often very direct. They tend to speak forcefully, with clarity, to "just come right out and say it." If you, as a white man, prefer a more indirect way of communicating, then such directness can be off-putting. As you individualize the way you coach black employees, consider providing corrective feedback and praise with a more direct verbal style, based on the employee's individual preference.

Coach all employees to improve their performance, by providing corrective feedback even-handedly, by focusing on behavior, by praising success generously, and by adapting your style to the communication preferences of those you coach.

And if your black employees are interested in life coaching, encourage them to seek more information from the Black Professional Coaches Alliance at www.blackcoaches.org.

CONVERSATION STARTER: *Who is the best coach you ever had? What did they do that causes you to rate them so highly? How did they affect your performance? How can you become that kind of coach to each of your employees?*

■ **83** ■

Be a mentor,
find a mentor.

In a healthy mentoring relationship, personal connection and professional learning serve as a potent mix for both parties. Many organizations have fueled diversity development through formal and informal mentoring programs. For instance, the mentoring program at General Mills matches newly hired people of color with experienced managers, white and otherwise. These new hires are also encouraged to explore peer mentoring, through participation in one of the company's seven employee affinity groups.

You have a lot to give and get in mentoring relationships. Here are four ways to mine the mentoring method.

Mentor (and learn with) a black employee. In a recent study, thirty-eight percent of black professional women indicated they had mentors. Only twenty-nine percent of those mentors were white men. If those same percentages hold true for black men, only eleven percent of black professionals are being mentored by white men, even though white men are a majority of the managers in most organizations. Those numbers need to change.

Look for structured and informal opportunities to build a mentoring relationship. As a wise and trusted adviser, you can support a black employee's development. And you should expect to learn a lot from them.

Explain "how we do it around here"; open the door to opportunities; expose them to leaders in other lines of business and levels in the company. Help them avoid mistakes and learn from setbacks.

Handle discussion about race with care. Because of the history rift (see essay 15) and perceptions around white male advantage (see essays 23–26), black employees may be guarded in how much they reveal about their thoughts and lives. An effective mentoring relationship requires personal transparency; disclose your learning and ask open-ended questions gently at the start: "I've been doing a lot of thinking and learning about what it means to lead as a white man lately, and I hope we'll have the chance to include diversity opportunities and challenges in our discussions." Focus on the work, not on diversity.

Mentor another white man who leads. As you move toward Relative Expertise in leadership as a white man, make sure you support other white men who are making the same journey. A generation from now, I hope black Americans will be able to expect white men to mentor other white men on diversity. Today, you'll stand out when you do this, and that, my friend, is a practical way to develop a sustainable collaborative advantage.

Find a diverse peer mentor. Mentoring relationships among people of the same generation can be very powerful. Much of my diversity learning has come from colleagues and friends who are similar in age, education, and vocation. Seek out diverse peers as mentors of mutuality; you help them grow professionally and personally, and they return the favor.

Find a senior mentor. If you can, build a relationship with a black man or woman of a generation senior to your own. My career was immeasurably enriched by my mentor, Bill Pannell, and he taught me a lot about leading as a white man. But what I learned runs much deeper than race and vocation: I seek to lead in a way that will honor Bill and make him proud of me. Deeper yet, I want my life to please Jesus, whom Bill helped me encounter up close and personal.

Make mentoring relationships a priority in your development as a white man who leads. A useful resource to help: Lois J. Zachary's *The Mentor's Guide: Facilitating Effective Learning Relationships.* Be a mentor, find a mentor, many times.

CONVERSATION STARTER: *Who are you mentoring? Who is mentoring you?*

■ **84** ■

Provide
performance-based development opportunities.

As managers, one of the most tangible promises we make to employees is to support them in their professional development. Yes, they are responsible for their success: we don't "develop" them. But the power of our position carries with it the duty and resources to help them achieve. We want the same support from our boss.

With the following tips in mind, equip black employees to develop:

- Encourage their networking skills, so they engage colleagues on cultural issues, customer needs, and growing the business.

Development opportunities often derive from relationships and business challenges outside their department.

- Be careful not to assume that black employees will not/cannot rise to meet stretch goals. Don't permit such an unfair expectation to creep into the corner of your mind. Give black colleagues every opportunity to show what they can do. Expect excellence, reward it, and coach when performance falls short.

- Offer the opportunity to lead or present at meetings as often as possible.

- Arrange for challenging and varied work assignments. For example, Fannie Mae has a job rotation initiative, which develops high-potential employees by assigning them to short-term projects. This builds their skills, heightens their visibility, and provides staffing flexibility.

- Ensure your black employees have the support they need to earn any professional certifications recognized in your industry.

- Assign them to high profile, business-focused projects. My bias: while involvement with United Way, diversity events, and community volunteering can be good for their visibility, it is a superior development opportunity when black employees participate in projects that actually make money for the company.

- Give people the chance to grow by giving them your honest feedback. Professor Martin Davidson recently noted in *Black Enterprise:* "Research tells us that it is typically challenging for African-American women to get direct feedback, because their peers are worried about being offensive. A lot of times African-American women are left to decode what they ought to be doing, or what they ought to be paying attention to."

Don't make employees guess about the priorities that can drive their development.

- Finally, remove barriers to development. For instance, black employees often report that their authority and credibility are questioned. Equip your black employees to handle such resistance. And ensure that coaching and diversity training in your organization communicates that every employee is expected to support the success of every colleague.

What's the best way to counteract anyone's suspicions that an employee was hired just because they were black? Fuel the development of your black employees, and all will see that they're doing a great job. Ultimately, it's not about diversity. It's about performance.

Conversation Starter: *What specific steps will you take to provide performance-based development opportunities for your black employees? How will you make sure your manager sees these efforts and the results?*

LEADING AMONG COLLEAGUES
■ 85 ■

Develop
a diverse team.

irst, a definition: a **team** is a group of individuals whose common purpose requires interdependent contribution. A team shares a clear mutual accountability, and each member's success depends, in part, on other members' performance. While we still lead people one by one (because they are "Like No Other"), we also get to grow the team subculture (a "Like Some Others" experience).

Differences among team members offer opportunity and drive conflict. Developing a diverse team will reward and test your competence to lead.

Here are ten tips for developing your diverse team:

1) Set the pace for diversity learning. Share with the team your three key diversity lessons from the past year, and how you are applying

this learning in your life and leadership. This is a good way to introduce due regard (see essay 30).

2) Get on the same page, stay on the same page. Clarify the team's common purpose, by asking, "What do we produce that our customers are glad to receive?" Establish ground rules for how you will behave with each other (three favorites: *Hear people out: don't interrupt. Seek feedback to get better every day. Find a way to play every day.*).

3) Secure diversity training for team members (see essay 88) to instill ideas (like the Fundamental Filter, essays 3–5) that team members can apply together. Ensure they are trained in the skills they need to use with diverse colleagues and customers.

4) Explore dimensions of diversity beyond race and gender. The most innovative teams build an environment where members feel safe, don't hide who they are, and know they will be rewarded for bringing their best to the team's work.

5) Build a schedule to have fun together, secure some budget for the fun, and make "play" one of the team norms. I have observed that adults who play together also produce better, fight less, and stay longer.

6) Speaking of conflict, establish a clear team expectation that conflict is normal and can be entered into with confidence that issues will be resolved in a way that strengthens relationships and moves the team ahead (see the next essay). Leverage conflict to drive learning, by helping people learn from their mistakes, by learning when you blow it, and by ensuring that the whole team learns from this pain.

7) Use the team trust tool in essay 65 as a springboard for diversity discussions.

8) Sometimes team members will cluster by race or gender. Make sure everyone remembers the power and comfort of "Like Some Others" within the team. If it turns cliquey, review the team's common purpose.

9) Remember safety issues. For example, check in with black colleagues before scheduling team-building events in rural or wilderness environments.

10) Develop entrance and exit protocols. What will teammates do specifically to welcome and orient new members, and how will they honor the contribution of team members who are moving on?

A white professional photographer shared this story. He was assigned to photograph a successful basketball team from a local college. When he lined them up in the gym bleachers, the six black players were sitting in a cluster, and the camera was not differentiating well between their dark features. You could visually distinguish between the white guys, but the black guys, one face to the next, weren't as easily distinguishable. So the photographer decided to have some fun. He explained the problem; the six black players and their black coach all knew what he was talking about. The white guys were surprised. So he alternated players and coaches, black and white. Everyone was visible in the photo, and the mixed composition drew a lot of positive comment. Even better, the coach used the experience to lead an overdue conversation about racial realities on the team. He made three points:

- Our team's diversity is visible for all to see, so let's make everyone proud of who we are together.

- We need to relate to each other as unique individuals, rather than as members of a different race.

- We need to commit to performing as a tight team on and off the court, because that's how we will win games and win in life.

Those are good rules to lead by as you develop your diverse team!

When you, as a white man, lead the development of a successful and diverse team, you will be seen as a diversity champion.

A resource to help? Study *Diverse Teams at Work: Capitalizing on the Power of Diversity*, by Lee Gardenswartz and Anita Rowe.

CONVERSATION STARTER: *What differences challenge the team you lead right now? How could such diversity be managed to strengthen the team's performance?*

■ **86** ■

Resolve conflict.

What binds us most strongly together
is our long history of conflict with one another.©

ASHLEIGH BRILLIANT

onflict by definition is rooted in differences: differences in opinion, experience, self-interest, and personality. The white man who leads should expect conflict; it comes with management responsibility, and it accompanies diversity.

We all know and fear the downside of conflict: simmering silence, hostile communication, broken relationships, derailed results. As leaders, we cannot steer clear of such outcomes by avoiding conflict. When you leave things alone in the hope that they'll get better on their own, how does that generally work out? Right, it's a mess.

So if conflict is inevitable, avoidance ain't much of a strategy. You need to hone your skills at resolving diversity-related conflict. Consider this approach.

First, buy and read Thomas Kochman's classic contribution, *Black and White: Styles in Conflict.* Study these 160 pages carefully, because his work is brilliant and practical. His analysis depends on generalizations, which some have criticized as stereotyping. As long as you remember the difference (see essay 19), this book will dramatically enhance your confidence as a white man who leads.

Second, get clear about private opinions versus employer expectations. Never forget for a moment that, as a manager, you have no moral or legal permission to tell your employees what to believe about diversity. It's a free country, as they say, and your coworkers have a right to believe whatever they want about human differences. For example

- they may think of younger workers as disloyal, or older workers as resistant to change;

- their family of origin may have instilled in them the opinion that people of color are inferior;

- ignorance may cause them to view people who speak English with an accent as less intelligent;

- the combination of being heterosexual and believing in the Bible's authority may cause in them discomfort in relating to gay or lesbian colleagues and customers.

Each employee's right to his or her own viewpoint presents you with a leadership challenge, because you know that an employee will be more effective if their personal beliefs are compatible with the organization's values.

So you may have to show some steel when an employee's private opinions conflict with the company's values. You *do* have the right and responsibility as a manager to insist and ensure that your employee's behavior at work demonstrates that they understand and accept the organization's commitment to diversity.

Many workplace conflicts find their source in this tension between private opinion and employer expectation. You need to get and stay clear about this in your own mind, because it takes skill and gumption to oblige your employees to express the company's values in the way they work, while avoiding intrusion into their private beliefs.

Third, build conflict resolution skills in three areas: *agree, agree to disagree,* and *disengage.*

- The preferable choice in conflict situations is to seek agreement among the parties. Lead through conflict intentionally, using a method like the one outlined below. Show people that you expect them to step up and operate with an open mind and heart, and then hold the parties to the conflict accountable for making things right and implementing the resolution.

- Sometimes agreement is not possible. When you resolve conflict by helping people agree to disagree, consensus is built around each party retaining their views in a way that still allows them to move ahead. While this doesn't feel as positive as outright agreement, sometimes it's a healthy interim step. And sometimes we just get to learn to live with the durable differences between us.

- There are moments of conflict that require disengagement: when emotions run high, when safety is at risk, when all that is in your mind and mouth will only damage the situation further. Let me be clear: we lead by disengaging *so that we can reengage.* We may take a break, or require others to do so, or change the subject, because that's what a volatile situation requires. But we can't run and hide as leaders. Disengaging serves the resolution of conflict by providing time or diversion, so that calm can prevail and goodwill can return. It's a great technique to use for de-escalation.

Fourth, follow a five-step method for resolving diversity-related conflicts:

1) If the conflict is high risk, consider help from a facilitator.

2) Explore causes and issues with all the parties. Get at the facts.

3) Build understanding and relationships. Explore and validate the feelings.

4) Develop options. Evoke creativity among all involved, seeking to identify how the interests of all parties can be addressed. Avoid the either/or positioning that drives so much conflict with false choices.

5) Try solutions. Experiment and follow up on both facts and feelings.

Fifth, for your black (and all) employees, you need to "have their back." Employees may undermine a black colleague's contribution by questioning his authority, doubting his knowledge or skill, going around him to someone else for information, excluding him from meetings or opportunities, or overscrutinizing his performance. Protect your black employees, by confirming their authority, redirecting work-arounds, and clarifying performance expectations for all.

When you, as a white man, lead people to resolve diversity-related conflict, you will stand out. That is to say you will be outstanding. Folks will follow you because you engage conflict with skill and confidence, and you equip them to do the same.

CONVERSATION STARTER: *As a leader, are you resolving conflict effectively? If so, help a peer to build the same skill set. If not, why not? Who can help you improve your conflict resolution skills?*

■ **87** ■

Recognize
and reward performance.

Black employees have the same need for recognition and reward as all employees. This is about honoring a person's contribution, it's about motivation, and it's about reinforcing priority behaviors and results.

You will not be surprised to find out that employees universally value money. Make sure employees are paid equally for equal work; this is foundational. See the discussion of comparable worth in essay 79. And extend spot bonuses and similar awards equitably among your direct reports.

Many companies reward managers financially for success with diversity goals:

- Denny's has turned around a poor reputation among black Americans since the 1990s. One tool: the chairman can issue a twenty-five percent discretionary bonus for senior managers who improve their hiring and promoting of minority employees.

- Procter & Gamble reinforces accountability through stock option awards based on diversity efforts.

- At Sodexho, ten to fifteen percent of their annual bonus is linked to success with diversity metrics. The funding does not depend on profitability, and in one recent year, seventy percent of managers earned the bonus.

- The executive chairman of Pitney Bowes, Michael Critelli, has been known to scale back a bonus for executives who don't demonstrate their commitment to diversity in the way they lead. Wal-Mart will also lower bonuses for managers who miss diversity targets.

Beyond compensation, recognition experts report that non–cash awards and incentives also keep employees engaged. So here's the rule of thumb: reward and recognize each person the way they want to be rewarded and recognized. Individualize.

For example, one West Coast exec found that his Asian-American accountant wanted a quiet, expensive lunch with the boss as a reward—and his Asian-American sales director wanted to explain his success at a staff meeting! He honored his employees by recognizing and rewarding them as they individually preferred.

Ensure that employees get the credit they deserve. If someone fails to recognize the contribution of a black employee, for example, by misattributing the employee's positive performance to another person, correct the record by making sure everyone understands the black employee's contribution.

Here are more reward and recognition ideas that may motivate:

- Advancement. Nothing reinforces performance like moving people into new and challenging responsibilities.

- Give them a plaque honoring an achievement. People may joke about such items, but they display them prominently, and never toss them out.

- Extra time off can be a huge reward. Combine a Friday and Monday off with a three-night gift certificate for their family at a nice local hotel or nearby resort, and you've solidified your relationship with a top performer.

- Provide merchandise or services that your company produces.

- Work with the employee to create a presentation about their successful contribution, and have them deliver it when your manager meets with peers. Create visibility.

- Do a little research on the employee's favorite music, and get them concert tickets.

- Identify their favorite food, and bring them takeout. I once found out from a colleague's wife that he was passionate about a certain style of ribs from a little place in Jackson, Mississippi. I found a way to get a slab delivered to his office one day at lunch; he was amazed at my resourcefulness and care, and it was a simple and fun thing for me to do.

You get the idea. There are many ways to reward and recognize employees for a job well done. When you're not sure how to honor an employee, just come right out and ask: "Omari, I want to honor you for your great work on the inventory report. What ideas do you have about how I could reward and recognize you in a way that would be special to you?" If he wants a Mercedes, laugh and ask for more ideas. People know their preferences for recognition and rewards.

Want to reward me? An excellent peanut butter milkshake will do the job almost every time.

CONVERSATION STARTER: *Experiment for the next month, by dramatically expanding your use of recognition and rewards with your employees. Keep it authentic (no fake enthusiasm), get creative, and individualize. Evaluate the impact a month from now.*

■ 88 ■

Ensure

that diversity training drives success.

I n a recent study, sixty-six percent of black women reported that their organizations have failed to address racism against black people. That's a sad commentary on corporate America's immense investment in diversity training.

I've designed and delivered diversity training for twenty years. Here's one thing I've learned: awareness education is a waste of time and money, unless it's connected to skills that help the organization grow.

Too many times I've heard this: "Awareness training is the remedy for the diversity issues we face." Yes, it is good to know enough about diverse people to avoid giving offense. But a training budget is a terrible thing to waste. Diversity awareness training may produce more conflict and no discernable bottom-line benefits, unless the training occurs as a tactic in a coherent strategy for managing the changes and opportunities that diversity brings.

I'm familiar with a Fortune 500 company that, for more than a decade, has mandated that managers attend a variety of diversity awareness courses without skill building. Their awareness of human differences, as an end in itself, is not generating much business value, and the company now pretends that leaders can be equipped to leverage diversity by completing a one-hour online module.

Don't mistake my point. Awareness is crucial (see essays 18 and 36). Here are two great training firms (see Resources for contact information):

- Stir Fry Communications offers a robust training approach to understanding racial differences, using the *Color of Fear* video.
- For training specific to white men, contact White Men as Full Diversity Partners, a firm based in Portland, Oregon. This training and consulting group is surprisingly seasoned in equipping white men to engage diversity as a personal and professional opportunity.

But awareness is just the beginning, not an end in itself. To be effective, diversity training must drive development of the skills a leader needs to build a business. Here's how.

Focus on communication skills. At JPMorgan Chase, managers attended "Micro-Inequities: The Power of Small." The program examined the scores of powerful and subtle messages we send to our colleagues that impact on their contribution, from nonverbals like a supportive nod or a disapproving glance, to small comments that eventually affect performance and retention.

Participants learned to observe and handle such microinequities, and to improve performance through positive micromessages.

Widen the scope. Training does need to delve into the foundational differences of race and gender. Since diversity involves many more dimensions (see essay 2), effective training should also extend, for example, to how differences in thinking and learning styles influence team dynamics and decision making. The Meyers-Briggs and DiSC tools are useful here.

Connect training to the business case. Training should link directly to diversity's business case: employees are right to ask why the investment in time and money is being made. A healthy organizational commitment to diversity lasers in on both employees and customers.

Develop skills that drive results. Training should lead directly to skill development that drives success on goals. For example, diversity training should equip the sales staff to open markets across cultural lines and reach more diverse customers.

Don't train the team when individual coaching is what's needed. It's a unique agony when a work group is subjected to training as a fix for one member's shortcomings. Provide effective coaching on diversity issues to the employees who need it. Professionals in the HR and Learning departments can help you with this.

Finally, you won't be surprised to find out that I recommend specific training for your organization's white men in leadership; see www.leadershipforwhitemen.com to find out about training built on this book. Black employees will benefit when training equips white men to lead effectively.

CONVERSATION STARTER: *What diversity training will improve how you lead? What diversity training will build in your employees the particular skills they need to deliver better business results?*

■ 89 ■

Prepare
high-potential employees for advancement.

One of your ultimate achievements as a white man who leads is helping high-potential black colleagues advance in their career. Or you may have the chance to support them as they decide to move out of the company to pursue another dream.

We're thinking about managing talent here: identifying performers with high potential, fueling their development, positioning them with career advice and visibility, promoting them when you can, and working to retain their services.

Here's why this matters: black colleagues (and prospective employees) evaluate the organization and their opportunities in part by whether there are visible black leaders in the company. It's a "Like Some Others" thing. In a study by Catalyst (a women's advocacy group), thirty-one percent of black women said that their organization's lack of black role models was a significant barrier to their career advancement and satisfaction. As white men, we expend precisely no energy looking to see if people who look like us are in senior positions. Because they always are. Our diverse colleagues see their faces in senior leaders much less often.

Like many other topics in this book, succession planning and talent management involve much more than a simple essay can address. Permit me to recommend seven modest methods you can pursue to help fill the leadership pipeline with talented black contributors.

1) If your organization has formal succession management practices, find out how they operate, for your own benefit, and so you can advise the high performers you lead. If such an emphasis does not yet exist in the company, explore William Rothwell's *Effective Succession Planning: Ensuring Leadership Continuity and Building Talent from Within.*

2) Equip your high-potential performer(s) to craft a career development plan.

3) Develop their global perspective and business acumen, and invest in your own learning about these areas. In a 2006 survey, ninety-one percent of corporate leaders agreed with the statement: "Competition for talent with global skills will become more fierce."

4) Connect them to mentors in the organization and marketplace (see essay 83). Aflac, for example, has a mentoring program for

minority agents, to diversify the talent available to move into senior management.

5) Find the budget to support high performers, so they widen their perspective by attending trade shows, visit company facilities, and work with international vendors.

6) Deepen their development through project work, job shadowing and rotation, and formal education and certifications.

7) When they're ready, open doors for them to serve on projects and present to senior leadership and key customers.

Some white men, otherwise known for their cultivation of leadership talent, have not succeeded in developing diverse leaders. Famed corporate leader Jack Welch, for example, moved few women and people of color into senior positions at GE. Here's your chance to best Jack. Commit to building a reputation for preparing high-potential employees for advancement.

CONVERSATION STARTER: *Are you ready to formulate a DRPO (see essay 76) with your boss to identify and prepare high potential employees (black and otherwise) for advancement?*

LEADING AMONG COLLEAGUES
■ 90 ■

Promote
high performers.

Every time a white man leads by participating in the promotion of a black employee, he crosses a threshold: potential developed, opportunity delivered. It feels good to promote high-performing people of every ethnicity.

Promoting diverse talent is also a competitive strategy. The parent company of Pizza Hut and Taco Bell takes seriously the opportunity to promote diverse leaders: more than forty percent of the company's restaurant managers are minorities. That's impressive for its intentionality.

If you, as a white man, lead successfully on several of the other topics in this section, then promoting high-performing black (and all) employees will occur naturally. Here are the connections:

- Recruiting: When the organization attracts people prepared to grow, the stage is set for advancement (see essay 77).

- Individualizing development: As your support for an employee's development is tailored to them individually, they emerge as high performers (see essays 78, 84, 89).

- Coaching and mentoring: Top performance will more likely emerge from people who receive effective improvement coaching and have career-building access to mentors (see essays 82 and 83).

Another way to come at the practice of promotion: remove barriers that may slow down or prevent black employees from moving ahead in their careers. Let's look at four impediments:

First, watch for and root out any perception that diverse employees are not as motivated to advance as white men. They may have more responsibilities at home: employed women and single mothers in particular carry the lion's share of homemaking work. Or a diverse colleague may doubt their chance for promotion, if they have observed other people of color or women being passed over.

Second, rigorously ensure access to job openings. We're all familiar with the difficulty of competing for a position that is not posted, and then filled before the "opening" is evident. Another door-closing message: only *certain* people are encouraged to seek select positions ("certain" meaning the boss likes you, or you look like the boss).

Third, deal with a particular challenge for promoting black employees: relocation issues. The job you want to move them into may exist in a community where it could be tough for them to find

- a neighborhood that will welcome a black family;
- people who want to care for black children;

- a suitable church;
- professionals who know how to care for a black person's hair;
- restaurants serving the food they prefer, and so on.

Take these issues into account in your relocation conversations with your employee.

Finally, opening promotional doors for black people is a challenge for white men *and women*. Frances Kendall, in *Understanding White Privilege*, writes: "For many men and women of color in corporations and academia, white women are seen as the primary barriers to promotion and tenure. They frequently form a broad band in the middle of the organizational hierarchy as middle managers and associate professors, making it very difficult for people of color to break through and move to the top." Food for thought and conversation.

Black Enterprise recently quoted recruiting exec Kenneth Arroyo Roldan: "Young African Americans are frustrated, because when they look up the ranks, they don't see anyone who looks like them." So when we promote high-performing black employees, we not only benefit from their expertise at a new level. We also expand the sense of opportunity among other black employees and recruits. And we widen the vision among all employees for the emerging face of leadership.

CONVERSATION STARTER: *How many black employees have you promoted in the past year? In your career? What will you do to help your organization promote more high-performing black employees?*

■ 91 ■

Terminate
with equity.

Employees leave under many circumstances. It's a positive event when they depart for another team and a new opportunity in the organization (even though we'll miss them). When a colleague leaves to pursue a dream or meet a need outside the company, we don't like to see them go, but we understand. Sometimes folks drift away and we never find out why. We may ask people to leave when the company reorganizes, even though their performance is adequate. And, in every leadership career, it is necessary to terminate employees for job performance or conduct problems. Often we've gone many extra miles to help them succeed, and it has become clear (at least to us) that they need to move to another opportunity.

As a white man in leadership, you may feel special concern when performance or conduct issues cause you to end an employment relationship with an employee who differs from you by race and/or gender. You want your departing employee to face up to his or her need to improve; you want to avoid accusations of racial or gender discrimination; and you want to protect yourself and your organization from a post-termination lawsuit.

The most effective way to secure these three wants, of course, is to already have built a relationship of respect with your black (and all) employees. Even if you relate to a diverse employee with equity, support, and candor, and even if you lead them as this book envisions, termination may still be required. But they will be much less likely to claim that a dimension of diversity is a cause for their performance or conduct problem. And even if they raise such concerns, your positive and proactive behavior as a diversity manager will be documented.

Did I mention earlier that I am not an attorney, and that this book does not dispense legal advice? That's still true. So I encourage you to consult with legal counsel before you terminate any employee. It is simply wise to contemplate risk, and to handle such situations by the letter of the law. This will demonstrate your respect to the departing employee and, in the case of future litigation, protect both you and your company.

Human Resource professionals are another key ally when you consider firing an employee. Hopefully, HR has ensured your documentation of all efforts to help the employee improve his or her performance or conduct, and your compliance with policy and the law. Even though everything can seem to take too long when we work with HR in such situations, their partnership is intended to guarantee that we do right by the employee and the company. That keeps us safe as well. And an effective exit interview by your HR partner will provide the departing employee, you as the firing manager, and the company with insight on improving for the future.

Being pulled into diversity-related litigation after a messy termination is only fun if you are already demented. But you *must* face up to the necessity of terminating a diverse employee when it becomes necessary. There are six good reasons why you *must not* permit an employee's skin color or gender to prevent a rightful termination:

1) You fail to give them the chance to improve in their next position.

2) You join them in perpetuating the wrong fight: the situation is not about diversity, it's about behavior.

3) Your team will continue to suffer from their poor performance.

4) You send the message that your incompetence with diverse employees is more important than their lack of performance. This is insidious, because we don't come to work to be diverse; we come to work to perform!

5) Employees who hear about the situation (and many will) may conclude that preference (i.e., immunity from rightful termination) accrues on the basis of race or gender.

6) Your manager will see, up close and personal, that you have abdicated your duty to lead. Maybe not an outcome you're looking for …

Obviously, it's just plain smart to lead effectively among diverse colleagues. You may never arrive at the moment when you have to factor diversity issues into a termination. But if such a situation does come to you, lead by securing help from your HR partners and legal counsel. Carry your commitment to diversity all the way to the end of an employment relationship. Terminate with equity.

CONVERSATION STARTER: *Have you ever had to terminate an employee who differed from you by race and/or gender? What did you learn from the experience? Are you avoiding or mishandling any situations that might lead to termination right now? If so, who can help you sort out the situation and get it right?*

Avoid litigation,
and lead beyond the law.

First, there is the law. It must be obeyed.
But the law is the minimum. You must act ethically.

IBM Business Guidelines for Employees

AVOID LITIGATION

Make no mistake, it is a good and measurable goal to avoid litigation over conflicts in employee or customer relations. Diversityinc reports that, for the average discrimination lawsuit, large companies drop $4 million on settlement and legal fees. Even worse, the average two-day loss in market value of a large company's stock following a major discrimination lawsuit is $169 million. These are not exactly best practices in managing corporate capital.

Every week the media reports a new mess. The day I sat down to write this essay, it was reported that Walgreens, the nation's largest chain of drugstores, agreed to pay $20 million to more than 7,500 black employees for discrimination in hiring and assignment decisions. This was not good news for their leaders or their shareholders.

Lawsuits also distract and embarrass managers; damage morale, performance and retention; and steal time away from serving customers and making money. Litigation doesn't offer much upside, although mounting an effective defense will remain a necessary capability, because even when the company has done nothing wrong, it will still get sued.

The risk of diversity-related lawsuits holds leaders accountable for managing diversity within the law. So whatever can be done to prevent litigation should be done. Successful tactics include a clear articulation of the diversity commitment and related policies, training managers in the requirements of law and policy, listening carefully and responding frequently to employee concerns, effective resolution of workplace conflicts, and actively educating managers to build trust and document carefully.

But don't delude yourself: a decrease in diversity-related litigation does not suffice as a vision for diversity at work. No one will applaud when it becomes apparent that "Don't get sued" is an organization's primary diversity objective.

One sad example: some companies are now purchasing liability coverage for losses related to claims of sexual harassment. It doesn't require much intelligence to recognize that this sends precisely the wrong message to women and men alike: "The company would rather buy protection from the symptoms of sexual harassment than root out its cause."

Such insurance cannot substitute for the hard work necessary to build a healthy environment for people on your team and in your organization. The premiums for these policies would be better spent on

- establishing policies to clarify and prohibit specific behavior;
- training managers and employees to implement the policies;
- identifying and supporting investments and practices that craft a climate where men and women of every color work well together.

Lead Beyond the Law

The law makes promises you must keep as a manager. No option there. But you have choices about *how* you implement these mandates. Take inspiration from two companies that leverage what they learn while managing *within* the law to lead *beyond* the law.

At Microsoft, a company that has never suffered a shortage of self-confidence, HR managers decided to consider the requirements of labor law a benchmark to exceed, rather than a distracting imposition. These leaders knew that the company's creative, chaotic, high-speed style would not embrace labor law for its own sake: diversity and legal mandates had to add value. The result? While Microsoft must comply with the law like every company (and they do not always succeed), this lemons-to-lemonade approach has directed their diversity investment toward meeting line managers' needs (e.g., help with recruiting, handling language issues in product development and project management, providing cross-cultural expertise to open and serve international markets). Microsoft's approach is refreshing: since every asset and agenda at the company is expected to contribute, compliance with the law was transformed from a burden to a baseline.

At Hewlett-Packard, during a plant's audit on issues related to the Americans with Disabilities Act (ADA), engineers received feedback that blind customers were unhappy with the design of their most popular printer: a number of key features could not be accessed without sight. Once these designers got over feeling defensive, they spoke with a number of these critics. In the end, several design improvements responded to the needs of their blind customers and, in fact, delivered a printer easier for all customers to use. In this instance the law did not require HP to make the accommodation, but they leveraged learning from complying with the ADA into product improvements and more satisfied customers.

An organization and its leaders send a powerful message when they surpass diversity-related legal mandates: "We will operate by the letter of the law, and we will leverage the law's intent." This is especially true for you as a white man, when your leadership exceeds the promises of the law. In doing so, you make it safe, and summon a maturing trust from your colleagues.

CONVERSATION STARTER: *Have you been trained to manage within the law, for the protection of employees, customers, and the company? What opportunities can you help your organization find for leading beyond the law?*

Pursue
the black marketplace.

C onsider these facts about the black marketplace:

- There are 14 million black households in America (81 million white).

- At more than 39 million people, the black population is growing about thirty-five percent faster than the U.S. population as a whole.

- Catalyst reports that "African-American buying power is predicted to increase from $318 billion in 1990 to $921 billion in 2008; an increase of 189%. This increase is significantly higher than the growth rate for white consumers, which is 128%."

- A 2005 study found that, even when the economy was uncertain, twenty-five percent of black Americans still intended to make a major purchase, compared with only sixteen percent of white people.
- Sixty percent of black Americans live in ten states: New York, Maryland, Michigan, Virginia, Illinois, Georgia, Florida, Louisiana, Texas, and California.

Depending on what your business sells, the growing number and clout of black customers offers opportunity you should pursue. Here's a cross-section of business trends in the black marketplace:

- It helps to understand the ethnic demographics of your customer base. For example, Merck Pharmaceuticals recognizes that African-Americans are a priority market for cholesterol medications, because they are at a higher risk for heart disease.
- The National Restaurant Association reports that black customers are more likely than white customers to purchase every meal except breakfast away from home.
- LIMRA, the trade association for life insurance companies, has highlighted the growth potential with people of color in the middle market (annual income between $50,000 and $100,000).
- A study from The Hartman Group indicates that African-American consumers are twenty-four percent more likely than the general population to consistently purchase organic foods. Former U.S. senator Carol Moseley Braun has founded Good Food Organics.
- Financial planning, home ownership, business development, and wealth management are of huge interest in the black community.

Peruse *Black Enterprise* magazine; you'll get an encouraging view into America's black middle class.

More women and people of color are leading in distribution channels as well.

- General Motors, through its Women's Retail Initiative, recruits and supports female owners of GM dealerships, which are as profitable as dealerships owned by men.
- Women and minority leaders operate more than forty percent of the McDonald's franchises in the United States.
- One more: The number of black-owned Toyota dealerships has doubled in the last decade.

Finally, don't overlook the link between serving black customers and attracting prospective black employees. Merchandising giant Procter & Gamble, for one, assiduously seeks referrals of minority employee prospects from customers and suppliers.

For more information on the emerging black marketplace, grab a copy of a book by Pepper Miller and Herb Kemp, entitled *What's Black About It? Insights to Increase Your Share of the Changing African American Market.*

CONVERSATION STARTER: *Has your organization attended to its opportunities in the growing black marketplace?*

Develop products and services *for black customers.*

As the black marketplace grows, products and services evolve in response. Black customers, employees, and suppliers can help your company innovate and evaluate new market opportunities. To stimulate your thinking, here are ten examples of products and services for black customers.

1) In 2003, L'Oreal opened the Institute for Ethnic Hair and Skin Research in Chicago. No other facility in the world conducts such research on the personal care needs of people of African descent.

2) Procter & Gamble leverages the connections its black employees have to the black marketplace. For example, their affinity group of black employees helped target black women with the "Pantene Total You" community-based beauty campaign.

3) Metropolitan Life launched a Clergy Compensation Planning Program, to educate leaders in black churches on financial management tools they can use personally, and in leading their congregation's business. The initiative operates in fifteen urban markets.

4) There are some surprisingly cool niche markets opening with black consumers. Two that intrigue me: DNA testing (like africanancestry.com) that helps black Americans trace their ancestry in this hemisphere and back to Africa, and Internet resources (like ancestry.com) that provide Web databases for genealogical research.

5) Monster.com provides a variety of Web pages focusing on the interests of black job seekers, including a fine list of African-American professional associations.

6) Health insurer Aetna, for two years running, has been honored with a national award for efforts to educate African-Americans and other consumers about reducing racial disparities in health care.

7) State Farm was the official sponsor for Dr. Ian Smith's 50 Million Pound Challenge program, seeking to improve the health of black Americans by shedding, yep, fifty million pounds. 11,000 State Farm offices offered free Challenge kits.

8) Wells-Fargo operates an African-American Business Services Program, which seeks to lend $1 billion to black-owned business over a twelve-year period.

9) AC Nielsen, the market research firm, offers the Homescan African-American Consumer Panel, featuring information about black consumers that combines "actual purchasing behavior with attitude, lifestyle, and health information."

10) Over decades, Historically-Black Colleges and Universities (HBCUs) have evolved to deliver higher education to African-American high school graduates. About ten percent of black college students attend an HBCU.

It will pay for your organization to deliver products and services to a black marketplace with a trillion dollars of buying power by 2010.

CONVERSATION STARTER: *Does your organization have opportunities to develop products and services for black customers?*

Handle issues
and opportunities in sales and marketing.

M ost services and products are not specific to ethnicity: laundry soap cleans everyone's clothes. The diversity investment should influence what diverse customers hear about and decide to buy. So sales and marketing also drives the development of a black customer base. Many companies are figuring out how to build share in diverse markets.

- Chrysler sponsored Patti LaBelle's gospel concert tour in black churches. Diversityinc quoted Chrysler's spokesperson, James Kenyon: "We're trying to meet this audience where they are, by taking our vehicles to their communities, rather than asking them to come to us."

- Merck discovered that black customers want to see people who look like them in advertising for pharmaceutical products. In 2003, Merck invested more than thirteen percent ($67 million) of its marketing budget in multicultural marketing.
- Subway featured black duo Herman and Sherman Smith as "The Subway Twins." Reportedly, they dropped a combined 215 pounds by eating Subway sandwiches.
- New York Life identified the African-American community as a significant market, and reached out through black agents serving as financial counselors to pastors in large urban churches, along with a partnership with the Rainbow/PUSH Coalition.
- In collaboration with Historically-Black Colleges and Universities, Honda and Ford sponsored tours featuring large music and sports events.

In 2000, U.S. companies spent $1.5 billion in advertising to black consumers. And it is targeted: one study showed that viewers of predominantly African-American prime-time TV shows saw sixty-seven percent more food commercials than did general prime-time viewers.

Ironically, the advertising industry itself has a miserable track record with diversity. The exclusionary hiring practices of Madison Avenue firms have been investigated by the NYC Commission on Human Rights. Of the half million employees nationwide in advertising and related services, only six percent are black. If your company works with an ad agency, hold your agency accountable.

And speaking of accountability: for six years, I observed the diversity marketing efforts in an outlet of a regional bank located in my local grocery store. There were forty-two large and excellent photos of diverse people featured in the branch. Sadly, the face of a black person has never appeared, not once, in all six years. I finally got tired of leaving the store upset at their thickheadedness. So I emailed the bank's president (ironically, a woman of color) and shared my concerns. Her HR vice president emailed me back; I was surprised and pleased. She indicated that all the photographs featured bank employees, and, even with a dozen branches and a decade of experience, the bank had never been able to hire a black employee. Groaning at their incompetence, I sent them some ideas about recruiting. Today there are only six people pictured, and none of them are black. The takeaway here: make sure you can market your diversity story with integrity.

Selling into the black marketplace has become big business: there's a tradeshow devoted to reaching black customers. For information, see www. targetmarketnews.com.

CONVERSATION STARTER: *What specific efforts does your business make to market and sell to black customers?*

■ **96** ■

Serve
black customers effectively.

Every customer wants to feel understood and welcome. When you expect culturally diverse customers to spend their money on your products and services, cultural competence is a frontline service issue. Great service grows the business; deficient service drives customers to your competitors. And it's not just a matter of having employees who reflect the diversity of your customers; every employee serving the customer needs cultural savvy.

Here are nine tips on what such savvy includes and excludes in serving customers across dimensions of difference.

- In general, treat black customers similarly to white customers. Don't question that they have the money to pay for an item, and don't steer them to inexpensive purchases because you think that's what they can afford. Train customer service staff to never ignore black customers, and to always serve them in the proper order, by observing who approached earliest. Research shows that black consumers choose to shop at stores where the prices are good, and where they will be respected.

• Starbucks, in a joint venture with Earvin "Magic" Johnson's Johnson Development Corporation, has more than 120 stores in urban neighborhoods. Customers return to these locations, like customers everywhere, because they receive excellent service for the product and price. And they see people who look like them behind the counter.

• Play in-store music that matches the generalized preferences of your customers. I worked with a black district manager at Wal-Mart, who was trying to figure out how to get R&B onto the corporately programmed music rotation in his eight stores.

• Ask black people for an ID only when you're asking white people for the same thing. And don't target black customers for special attention from security, unless they are actually behaving suspiciously. If you manage in a retail store, you have the power to make sure that black customers don't experience the dreaded "shopping while black" dynamic on your watch.

• Do not avoid touch with a black customer (for example, when placing change in their hand at a cash register), when you would not avoid it with a white customer. They notice, and are understandably offended.

• Be prepared to extend your diversity commitment in situations where customers resist it. Examples include an older gentleman who doesn't trust a younger woman to handle the funds in an estate account, or the challenge to assign a woman to lead a project in a country where the culture may not readily accept women in leadership.

- Treat black customers like the individuals they are. Monitor any tendency (in you or your staff) to stereotype. If your experience with an ethnic group is limited, it may be hard for you to distinguish between customers from that culture. But if you actually want to build a profitable connection, you must encounter each customer as a distinct individual. Grow the habit of learning and pronouncing unfamiliar names; in a global marketplace, this is simply good customer service.
- Track customer service complaints to diagnose trends that need training. Identify and reward service staff who excel at serving diverse customers.
- Avon turned around its sales in urban markets, by assigning black and other ethnic managers to ensure that diverse customers were served with cultural competence.

There are many ways that customer service affects leadership on diversity. At Pitney Bowes, they tell this story: in 1947, Chairman Walter Wheeler, a white corporate leader who despised discrimination, refused to stay at a hotel that denied entry to a black Pitney-Bowes salesman. For Mr. Wheeler, that was a pretty simple response to poor customer service. But that small act sent a powerful message throughout the company. And here we are, still talking about it sixty years later.

CONVERSATION STARTER: *In what ways do your black customers expect exactly what all your customers want? Does the company need to address any particular service issues and opportunities distinct to black customers?*

■ 97 ■

Manage relationships
with diverse suppliers.

I n addition to attending to black customers, many successful American organizations widen their diversity commitment by building supplier partnerships with small businesses owned by black leaders and other diverse business people. This movement gained significant momentum in the past decade: in the mid 1990s, supplier diversity was small potatoes in the diversity discussion. By 2005, the nation's largest companies spent $70 billion (four percent of their procurement budgets) with small businesses owned by people of color or women. The potatoes are larger now.

What are the benefits to managing relationships with diverse suppliers? Let's consider four.

First, investing in high-performing small businesses secures superior and stable supplier support for your company. This helps you stay agile and competitive. Diversityinc recently reported that "businesses owned by women and people of color are growing at more than triple the rate of those owned by white men." Many corporate supplier initiatives also provide training and mentoring programs, equipping their diverse vendors to grow their businesses. In 2002, four percent of Eastman Kodak's suppliers were owned by women or minorities. In 2008, the company expects that figure to be close to twelve percent.

Second, when you build high-quality vendor relationships in a local community, you open the door to talent. Suppliers promote your company, and prospective employees consider coming to work for a company that invests locally. Long-term supplier relationships can open a recruiting pipeline to diverse employees.

Third, if you're in a business that sells to business, your vendors can also become customers. Wachovia takes this approach: the bank is expanding into diverse California communities by inviting local business owners of color to supplier diversity seminars, intent on doing business in both directions. In a market like California, where there is no ethnic majority, such a leveraging strategy can secure market share from less-agile competitors.

Finally, clients want to see that a company is investing in small businesses owned by women and people of color. In 2003, San Antonio's SBC spent fifteen percent of its procurement budget with 1,052 companies owned by women, people of color, and disabled veterans. The company reported that "public- and private-sector customers are increasingly demanding *supplier* diversity plans and results from their strategic suppliers. Promoting the participation of a diverse supplier base not only provides good business solutions, it also cultivates customer loyalty, bidding advantages, and public policy support in the communities our company serves."

Two excellent resources on diverse supplier programs are the Women's Business Enterprise National Council (wbenc.org) and the National Minority Supplier Development Council (nmsdcus.org).

CONVERSATION STARTER: *Does your company have a strategy for working with diverse suppliers? If so, how can you expand it? If not, how can you help launch such an approach?*

■ **98** ■

Calculate

diversity's real return on investment.

I t is notoriously tough to measure the return on investing in diversity at the enterprise level. For instance, some have made the case that public companies can improve share price by following selected diversity practices. But a correlation is not a cause. While the diversity investment contributes to financial success, by misstating such a contribution we fail to calculate diversity's real return on investment.

Let's avoid that failure. Start by reviewing definitions of two key ideas: character (see essay 59) and transformation (see essay 16). **Character** is the intrinsic values, qualities, and gifts that find expression in a person or organization's behavior. **Transformation** is dramatic growth in an individual or organization's character and performance. I suggest we think of character as a way to measure qualitative progress, and performance as a way to evaluate quantitative growth. So when we lead on diversity, we produce results through being (character) and doing (performance).

Using these definitions, consider this scorecard for calculating diversity's real return on investment. Each of the eight numbered cells will contain data that tells the story of results (the ROI) emerging from investing time, money, and other resources in diversity. I call this tool the *Eight-Cell Scorecard.*

Return

Investment	Character*	Performance*
Self	Cell 1	Cell 2
Colleagues	Cell 3	Cell 4
Customers	Cell 5	Cell 6
Company	Cell 7	Cell 8

Figure 98-1

*A Note on Data:

If you want to measure the full benefit of investing in diverse employees and customers, you must be able to demonstrate through hard-nosed research how these initiatives strengthen the bottom line. This will include numbers that measure what matters (employee headcount, value in dollars from sales to diverse market segments, decrease in litigation costs, number of new stores opened in international markets, and so on).

A second imperative: leverage the power of qualitative information (e.g., competencies, culture, employer brand, customer loyalty). While such data cannot be distilled into simple numbers, it offers critical competitive information. Candidly, some of your competitors ignore qualitative data because it's "soft." Don't make their mistake; ROI efforts show how diversity drives dramatic growth in the character *and* performance of an organization and its people.

Like any good tool, the Eight-Cell Scorecard is designed to do a specific job: in this case, to evaluate what you (as a white man who leads) and your organization can get from investing in diversity. And, like any good tool, it will take some time to learn how to use this ROI instrument expertly.

There are hundreds of diversity metrics. Here's how you prioritize among them:

- Work with your manager to identify your own diversity-related performance objectives (DRPOs: see essay 76). Connect them to goals that have cascaded down to you.
- Develop DRPOs with each of your direct reports.
- Collaborate with your peers to help them formulate their own DRPOs.

To help you move ahead, I've identified eight examples of measurable diversity results for each scorecard cell. These are illustrative; you need to craft the measures that matter to you. The word *diverse* appears as a marker for a specific dimension of diversity; you might, for example, insert *women* or *black* in its place, depending on your actual objectives.

Here are sample metrics in the format of the Eight-Cell Scorecard.

Cell 1   Growth in your personal character as a leader

I met with my manager monthly to discuss our mutual diversity learning

I actively led with Adventurous Competence on matters related to race and gender, when I … (specify action)

I met weekly with both my diverse mentee and two peer mentors

I emerged from Pre-Awareness on homosexuality, realizing that my religious beliefs may be limiting my relationships with gay colleagues and customers (I'm now in the Necessity stage)

I was selected to lead a project over two other white men, and was told the deciding factor was my diversity experience

Due regard is a concept I am consistently applying to situations in diverse relationships (for example, …)

I'm cultivating a closer friendship with a black friend at church

I've encountered two situations the past month where inappropriate racial language was used; I responded effectively in one, and chickened out in the other

Figure 98-2

Cell 2 Growth in your performance as a leader

I identified budget for our diversity work, and made certain my
supervisor, peers and employees knew about the investment

On each of my DRPO's, my manager rated my performance as
'exceeded expectations', and I earned my full diversity bonus

At no time in the previous quarter did I withhold corrective feedback
from a diverse employee for fear of diversity issues being raised

I ensured that we interviewed diverse candidates for 100% of my
openings this year

The percentage of diverse employees in my unit exceeds by 10% the
percentage of diverse employees company wide

For every major decision last quarter, I involved my team in the
process at the highest level of inclusion possible

I promoted two female team leads into supervisory positions last year

I'm talking less and listening more, based on employee ratings

Figure 98-3

Cell 3 Qualitative growth in your colleagues (reports, peers, manager)

We saw improvement in team trust over four quarters, based on quarterly use of the Team Trust tool (Essay 65)

Employees have resolved four diversity-related conflicts between themselves this year, rather than bringing them to me

My direct reports received targeted diversity training, and rated the training's success above a 4.5 on a 1-5 scale

Members of my team now regularly raise diversity-related questions and concerns

The youngest members of the team stepped up to lead the orientation process with new hires

I advised and partnered with the women on my team to decrease the amount of interrupting during team meetings

My manager asked me for my perspective on a diversity issue she was having with her boss

My peers and I now regularly develop DRPO's with colleagues across the organization

Figure 98-4

Cell 4   Performance improvements among colleagues

Cultural competence training and coaching with my CSR's contributed to a customer satisfaction rating increase from 3.2 to 3.7 on a 1-5 scale

Mid-year and annual reviews included ratings and discussion on unit diversity goals with each employee in the facility

Our team's members in the black employee affinity group participated in 42% more candidate interviews than last year

In the division, we ended employment relationships with 58 employees in the first half of the year, and there were no lawsuits filed following these terminations

I worked with my manager's manager to put together a presentation for the Board on the diversity results in our department

I worked with Compensation to ensure that the 16 women in our unit are paid equally for equal work

I helped my manager develop a "Coaching in Support of Diversity" module, which he is now rolling out across the department

I succeeded in moving my top black employee into "The Future of Leadership" program for high-performers

Figure 98-5

Cell 5 Qualitative improvements in working with customers

Diverse customers complained less and indicated higher levels of satisfaction

I trained and coached with my manager and peers to handle situations when customers resist our diversity commitment

We improved the quality of product and service improvements achieved in response to feedback from diverse customers

We improved language capacity among employees in Spanish-speaking markets who now can serve customers with at least vocational Spanish

We conducted research with diverse prospects in the Southeast Asian market

I worked with quality assurance to figure out how to capture diversity information from customers, so we can measure diverse customer service

I put my sales team through training in culturally-competent influence skills; we're seeking to apply it by closing 20% more sales with diverse customers in the coming quarter

We researched a competitor's ability to work with India-based CSR's in a manner that maintains high customer satisfaction

Figure 98-6

Cell 6 Performance improvements with customers

We increased the number of new diverse customers by 22%

48% of diverse customers returned to the store within 60 days

We won 14 new accounts in Africa

The sales value of products targeted to black customers in the store grew 27%

The three serious complaints involving diverse customers were all resolved within two hours

I generated 15 leads through networking with diverse suppliers

A new ad campaign to black college students increased sales in that product channel 18%

For the first time, in each of the 44 outlets where diverse customers make up a majority of the clientele, the manager brings direct experience with these customer's culture and needs

Figure 98-7

Cell 7 Qualitative growth in the organization's culture and character

We improved the caliber of innovative ideas in service and product development, by collecting diverse input

The company-wide employee attitude surveys show improvement in the diversity-related indicators

We increased the number of diverse employees participating in employee affinity groups

We saw an increased frequency and focus in the CEO's expressed commitment to diversity

There was a 12% increase in the number of diverse candidates identified through employee referrals

30% more employees volunteered in organizations serving communities of color

57% of white male executives at VP level and above participate in mentoring women and people of color

People of color, in proportion to their percentage in the employee base, were 23% more likely to be promoted

Figure 98-8

CELL 8: IMPROVEMENTS IN ORGANIZATIONAL PERFORMANCE

Cell 8 measures tend to dominate diversity literature, because they can describe enterprise-wide progress. Such data fits well into articles and annual reports, providing essential talking points.

The limitation: Cell 8 metrics tend to be summative, bottom-line. Cells 1–7 should not be ignored, because they produce and they tell the actual diversity ROI story that Cell 8 metrics summarize.

Cell 8   Improvements in organizational performance

61% of new hires last year were white women or people of color; our company-wide headcount is now 51% white women and people of color

27% of the total marketing budget is targeted to diverse markets

We increased sales revenue from diverse customers by 14% across all products and services over the same quarter last year

We decreased the number of diversity-related lawsuits by 27%, and related legal costs by 47%

There was an 8% increase in diverse senior leaders (VP and above) over last year

78% of managers were eligible to earn the bonus for meeting diversity goals

9% of total procurement budget went to diverse suppliers, up from 7%

The company was mentioned as a diversity leader in the national media 13 times

Figure 98-9

One of the most original thinkers about measuring diversity's ROI is Edward E. Hubbard. His book, *The Diversity Scorecard: Evaluating the Impact of Diversity on Organizational Performance*, is a gift you should give yourself.

You will learn more and faster about diversity's ROI when you network with your organization's diversity stakeholders in HR, learning, diversity, affinity groups, the supplier program, sales and marketing initiatives, and external consultants. They will value the partnership of a dedicated white male leader, and such relationships can open doors for you.

Learn to calculate diversity's real return as a core skill. Commit to measuring what matters, and you'll be able to articulate the value that your investment in diversity delivers to your organization.

CONVERSATION STARTER: *Who can you work with on developing an Eight-Cell Scorecard, in order to track and tell the story of diversity's ROI for you and the organization?*

■ **99** ■

Lead
with a transformative vision.

I believe America taught our son's killer to hate African-Americans. After Mikhail Markhasev killed Ennis William Cosby on January 16, 1997, he said to his friends: "I shot a n———. It's all over the news." All African-Americans, regardless of their educational and economic accomplishments, have been and are at risk in America simply because of their skin colors. Sadly, my family and I experienced that to be one of America's racial truths. Most people know that facing the truth brings about healing and growth. When is America going to face its historical and current racial realities, so it can be what it says it is?

DR. CAMILLE COSBY
USA Today; *July 9, 1998,*
after Bill and Camille Cosby's son was murdered by a white immigrant

I wrote this book to challenge you to answer Dr. Cosby's plaintive question, by leading with your own transformative vision.

We have considered **transformation** as dramatic growth in an individual or organization's character and performance. In the previous essay, we glimpsed dozens of potential metrics for such growth, each one a sample piece to the diversity puzzle we seek to solve as white men who lead.

A vision is like the boxtop for a jigsaw puzzle; it's the picture of the desired future to which we refer, as we piece together the present opportunities on the table.

In a nutshell, here's my transformative vision for leading on diversity:

In 2024, the year I turn seventy,
I want to hear black American leaders say out loud:
"Today we see what we never thought we would see—
a generation of white men partnering with us to lead on diversity."

I hope this book, and my life's work, will contribute to the realization of this vision. The Cosby family, and each black family under God's sun, deserves no less.

If you need any more motivation, here's a data point that will get under your skin. A decade after Dr. Cosby spoke, the National Urban League, in their 2007 "State of Black America" report, found the economic status of black men was fifty-seven percent of white men, taking into account such indicators as annual median income, employment issues, poverty, housing, wealth formation, transportation, and the digital divide. This should raise a question that will fuel your transformative vision: What will you do, what will we do together, to equalize such a shocking disparity?

I seek transformation. I want to grow dramatically, in my person and in my profession. I want to be a source for such growth in others. I hope you'll join me. As white men, we can learn to lead with transformative effect.

CONVERSATION STARTER: *What is your transformative vision for leading on diversity?*

Lead yourself
to expertise.

It has taken me forty years to prepare for this book. I've still got much to learn, even with my Relative Expertise.

Remember, relative means you hold your expertise with humility. You lead on differences from your side, always remembering your limits so that you honor others' experiences and evoke their contribution.

Lead from the inside out on diversity. You also honor your own experience, and choose to contribute from character. The thread for such personal transformation weaves through this book in clusters of essays. Permit me to retrace a nine-step staircase that you can climb to Relative Expertise.

Step One: *Stages of Growth*

The Transformation Curve (see essays 16–18 and 31–35) lays out the path for dramatic growth, as you learn to lead on diversity as a white man.

Step Two: *Motivation for Change*

Sustainable collaborative advantage (see essay 8) and the business case for diversity (see essays 7, 74, and 75) introduce thirteen reasons to learn to lead as a white man, and twelve trends and motives for your organization to invest in diversity.

Step Three: *Understanding Human Differences*

A straightforward and pragmatic approach to defining diversity provided a foundation in essays 2–6, outlined in the Fundamental Filter.

Step Four: *Own Your Advantages*

The heart of personal responsibility as a white man who leads may be found in the way you assess and leverage your power, privilege, opportunity, and views of preference, as proposed in the Advantage Complex, essays 23–26.

Step Five: *Sort Diversity's Significance*

In Essay 30, the concept of due regard suggests that a manager needs to demonstrate "the ability to distinguish among the attributes and cultures of their employees, peers, superiors, and customers, so that they encourage each person's contribution." This avoids both the ignorance and exaggeration of human differences.

STEP SIX: *To Thine Own Self*

Emerging from the vital skill of self-monitoring (see essay 36), a white man who leads must proficiently face and manage the emotions that accompany a commitment to diversity: denial, fear, guilt, shame, and anger (explored in essays 37–40).

STEP SEVEN: *Engage Culture*

Diverse humans operate in groups, the "Like Some Others" reality, so it is essential to become a continuing student of cultures. Essays 46–50 offer a start in considering cultures at work.

STEP EIGHT: *Guard Your Tongue*

For a white man in leadership, landmines lie along the road to Relative Expertise. We can explode them with words that wound, and hurt everyone whose journey intersects with our own. Essays 54–58 offer words to the wise.

STEP NINE: *Make and Keep Promises*

Bridges across the diversity divide are built with trust, and trust is composed of promises, made and kept over time. Essays 61–65 consider the construction of trust.

These are nine steps in your journey to diversity expertise. You will lead by getting things done with diverse colleagues and customers. Essays that focus on behavior, from 59–98, provide ideas for action.

Lead yourself to expertise. You can only lead others where you are willing to go yourself.

CONVERSATION STARTER: *What are the next steps you will take to learn and lead on diversity?*

LEADING TRANSFORMATIVELY
■ 101 ■

Lead your organization
to success.

I n a recent study by the University of Minnesota, seventy-four percent of white Americans said their racial identity is important to them. Eighty-three percent identified that their "white advantage" came from access to education and social networks. White Americans are engaging diversity like never before, and our nation's progress with inclusion is breathtaking. Yes, we still have a long way to go. But the white community is ready to walk the talk.

Meanwhile, diverse colleagues and customers are walking in your door, every day.

Today Is the Day

Now is the time for you to lead on the diversity commitment in your organization: time to articulate the business case, time to protect and defend black colleagues, time to open the doors of opportunity for all, time to grow in a global marketplace. Here's an excellent resource for leading a diversity initiative across the enterprise: *Designing & Implementing Successful Diversity Programs*, by Lawrence M. Baytos. This book provides a great strategic perspective on managing diversity.

It is a good and worthy end in itself to learn about differences in race, gender, and other human distinctives. But it's not enough; we have to lead as we learn. In essay 12, I defined **leadership** as achieving results by developing people through work. So this entire book can be distilled down to two questions for you, as a white man who leads:

- *What results do you need to achieve?*
- *How will you develop diverse colleagues and reach diverse customers to achieve these goals?*

I hope you will dare to become the sort of leader your black colleagues have not seen before and do not yet expect: a white man who leads on diversity, with an open heart, a teachable mind, a careful tongue, and the discipline to hold diversity accountable for business results.

This won't be easy, but it will be good.

Years ago my sister gave me a shirt that featured a simple message: *We are meant to be here together*. All the differences that test us can also be sources of learning. Deep in my spirit, I believe that God intends us for one another, across every dimension of difference.

We share an honorable vocation as white men: to lead and learn with others through diversity. I invite you to travel deeper into this work of transformation.

CONVERSATION STARTER: *What results do you need to achieve? How will you develop diverse colleagues and reach diverse customers to achieve these goals?*

■ DEFINITIONS ■

55% Rule. Each person is responsible for fully holding up their 50% (no easy thing), and each person can expect the other to extend an extra 5% for the sake of the relationship.

anger. A strong feeling of displeasure or hostility.

awareness. Recognizing and understanding individual and cultural differences and similarities among colleagues and customers.

bias. An inclination that opposes or supports a person or idea.

character. The intrinsic values, qualities, and gifts that find expression in a person's or organization's behavior.

collaboration. To co-labor, to achieve business results *with* your colleagues, for your customers.

courage. Facing fear and managing conflict with self-possession and resolve.

culture. The assumptions, values, and behaviors a group of people develop as they share experiences over time.

dimensions of diversity. Twenty differences that distinguish humans as individuals and in cultures.

diversity. All the qualities that differentiate us from one another.

Diversity Point of View. Your evolving personal perspective on twenty dimensions of diversity, filtered through the saying: Each one of us is like all others, like some others, and like no other.

Due Regard. A manager's demonstrated ability to distinguish among the attributes and cultures of their employees, peers, superiors, and customers, so that they encourage each person's contribution.

ethnicity. A cultural group of which you are a part, which may be distinguished by such common traits as family, geography, appearance, demeanor, language, race, religion, and economics.

fair treatment. Consistent, individualized treatment, rather than the exact same treatment for each individual.

feminism. The belief that God gives all humans, male and female, the freedom to be authentic, and gifts to share with everyone.

Fundamental Filter. A saying to help us clarify levels of human identity. Each one of us is: Like All Others, Like Some Others, and Like No Other.

generalization. A useful but imprecise statement about widely observable tendencies among a group of people.

groupism. The unthinking presumption that cultural connections determine individuality rather than shape individuality.

guilt. Being responsible and feeling remorseful for wrongdoing.

integrity. The positive congruence between who I am and what I do.

leader. A person who achieves results by developing people through work.

leadership. Achieving results by developing people through work.

merit. Access to advantages and benefits earned through performance.

motivate. To impel to action.

norm. A standard or model operating in a group.

political correctness. The lazy and empty label that distracts us from the discussion we should be having, on the inherent tension between speech that avoids giving offense and speech that is free and candid.

power. The opportunity and ability to see, make, and carry out choices.

preference. Selecting one person over another.

privilege. Access to special advantages, benefits, and opportunities.

promise. A vow that creates expectation and accountability.

race. Skin color and other physical traits that influence complex social meanings and practical knowledge.

racism. Belief and behavior that discriminates against people of a different race.

respect. The art of showing deferential esteem.

Self-Interest in Diversity. A healthy attention to your own motivations and needs, as you work with diverse people.

self-monitoring. The skill by which we watch ourselves during our interactions, and make effective choices about how we think, feel, and act toward the Other.

shame. Guilt publicized, a deserved or perceived disgrace for behavior that dishonors.

stereotyping. Applying a generalization with bias to an individual.

Sustainable Collaborative Advantage. The tangible benefits that accrue to the white male manager who invests in developing his diversity competencies.

teachability. Being ready, willing, and able to learn diversity's lessons fast and well, so you develop the reputation for instructability among people who are "different" from you.

team. A group of individuals whose common purpose requires interdependent contribution.

transformation. Dramatic growth in an individual's or an organization's character and performance.

Transformation Curve. The five stages for developing competence with human differences, which include Pre-Awareness, Interest and

Necessity, Careful Skill Progress, Adventurous Competence, and Relative Expertise.

trust. The making and keeping of promises over time.

■ RESOURCES ■

BOOKS

Baytos, Lawrence. *Designing and Implementing Successful Diversity Programs.* Englewood Cliffs, NJ: Prentice-Hall, 1995.

Bellman, Geoff. *Getting Things Done When You Are Not in Charge.* San Francisco: Berrett-Koehler Publishers, 1992.

Brilliant, Ashleigh. *I May Not Be Perfect, But Parts Of Me Are Excellent.* Santa Barbara, CA: Woodridge Press, 1985.

———. *We've Been Through So Much Together, And Most Of If Was Your Fault.* Santa Barbara: Woodridge Press, 1990.

———. *All I Want Is A Warm Bed And A Kind Word.* Santa Barbara: Woodridge Press, 1992.

Correspondents of the *New York Times. How Race Is Lived in America.* Times Books: New York, 2001.

DePree, Max. *Leadership Is an Art.* East Lansing: Michigan State University Press, 1987.

Dingle, Derek T. *Black Enterprise Titans of the BE 100's: Black CEOs Who Redefined and Conquered American Business.* New York: John Wiley & Sons, 1999.

Friedman, Thomas. *The World Is Flat: A Brief History of the 21st Century.* New York: Farrar, Straus and Giroux, 2005.

Gardenswartz, Lee, and Anita Rowe. *Diverse Teams at Work: Capitalizing on the Power of Diversity.* Chicago: Irwin Professional Publishing, 1994.

Hacker, Andrew. *Two Nations: Black and White, Separate, Hostile, Unequal.* New York: Scribner, 1992.

Hallesby, O. *Prayer.* Minneapolis: Augsburg, 1931.

Hillman, James. *The Soul's Code: In Search of Character and Calling.* New York: Warner Books, 1996.

Hubbard, Edward E. *The Diversity Scorecard: Evaluating the Impact of Diversity on Organizational Performance.* Burlington, MA: Elsevier Butterworth-Heinemann, 2004.

Jacobs, Bruce. *Race Manners in the 21st Century: Navigating the Minefield Between Black and White Americans in an Age of Fear.* New York: Arcade Publishing, 2006.

Jacobson, Matthew Frye. *Whiteness of a Different Color: European Immigrants and the Alchemy of Race.* Cambridge, MA: Harvard University Press, 1998.

Johnson, Allan G. *Power, Privilege and Difference.* Boston: McGraw Hill, 2001.

Johnston, W. B, and A. H. Packer. *Workforce 2000: Work and Workers for the 21st Century.* Indianapolis: Hudson Institute, 1987.

Katz, Judith H. *White Awareness.* Norman: University of Oklahoma Press, 1987.

Kendall, Frances. *Understanding White Privilege: Creating Pathways to Authentic Relationships Across Race.* New York: Routledge, 2006.

Kivel, Paul. *Uprooting Racism: How White People Can Work for Racial Justice.* Gabriola Island, BC: New Society Publishers, 2002.

Kluckhohn, Clyde, and Henry A. Murray. *Personality in Nature, Society and Culture.* New York: Alfred A. Knopf, 1950.

Kochman, Thomas. *Black and White: Styles of Conflict.* Chicago: University of Chicago Press, 1981.

Kotkin, Joel. *Tribes: How Race, Religion and Identity Determine Success in the New Global Economy.* New York: Random House, 1992.

Lee, Blaine. *The Power Principle: Influence with Honor.* New York: Simon & Schuster, 1998.

Liu, Eric. *The Accidental Asian.* New York: Random House, 1998.

Livers, Ancella B., and Keith A. Carver. *Leading in Black and White: Working Across the Racial Divide in Corporate America.* San Francisco: Jossey-Bass and the Center for Creative Leadership in Greensboro, 2003.

Lui, Meizhu, Barbara Robles, Betsy Leondar-Wright, Rose Brewer, and Rebecca Adamson. *The Color of Wealth: The Story Behind the U.S. Racial Wealth Divide.* New York: The New Press, 2006.

Lynch, Frederick R. *The Diversity Machine: The Drive to Change the "White Male" Workplace.* New York: Free Press, 1997.

Marable, Manning. *The Great Wells of Democracy.* New York: Perseus Books, 2002.

Miller, Pepper, and Herb Kemp. *What's Black About It? Insights to Increase Your Share of the Changing African American Market.* Ithaca, NY: Paramount Market Publishing, 2006.

Myers, Jim. *Afraid of the Dark: What Whites and Blacks Need to Know About Each Other.* Chicago: Lawrence Hill Books, 2000.

Patterson, Kerry, Joseph Grenny, Ron McMillan, and Al Switzer. *Crucial Conversations: Tools for Talking When Stakes Are High.* New York: McGraw-Hill, 2002.

Prochaska, James, John Norcross, and Carlo Diclemente. *Changing for Good*. New York: Avon Books, 1995.

Rothwell, William. *Effective Succession Planning: Ensuring Leadership Continuity and Building Talent from Within*. New York: Amacom, 2005.

Salter McNeil, Brenda, and Rick Richardson. *The Heart of Racial Justice: How Soul Change Leads to Social Change*. Downers Grove, IL: InterVarsity Press, 2004.

Schnarch, David. *Passionate Marriage*. New York: Henry Holt and Company, 1997.

Shapiro, Jerrold Lee. *The Measure of a Man*. New York: Berkley Publishing Group, 1995.

Steele, Shelby. *The Content of Our Character*. New York: St. Martin's Press, 1990.

Steinhorn, Leonard, and Barbara Diggs-Brown. *By the Color of Our Skin: The Illusion of Integration and the Reality of Race*. New York: Dutton, 1999.

Tannen, Deborah. *Talking From 9 to 5: How Women's and Men's Conversational Styles Affect Who Gets Heard, Who Gets Credit, and What Gets Done at Work*. New York: William Morrow Company, 1994.

Terkel, Studs. *Race: How Blacks & Whites Think & Feel About the American Obsession*. New York: Anchor Books, 1993.

Wagner, Rodd, and James, Harter. *12: The Elements of Great Managing*. New York: Gallup Press, 2006.

Watson, Joe. *Without Excuses: Unleash the Power of Diversity to Build Your Business*. New York: St. Martin's Press, 2006.

West, Cornel. *Race Matters*. Boston: Beacon Press, 1993.

Williams, Lena. *It's the Little Things: Everyday Interactions That Anger, Annoy and Divide the Races*. New York: Harcourt, 2000.

Zachary, Lois J. *The Mentor's Guide: Facilitating Effective Learning Relationships*. San Francisco: Jossey-Bass, 2000.

Selected Books on White Studies

Feagin, Joe, and Eileen O'Brien. *White Men on Race: Power, Privilege, and the Shaping of Cultural Consciousness.* Boston: Beacon Press, 2003.

Ipsaro, Anthony. *White Men, Women & Minorities.* Denver: Meridian Associates, 1997.

Articles

Ely, Robin, Debra Meyerson, and Martin Davidson. "Rethinking Political Correctness." Harvard Business Review, September 2006.

McIntosh, Peggy. "White Privilege and Male Privilege." Center for Research on Women, Wellesley College, 1988.

Witzig, Ritchie. "The Medicalization of Race: Scientific Legitimization of a Flawed Social   Construct." *Annals of Internal Medicine* 125, no. 8 (October 15, 1996): 675–8.

Videos and Films

A Time to Kill. Theatrical release directed by Joel Schumacher: Warner Brothers, 1996.

An Unlikely Friendship. Educational video produced by Diane Bloom: www.dianebloom.com, 919-929-8941, North Carolina.

Open Range. Theatrical release directed by Kevin Costner: Touchstone Pictures, 2004.

The Color of Fear. Educational video from filmmaker Lee Mun Wah: stirfryseminars.com, 510-204-8840, California.

Organization	www. (2008)	Phone	HQ
African Ancestry	africanancestry.com	202.723.0900	DC
Black Professional Coaches Alliance	blackcoaches.org	888.690.3456	CA
Catalyst	catalyst.org	212.514.7600	NY
Center for Creative Leadership	ccl.org	336.545.2810	NC
Development Dimensions International	ddiworld.com	800.933.4463	PA
Diversityinc	diversityinc.com	973.494.0500	NJ
Employment Learning Innovations	eliinc.com	800.497.7654	GA
MyFamily.com, Inc.	ancestry.com	801.705.7000	UT
NAACP	naacp.org	877.622.2798	MD
Nancy D. Solomon, LLC	nancydsolomon.com	253.265.3240	WA
National Urban League	nul.org	212.558.5300	NY
National Minority Suppliers Development Council	nmsdcus.org	212.944.2430	NY
Salter McNeil & Associates, LLC	saltermcneil.com	773.583.8085	IL
Sojourners	sojo.net	202.328.8842	DC
Southern Poverty Law Center	splcenter.org	334.956.8200	AL
Situation Management Systems	smsinc.com	603.897.1200	NH
White Men as Full Diversity Partners	wmfdp.com	503.281.5585	OR
White Sand Consultants	whitesandconsultants.com	888.266.1199	CA
Women's Business Enterprise National Council	wbenc.org	202.872.5515	DC

■ ABOUT THE AUTHOR ■

Chuck Shelton has developed leaders at Microsoft, Wal-Mart, Key Bank, Comcast, Safeco Insurance, and in more than thirty other organizations. Since 1981, he has coached, trained, spoken, and consulted on leadership development and diversity management nationally, through more than 250 presentations and projects. As the managing director for Greatheart Leader Labs in Seattle, he calls the signals at leadershipforwhitemen.com, the premier online resource equipping white men to lead more effectively.

A leader his entire life, Chuck earned degrees from a progressive college (Evergreen) and an evangelical seminary (Fuller). With a dozen training certifications, his professional memberships include the National Speaker's Association, the Society for Human Resource Management, and the Association for Training and Development.

Chuck lives near Seattle with his family and an intact sense of humor.

Contact him at:

chuck@leadershipforwhitemen.com

or

chuck@greatheartleaderlabs.com

455

■ BONUS ■

Ready to transform the way you lead?
Go to leadershipforwhitemen.com

The only online resource dedicated to white men who lead for a living

Sign up for your free monthly newsletter
— a $239 value.

◆ Download free management tools

◆ Find out about leadership training built on this book

◆ Encounter other white men who lead for a living

◆ Learn from the blog and teleseminars, and order learning resources

◆ Explore speaking and consulting services that equip white men to lead

And go to greatheartleaderlabs.com

The leadership development company that brought you
Leadership 101 For White Men:
How to Work Successfully with Black Colleagues and Customers

Transform the way you lead.